PRAISE FOR HAROLD RHENISCH

With *Tom Thomson's Shack*, Rhenisch proves that the unique adaptation of a magic-realist style to non-fiction, combined with an episodic structure that would be quicksand to most writers, wasn't just a brilliant fluke in *Out of the Interior*, but a technique he has mastered completely.
—Vancouver Sun

His "surreal linkages" and "delicate observations of nature" are really discoveries of cultural promise; they are a poetry of place afforded by this landscape and the potential for meaningful life within it.
—BC Bookworld

Rhenisch speaks frequently about history because he distrusts history of the textbook variety, with its continuum of predictable cause and effect. . . . Hence there are many forms and at least two levels of history budding in this book. One is the satisfying detail of the orchard economy, a subject little written into British Columbia literature. The other is the lyric of compounds and mixed metaphors and variations of light that write history as verbal impressionism.
—BC Studies

What gives Rhenisch's work its uncommon depth is the constant tension between the natural world and the world of words and ideas in which he is equally at home.
—Vancouver Sun

I find it difficult to categorize what Harold Rhenisch has done with *Out of the Interior*. . . . He has given us excellence of craft and a depth of understanding that I haven't come across in prose in a considerable length of time. . . . All the world is in this book.
—Prairie Fire

The Wolves at Evelyn
Journeys Through a Dark Century

HAROLD RHENISCH

© Harold Rhenisch 2006

All rights reserved. The use of any part of this publication reproduced, transmitted in any form or by any means, electronic, mechanical, recording or otherwise, or stored in a retrieval system, without the prior consent of the publisher is an infringement of the copyright law. In the case of photocopying or other reprographic copying of the material, a licence must be obtained from ACCESS the Canadian Reprography Collective before proceeding.

Library and Archives Canada Cataloguing in Publication
Rhenisch, Harold, 1958-
The wolves at Evelyn : journeys through a dark century / Harold Rhenisch.

ISBN 1-897142-10-2

I. Title.

PS8585.H54Z477 2006   C814'.54   C2006-904311-6

Cover image: On Travel by Rémy Markowitsch. Courtesy: Galerie EIGEN + ART, Berlin / Leipzig. © 2005 by Rémy Markowitsch, Berlin. "On Travel", 2004, published by Verlag für moderne Kunst Nürnberg. www.markowitsch.org

 Canada Council   Conseil des Arts
for the Arts   du Canada

Brindle & Glass is pleased to thank the Canada Council for the Arts and the Alberta Foundation for the Arts for their contributions to our publishing program.

Brindle & Glass is committed to protecting the environment and to the responsible use of natural resources. This book is printed on 100% post-consumer recycled and ancient-forest-friendly paper. For more information, please visit www.oldgrowthfree.com.

Brindle & Glass Publishing
www.brindleandglass.com

1 2 3 4 5 09 08 07 06

PRINTED AND BOUND IN CANADA

for Auguste, Charlotte, and Dorothy

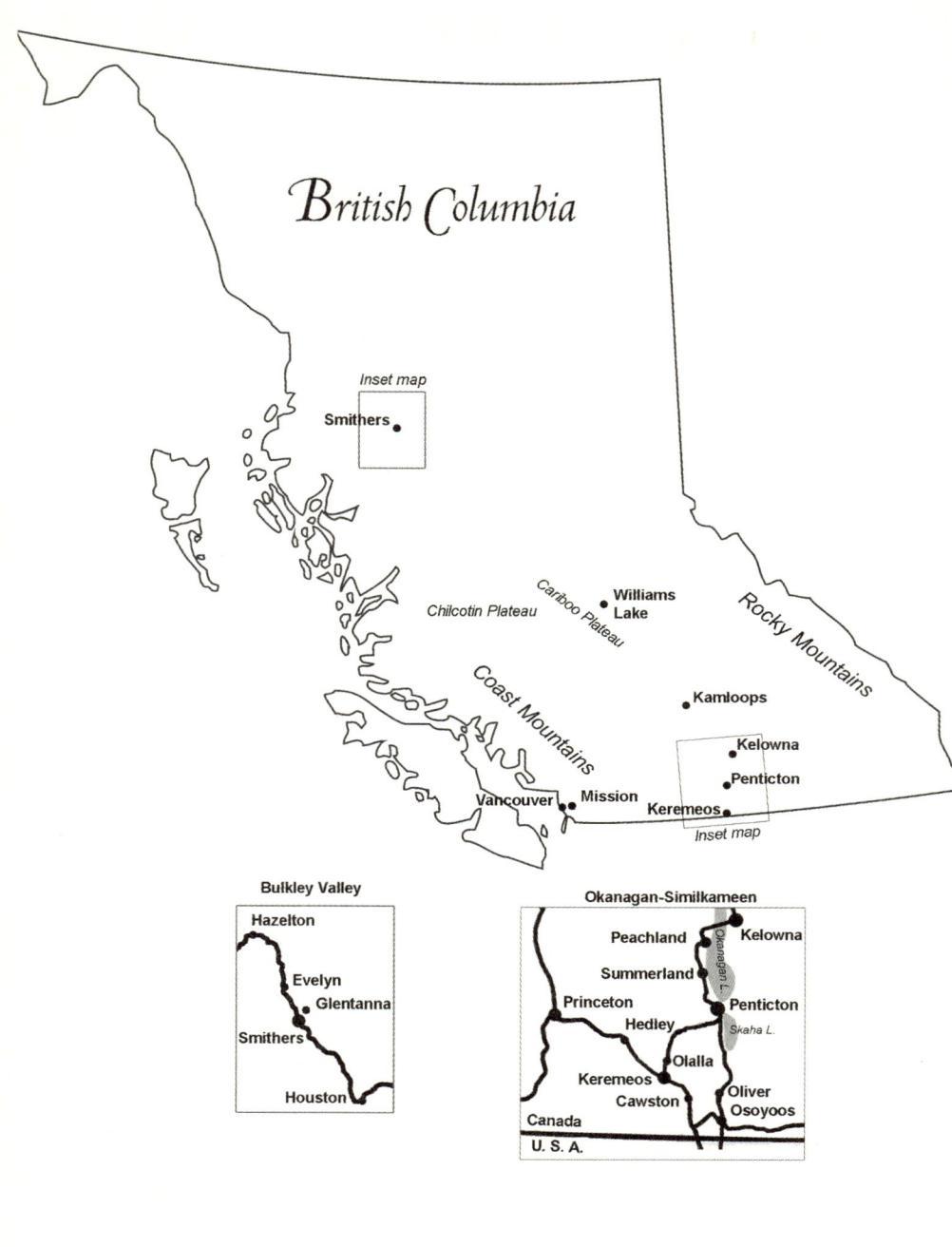

~The House on the Hill~

*E*uropeans came to British Columbia by the boatload to walk freely on the earth, and like the rats that came in the holds of their ships and the string quartets that played in their heads, the idea of land came along, too. It gave us the Indian reserve system and the system of fences and water rights that turned the wild earth into a contract that could be bought or sold. Incredible, isn't it? Contracts can be traded, but not land, surely. We do trade it, though. In fact, land and the history tied to it is traded around so much that the idea of land has even defined how native communities view their, well, land. You see how it is. It's the only word we have left to sum up our relationship to the earth and to the interface between our perceptions and our society. In fact, we use it so much we don't even talk about that interface.

Well, we do now.

On February 7, 1945, seven hundred American and British planes dropped approximately four million pounds of explosives on the centre of Dresden, hand-shaping the old streets by the river, the opera house, the pleasure palace, and the cathedral into a blast furnace, and then into a rock quarry. Before the bombs fell, Dresden had been a city of narrow alleys and tall thin houses with Renaissance doorways. The doorframes of the pleasure palace on the muddy north bank of the Elbe were decorated with naughty little mussel shells in honour of Venus, the goddess of love. Walking through the doors was like walking under a sprig of mistletoe on New Year's Eve. Today, the ruins are graded under wide avenues and parking lots. The rows of statues of the randy, pipe-playing, violin-fiddling goat-footed god Pan have been propped back up against the walls of the palace, looking in over the romantic walkways and the sculpted lawns—edged with steel because these days no one can afford to sculpt the sod by hand.

Back when the European aristocracy shipped half the wealth of Europe to Beijing, though, to pay for Ming Dynasty vases and blueware and the bribes to get it past the warlords of Afghanistan, the Saxon King August the Strong gave his cousins cheaper china (but not that much cheaper!). He hired peasant women to decorate it with flowers from the meadows along the Elbe. He gave his cousins new forms, too: chocolate cups and teacups, creamers, sugarboats and coffee services, and little figures of Chinese monkeys playing the drums. It all went up in the name of Freedom; its loss showed us, before Hiroshima, the effects of a firestorm and how many people could suffocate from lack of oxygen as the fires drank the atmosphere for miles around.

Nineteen years later, my mother was still hiding from that firestorm. It was 1964. It was still bad luck to have German blood in your veins. My mother, who had grown up in the British Columbian bush and had never seen a piece of Meissen china, watched the wind rise up the valley wall in the morning and fall back again in the night. I was five years old and watched scorpions on our back lawn. Those were big scorpions, the length of a finger. Smaller scorpions strutted across the linoleum of my mother's kitchen. When I found them, I dropped them into canning jars and set them on the counter next to the jar of Ivory Liquid and the single eighteen-inch window from which my mother saw most of the world. The world was like a watercolour painting. The scorpions tried to sting the glass. Venom ran down it in beads.

The linoleum of my mother's kitchen was gouged by the hobnailed boots of the loggers who had rented the house before we moved in. In between the gouges, the linoleum was chequered, white and red like an Italian tablecloth in Walt Disney's *Lady and the Tramp*. I just knew we had found true elegance.

"Stupid loggers!" my mother said over and over again, on her hands and knees with a rag, scrubbing that floor clean in big circles, her hair tied up in a blue and white kerchief while it dried in its rollers. "Look at me. I'm just like an Irish washerwoman. All they had to do was take off their boots. Boors. What were they, raised in a barn?"

Thing is, she pretty nearly was.

"You have to scrub inside your ears or the potatoes will grow there," my mother said as she sudsed me up in my bath. "Oh, look at that! A carrot!" I shrieked—every time. I was proud, though, to have potatoes growing in my ears. I could hold my head up high when I went to school the next day and the tough kids beat me up: I was a farmer, and not just any farmer, but one who had it in his heart, one who was chosen by God, who had a magical touch that would cause plants to grow out of barren soil. I liked this kind of madness.

The Germans who came to drink beer and talk about the "Old Country" always came up very close to me in their tweed and wool and silk, in their plain cotton dress shirts stained with gravy, in their cigar smoke and beer and sunken blue cheeks, with their yellow teeth and all their sweet words. I was something of a novelty to them—a little German boy in this land at the end of the earth. They loomed over me, and tousled my hair. These were not Germans bred to order and discipline and obedience. These were Silesians, old communists who had come to Canada in 1929, who had been stranded by the war and dispossessed by the ethnic cleansing that followed it, which wiped their old land off the map. To our ears, today, they would seem more Yiddish than German. They were the last of their kind.

In the summer of 2003, my uncle Eberhard took my daughter, Anassa, and me on a trip to Dresden and Berlin.

"Look at these factories and industrial parks," Eberhard said, driving slowly through a two-kilometre-long loop of new buildings edged in yellow and green plastic moulding—trucking companies and engineering firms circling Kesselsdorf, a small farming town on the western outskirts of Dresden. Five years earlier, the town had tried to transform itself overnight from pig sties and tiny apple orchards into Mississauga: the Autobahn was coming to town and Kesselsdorf was going to cash in. By the time we got there, most of the industrial park was surrounded by chain link fences, many permanently closed by rusty chains and big padlocks.

The car eased to a stop in the middle of the street. Eberhard leaned across the steering wheel and pointed over my chest. "They were dreaming. If you came up with a business plan you were given all the money you wanted. No one checked on how the money was spent." Eberhard's breath on my cheek smelled of cologne. He was pointing at the roses planted to greet the crowds coming into the two-storey glass-fronted showroom of a plumbing warehouse. The warehouse was abandoned. The roses had grown matted and wild, like the wall of thorns around Sleeping Beauty's castle. "My friends get together in the pub in the evening and they say it's time we put the damned Wall back up to keep those bastards away from us. They ruined their country. Don't let them ruin ours."

Later that night, Barbara, the young woman behind the bar of our hotel, poured us beer in tall thin glasses. She had long black hair like coal and wore a deep blue dress, which set off her fair face and her cool, appraising eyes. Except for a group of Mexicans touring Dresden with an Italian tour company, we were the only guests in her hotel. Barbara didn't let her disappointment show. She joked with us in her Saxon dialect. The dialect pushed most sounds to the front of her mouth, so that with every word she spoke she sounded as if she was laughing good-naturedly, shaping her lips into a small grin. I was charmed.

"You don't understand," Eberhard said, as Barbara washed glasses, waiting for us to finally go to bed. Little did she know she was going to have a long wait: Eberhard loves nothing in the world more than closing down a bar—that sense of being the last celebrant in the silence of the night is his idea of civility, something he learned when Germany was just a pile of bricks between the pile of bricks that was Poland and the pile of bricks that was France. This was a challenge Barbara was not going to win. Those glasses were washed and straightened up again and again. "Germany used to be the most powerful country in Europe," Eberhard went on, after calling Barbara over to pour us another beer. "Economically. Now France is."

I blew the foam off my beer and took a sip. Barbara had begun to set up the tables for the Mexicans' breakfast.

The next day, we sheltered from the July heat at a streetside table in a shady Dresden alley. A few tables back, a band was practising, cutting into shreds every tune they knew. We were trying to talk over the noise. Eberhard motioned the waiter over and asked him to shut the band up. The waiter just stared blankly and walked past. Eberhard turned to me. "It's just like 1950 in the West. They played shit like that then, too."

I was thinking of our trip east and of the McDonald's signs towering seventy metres over the small towns in Thuringia to be visible to cars passing at 190 km/h on the Autobahn—or faster. Anassa, who had spent every school night during the preceding five months playing trumpet in a concert band, a touring band, a jazz band, and a stage band, was smiling and tapping along with her toe. The waiter swept past towards the musicians with another tray of beer. I winced at an especially loud trumpet solo. *Jingle Bells.*

"Jingle Bells! I don't believe it!"

Eberhard made a dismissive gesture in the band's direction, and cupped both of his hands around his beer glass. Anassa had broken down into laughter.

"What has the West given up?" I asked. "You can't expect the Ossies to make all the movement. They will see reunification as Americanization." Sweat beaded on Eberhard's forehead. Anassa had a glazed-over look. I soldiered on. "The younger generation will heal it all," I said, hoping to catch Anassa's attention. I didn't. "It will just take time."

"We used to be the richest country in Europe." Eberhard's words were muffled by the band. His sad Silesian eyes hung down. "We had the strongest economy."

"It doesn't matter. Look at what you have gained. There's never been a country that has had this chance before."

Eberhard looked up in obvious distress. He spoke quietly, almost as if throwing the words away. "It matters to me." You could have cut the air with a knife.

In my own country, when I was two years old and my brother was three, we found a big rattlesnake in the weedy grass. We didn't know that it was dangerous, and started poking it with a couple of sticks. The snake struck at the sticks, and rattled, and we giggled and poked it again, and again and again. We kept poking, the sun kept shining, the snake kept striking and rattling, like a rattle you give to a baby in a stroller, except a lot more fun.

That's when our mother came walking towards us in her red and black logger's shirt and tan slacks. Then she screamed. Before we knew it, she ordered us into the house and told us not to come out for a week. The scene burned into me: my face pressed up against the cold glass, the bright sun on the dust, my mother beating the snake over and over again with a straw broom. The broom came down on the snake and the snake flew up in the air, and the broom came down on the snake and the snake flew up in the air, and it went on and on and on in silence.

Within five minutes my father burst in running from the trees. He grabbed a shovel and chopped off the snake's head. My mother collapsed sobbing into his arms.

—

It was the Wild West. The road leading east to Osoyoos was the old stagecoach road. It wound around boulders, snaked over hills, and washed out in the rains. In the summers, fans of dust streamed behind us; we slid out on all the corners. In the winters, the car spun out on the black ice, doing long loop-de-loops on the hills, spiralling down and down and down, like a figure skater making a perfect triple jump as the lights of the town rose up to meet us in a sparkling necklace along the lake. If my father had to fix a flat tire—and there were often flat tires—he first stuck his head out of the window and checked for rattlesnakes. There were often rattlesnakes. My father used to joke that they were responsible for a lot of the flats when they struck out at the tires.

—

Those were the days when the "British" in British Columbia really meant something: wool coats with wooden toggles, maypole dances to usher in the windy spring, lipstick, Marmite. The rest of it was just gas stations, hot cars, drive-ins, corn on the cob, baseball: American. In all of that, to be Canadian meant rather little—the mountains perhaps. When my uncle Michael came over from Germany in 1974, my father took him to meet some cowboys and Indians. In this country, cowboys don't go around in ten-gallon hats, with spurs and chaps. They wear blue jeans and baseball caps that say "John Deere" and "Cat." The Indians wear the cowboy hats, but they also wear blue jeans. It's hard on tourists. After fifteen minutes at the K-Mountain Inn, as the billiard balls clacked against each other while cool glasses of pale yellow beer trembled gently on the felt corners of the table, Michael asked, "Why do you get all these tourists here in your bar?"

"They aren't tourists. They're Canadians."

Michael was not going to be put off that easily. He had a pretty good ear. "They're all speaking differently. Where are they from?"

"Well," said Michael to me thirty years later, "your father pointed to one guy playing pool and said, 'He's from France,' and to another guy and said, 'He's from Italy,' and this guy was from Hungary and that guy was from Russia, and they all spoke a different kind of English. I could hardly understand them. 'They're all Canadians,' your father said. I could hardly believe it."

In those days, government clerks had English accents. The announcers on CBC Radio spoke with BBC élan. Anyone with a position of governmental authority spoke with an Oxford tweak. Men wore Harris Tweed, white dress shirts, and striped ties. Vauxhalls and Mini Minors rolled down the highways among the Chevys and Studebakers. Every day at school we sang "God Save the Queen." We learned "God Save the King," just in case. We learned to draw the Union Jack. We did not consider England to be a part of Europe. Kids in high school, with their heads full of milkshakes and drag races by the river, were still reading John Keats as if he were a modern poet and one of our own. He was. We weren't singled out for this treatment, either. This was the same message that was given to generations of school kids throughout the British Empire, from Cape Town to Nairobi to Peshawar, from Singapore to Halifax. All of them had lives and worlds around them desperately needing to be understood, celebrated, and put into art, and all of them learned that one lesson of what art, in the Empire, really was. My Grade 6 teacher proudly showed us the world, stabbing at the map with a long wooden pointer, here and here and here, to demonstrate to us how one quarter of the earth's surface was pink. "That is the British Empire," he told us—while Tet was coming down in Vietnam.

The mothers of my friends went around in wool coats, silk scarves, bobbed hair, and bright red lipstick: the tricks that had won them their devil-may-care soldier husbands. We ate English breakfasts of eggs, sausage, bacon, and toast. The bacon had to be fried to a crisp. That was the rule. We ate canned peas out of a tin—a tasteless paste. Although none of us could pronounce Worcestershire sauce, it was available in every grocery store, along with HP Sauce, Keen's Mustard, and McIntosh's Toffee. The 5 Cents to a Dollar Store in Keremeos sold English galoshes, with silver buckles and a lot of loose, flapping rubber. They were terribly cold when the weather got down to thirty-five below. We read *Blackie's Boys' Annual*. We sang "It's a long way to Tipperary." The training was pretty intense.

We were like nineteenth-century Welsh peasants, never journeying over the hill, never moving more than an hour's walk from home in their lives. We had extended the distance to about a half-hour's drive, but that was it. We even had our own dialect. It was a subtle thing, raspy and windy and full of grass and dust like the valley, flattened out, slow and drawn out from butting up against Washington for so many years. When I went to Victoria in 1975 to study theatre, I was given a voice coach straightaway to teach me how to speak English. Friends who had grown up on Saltspring Island and Vancouver Island could hardly believe the way I talked.

"You sound like you come from a foreign country," they said.

―

Within the limits set by our tiny bit of England, we lived a cosmopolitan life. We listened to Petula Clark on the radio, singing about the bright lights of London, while we rode into town on the slick grey vinyl seats of the fruit truck, with five tons of apples or pears or tomatoes stacked up behind us and my father going through the gears on the way past the hayfields and orchards—and sometimes losing a half ton of tomatoes in a big splat on the road, or driving through the mess of someone else's dropped load: the big news of the day. On Friday nights, downtown Keremeos was as brightly lit as Broadway. For those end-of-the-week, let-your-hair-down trips to the Lucky Dollar Foods and the 5 Cents to a Dollar Store and the Rexall Drugs, we had a bath, slicked our hair back with Brylcreem, and put on our best clothes—black pants and white shirts and shiny black shoes. This was church. It might only have been a trip five miles up the valley, but in those days coming down the big hill into Keremeos, that welfare and service town of eight hundred and fifty souls, was like landing in West Berlin during the blockade. No trip to Vancouver or Toronto or San Francisco today, with a stretched white limo bringing you in from the airport, was more exciting than the golden light shining out of those shop windows into the night.

―

Hollywood casts the 1960s with bell bottoms and psychedelic green stick-on flowers, peace symbols, long-haired men, women in gingham dresses, sex, drugs, the Beatles, the Rolling Stones, assassination, war and protest. In the mountains of British Columbia, it wasn't quite like that. In the back of the 5 Cents to a Dollar Store there were shelves of gumboots and GWG work boots, racks of cheap clothing, bolts of fabric, skeins of wool stacked up in rainbow colours like Easter eggs, sewing notions—buttons on paper cards—children's games and puzzles, models of battleships and tiger tanks, Sopwith Camels and Spitfires, Lancaster bombers and Messerschmitts, B-52 bombers and Stuka dive bombers, with little jars of paint to add ocean or desert camouflage; there were linens, tablecloths, and plain white pillowcases that my mother embroidered in the afternoons. A generation earlier, penniless in the Depression, her mother, who had received needlepoint lessons as a girl, was sewing flowers onto flour sacks. By 1970, my mother had switched over to Liquid Embroidery®, painting the needlepoint on from a collection of tubes with ballpoint tips.

The front of the store was devoted to a whole table laid out with titles by Enid Blyton. By the time I finished a childhood of watching rockslides crackle down the slopes in the spring and mountain goats drift across the cliffs like scattered patches of snow, I knew more about being a child in England than I did about being one in Canada. I went on summer holidays on the Welsh coast. I picked eggs from puffin nests as the sea spun away dizzyingly below. I watched dogs herd sheep in the Dales. I wore scratchy tweed. Storms rattled the black-casemented windows and boys and girls stole out in rowboats in the night. Robin Hood was my brother. Guy Fawkes was my name. And I didn't skate. I had heard that it was a Canadian thing to do, but skating was a ridiculous proposition in the lower Similkameen, where the only ice was on the slough—only safe to skate on for a week, rough with upwellings of algae, with stumps and logs sticking through to trip you up, and little fish frozen in the ice.

Instead, I knew a lot about English school holidays, ancient treasure washed up from the Spanish Armada, King Arthur, the Isle of Man, the

Irish coast, and the loneliness of English public school life. I grew up in England. Canada didn't exist beyond the valley walls.

In the afternoons, my mother typed letters for the farm, hunched over her Arborite table cooking the books like an accountant in a backroom in Chicago. She added endless streams of numbers on an old manual adding machine. The total always came out in red.

When the table was finally cleared away on those bill-paying afternoons, my mother cooked: macaroni, ground beef, garlic sausage, pork and beans, potatoes—three of them boiled, the rest stirred up in a blackened cast-iron pan. If it was lunch time, it was Kraft Velveeta cheese on white bread. The cheese came in big bricks, next to the lard, on the bottom of the dairy cooler. The bread came in bigger, but lighter, bricks, from a shelf near the till. It was as weightless as angel food cake. Sometimes there was summer sausage, with its mustard seeds. I spit that stuff back out. There were no onions or garlic. The main spice in the house was ketchup. Needless to say, I was a skinny runt. As my brother and I grew older, my mother used to lay a big butcher knife between her plate and the dessert, which she had set down on the table to her left: a marble cake, usually. There was no icing. This thing was going to be gone too quickly for the effort of making icing to be worthwhile—or even for taking the cake out of the pan. My mother thought in efficiencies like that.

"You can have as many pieces of cake as you want," she said, "as long as you are quicker than my knife." That knife was quick. And it was no bluff—she meant it, bringing the sharpened blade down on the table with a big whack when we reached for a second piece.

My mother was not one for weakness or irrationality. She had the hard core of a judge on the Supreme Court Bench. When I left home, for instance, she decided I'd have to learn to look after myself. She taught me to scramble an egg and to make a box of Kraft Dinner.

"There," she said. "Now I've done my duty as a mother. Now I know you won't starve to death."

My mother had wanted to be a lawyer, but had the opportunity snatched away from her by society, children, marriage, and too many years spent stirring her tears into the fried potatoes. The air was ripe for revolution. When I was fourteen, the revolution came. Women's Liberation was in the air and the conversation around my mother's hair-dressing mornings with her friends changed overnight—became cynical, even conspiratorial, like that of a communist cell in Germany during the 1920s.

My mother went on strike. She presented my father, my brother, my sister and me with a list of work to be done around the house, neatly typed on her old Olympia. It was a long list. She must have spent the whole previous afternoon typing it up in a cool rage while my brother, my sister and I were at school and my father was out wheeling and dealing in apple politics. My mother wrote a manifesto. She had obviously improvised freely on the account ledgers she was supposed to be balancing. One column of her balance sheet was headed "Slave." The other was headed "Everyone Else." Slave's column was full to the bottom of the page, with a range of duties including bookkeeping, secretarial work, shopping, making coffee, cooking meals, doing dishes, sweeping, vacuuming, mopping floors, sewing, and laundry. Everyone Else's column was empty.

That night, my father cooked spaghetti with ketchup—his specialty—tinned mushrooms fried in butter, and potato pancakes with lots of salt, blowing his whole repertoire on one meal. My mother did not eat with us. She had already cooked herself a tin of Campbell's Cream of Mushroom Soup and had taken to bed.

As the years went by, Country and Western albums about tumbleweeds and little dogies, on a rack by the Lucky Dollar meat counter, were replaced by the soundtrack to *The Green Berets*. I fingered the albums, then walked on past the frozen rump roasts; even though I had watched marines being shot, wounded, and medevacked out every night at dinner since TV first came into our house in 1963, I had no idea what a Green Beret was.

Every October, the Five Cents to a Dollar Store next door pulled out all the stops: costumes of Indian braves with chicken-feather headdresses, costumes of pirates with black eye patches, costumes of gypsies with black veils, and costumes of princesses with tiaras and pink gossamer, all hung on a rack by the front door. On Hallowe'en, children tramped from farm to farm, or among the tumble-down houses in town, dressed in that English country fair finery. Old ladies asked us to sing for our candy. That was unbearable: children in our time did not sing! That was something out of a distant, fusty past, and it terrified me speechless—and motionless. Other kids with more wherewithal just bolted and ran.

The "Trick" in "Trick or Treat" was the important part of Hallowe'en in the '60s. Our first year on the farm, Hallowe'en lost us the mailbox from the end of our driveway. At first, my father thought he had been singled out for being German. A few phone calls cleared that up: some kids had driven down the road in the starry dark and had lassoed everyone's mailbox from the back of a pickup. The boxes showed up the next day twenty miles away, floating and sinking in Richter Lake, on the stagecoach road halfway to Osoyoos. Men from town drove down there together and hauled them out. Every year, high-school boys dismantled the pile of five hundred cinderblock bricks beside the irrigation building, nestled in the cactus a quarter mile down the road from our orchard, and set them in a wall across the asphalt. Anyone driving along had to keep their wits about them: the wall could show up at any time.

That became the town prank. Everyone in Cawston knew that at some point on Hallowe'en the wall was going to be built, but never by whom, and never exactly when. Every year a new group of fathers prowled the roads, trying to put an end to it, not knowing if their own sons were involved or not. It was so dark those nights they wouldn't have been able to identify them anyway. At best, they'd make out black shapes loping off into the blacker night and melting away among the trees. Other men, not necessarily fathers, banded together and roamed in groups, trying to protect their property. Phones rang off the hook as men passed sightings down the road. Men slammed down their phones, leaped out of their doors, and tore off in their trucks to intercept the culprits on the roads. Vigilante groups formed to stop all kids driving around that night, and to grill them about what they were doing. Hazards on the roads included thirty- and forty-foot aluminum irrigation pipes dragged out of orchards to block traffic and lines of flaming gasoline ignited on the asphalt. There were smashed fences and houses pelted with eggs. Every year, all the windows at the school were whitewashed with soap. On November 1 every year, the town looked like a war zone. People drove around to see just what damage had been done.

Our days at the end of Empire were numbered, though, because while my mother was making small talk with the Italian grocer in the Lucky Dollar, or while the whole family was window shopping at Blakeborough's Appliances, behind our backs on Main Street sixteen-year-old boys were cruising up and down the two blocks of downtown in their hopped-up Fords and Chevys. They made U-Turns at the Tastee Freez, then rumbled into the Victory Hall for the Thursday Night Teentown dances. It was straight out of *American Graffiti*. That was the deal about living in a border town: there were high-speed drag races up and down the eighteen miles of road that curved north along the river, curling around tiny native graveyards, following every bend and oxbow to the old mining town of Hedley. Cars crashed. Boys died. Not surprisingly, under this onslaught, and under the pressure of the tens of thousands of young Americans who hitchhiked through the valley from 1969 to 1973, by 1975 the chintzy English kitsch had vanished from the Five and Dime. I accepted the disappearance of the gypsies and pirates and of Enid Blyton from the counters in the same way I welcomed the end of childhood. I was glad to accept the gradual replacement of these old favourites with a whole army of toys by Mattel, all certified authentic because they had been advertised on TV. You just couldn't top that. As far as the "British" in British Columbia went, well, that was just old history. For us, the border that ran across the valley twenty minutes south of town was invisible. In the battle between Scotland Yard and the Fonz, the Yanks had won.

Or so it seemed, until I toured the English Midlands in 1999, reading poetry to diplomats, ex-pats, librarians, teachers, the elderly, and even a few poets who poofed their hair like John Lennon. Many of them came up to me after my readings and told me that they had been very glad to have heard me, that my poetry gave them hope. "So much poetry in our country is bloody depressing," they said. "English poets can only write poetry when they are in a funk, but you write it when you're happy. We can't relate to American poetry; English poetry leaves us cold. Yours lies in the middle: it is recognizably English, yet it has a spark of the American in it."

As soon as I landed in Britain I had known I was home. If it hadn't been for a few old buildings (and surprisingly few), I could have been back in British Columbia, except that in England I felt a stronger sense of belonging. With a few spare hours in Derby, on my last English afternoon, I searched for presents to take back to my girls. I found a lovely pink feather boa for my youngest, so she could dress up and pretend to be her deepest dreams, even, perhaps, a fairy. Not long after that, I found my childhood. There on the back streets of Derby, a few blocks north and east of the overpriced antique and souvenir shops, away from the Stalinesque shop selling crafts from utilitarian wooden racks in a big warehouse, and the myriad sheet, towel, and home decor merchants, I found not one but three trick-and-joke shops, selling stink bombs, itching powder, hand-staining black soap, whoopee cushions, costumes of Indian braves with chicken-feather headdresses, costumes of pirates with black eye patches, costumes of gypsies with black veils, and costumes of princesses with tiaras and pink gossamer. Every last dazzling bit of English kitsch that had decorated my dreams when I was a boy in the British Columbia desert was there—still alive, still produced, and still filling the dreams of children. The Fonz was not triumphant after all. All those stories of gypsy story-tellers and Punch and Judy and caravans in Ireland came back to me, Enid Blyton filled my head, and I suddenly understood that those gimcracks had not been replaced by a natural growth out of childhood. Instead, in British Columbia, rather than gaining our independence from Empire, we had simply traded one empire for another.

Mozzarella, Gorgonzola, Camembert, Cervelat, kielbasa, sourdough, and ciabatta were all unknown in that valley, where the rattlesnakes used to lie out on the roads along the bluffs, catching a little sun. You had to watch it when you came around the corner on your bike. All around the world, people were eating food that was a delight. Rushing home on our bicycles from changing our sprinkler lines after school, we were eating the products of industrial test kitchens: Velveeta, Cheez Whiz, Dream Whip, Wonder Bread, Spam, Bologna. War rations. We were being fed to keep us from starving to death.

Money was tight. My friends' mothers came over once a month to do each other's hair with Clairol Home Permanent kits. A perm down at the beauty salon was out of their budgets, but one of those Clairol jobs cost a quarter the price. The women sat around my mother's kitchen table all afternoon, putting each other's hair up in curlers, drinking thin percolated coffee, smoking cigarettes, and eating little egg salad and tuna sandwiches cut into triangles, with the crusts trimmed off, just as they had all learned in Grade 10 Home Economics. The table was covered with bowls and towels, with scissors and scraps of hair, and with bags of curlers, like torture instruments. The air stank. The kitchen became an alchemist's workshop in sixteenth-century Prague. I had never had sandwiches like those ones, either, and tried one when it was offered. They were virtually flavourless and almost completely textureless—unless their pastiness between the teeth was deliberate. The women laughed and tossed them back. With their wild, alien heads done up in curls and their red-stained fingernails holding smoking cigarettes, they looked like models. They were all *so* nice. I never could understand why they would light a cigarette and then let it burn away between their fingers as they talked and talked and talked, but they did, only butting the cigarettes out in an ashtray when it looked like the ash was going to collapse on its own. Their cars cluttered the driveway. On those days, my father didn't even come in for coffee. He said his yard had been turned into a used car lot.

—

With my father, it was different. Down at the garage, I scuffled around in the weeds out back, while he drank moonshine with the mechanic who fixed his tractor, patched his tires, and welded his steel water mains when they rusted through and turned the orchard into a sinkhole. Strange gears poked out of dirt. With the moonshine, there was always a lot of time to explore. A trip like that could take half the afternoon.

"Helping your Dad?" the mechanic asked, a cigarette hanging out of blue lips, a grizzle of beard on his chin, oil soaked into the skin of his fingers, as he emerged, bottle in hand, from the back of the deep gloom.

I nodded and said in a very quiet voice, "Yes," and he brought me a bottle of cream soda from the pop cooler, with the pop on racks in ice water. He wiped it off with an oily rag, flipped off the cap with a pair of pliers and handed it to me. I sat down among the weeds and drank while the moonshine did its work.

On a cold December night when I was in Grade 2, stars filled the narrow band of black sky between the mountains. In the warm, echoing school and the smell of oil heat, among pink, blue, and yellow flowers tied out of tissue paper, I saw angels that night. I heard them sing old songs that men have sung for a thousand years, angels with wings of wire and tinsel, who looked remarkably like the girls from Grade 7. They moved effortlessly among us Brylcreemed boys. We were scared to be alone in the cold classrooms, while they slipped in and out, running down the halls, singing snatches of holy songs. That night, the moon hung suspended on a string, the stars were cut from cardboard, bright with tinfoil, and we shivered, uncomfortable in our pressed white shirts and bow ties, somehow far too formal for that smell of chalk, as the dark pressed its mouth against the glass, trying to get in.

What saved that night was the thin voices of the girls from seventh grade singing on the stage as the light shone in their eyes and people watched and sang along behind the light. We all needed that belief. Every night we ate our roasts, poured gravy, kept our elbows off the tablecloth, and watched the war in Vietnam, the young men dead, who would soon be us, the blood held up in bags, yet there we were, singing angels on the night they said God was born and man was raised from folly. I have never heard any song more beautiful than those angels—except maybe my mother singing *Good King Wenceslas*, when the girl in her came out in her voice, all the freedom of that song and the heartbreak of her childhood, giving a depth to my year and binding me with time.

Sometimes my mother told me *Goldilocks and the Three Bears* or *Little Red Riding Hood* or about the dog she had when she was a girl. Night after night she read me stories from *The Fairy Tales of the Brothers Grimm* and *The Fairy Tales of Hans Christian Andersen*, with tipped-in coloured plates and golden vines and flowers twining around the spines—the last gasp of the nineteenth century. The plates were rarely set in at the same place as the stories, and I spent many hours in the afternoons paging through the books to locate the pictures and studying them in great detail. There was also a copy of *Struwwelpeter,* the terrifying German children's book, with misbehaving children being cooked and turned into little cookies and pecked up by chickens, along with Struwwelpeter himself, his fingernails growing as long as scimitars, and his wild golden hair. The chickens were served up for Sunday dinner.

My mother was fearful of power and force and the unknown, and brave in the face of it. She was dismissive of people who did not have jobs or homes or who were otherwise not respectable; they had not shouldered their responsibility to make society work, had not tied themselves with the webs of small-town relationships. My mother's distrust was profound. In a valley in which no one locked their doors, she locked hers, so that the hippies who picked our fruit could not sneak in and steal the jewellery off of her dresser, where it sparkled dully among the cold cream jars, in that room where the curtains were always pulled shut.

And there were hippies. They blew through the valley like a wind.

Living in the Similkameen in those years was like being in Haight-Ashbury. The young people of the world were on the road. They came from the choked industrial cities of the United States and the communes of California, they hitchhiked from Montreal and Toronto and Hamburg, with red bandanas wrapped around their foreheads; they came from Tel Aviv and Dublin, they came in military coats, with sergeant's chevrons on their sleeves, straight from peacekeeping on Cyprus; they came from London and Copenhagen, from Sydney and Cape Town, and they all passed through our valley on their way to India, on their way to the Kibbutz, on their way to Heidelberg and Gdansk, or on their way back, looking for work to keep them on the road or to take them home again or to buy them their next hit of acid. They had no ties to us or our way of life, except in our ability to fit them into late colonial agricultural society, with which they were familiar from Kenya and Australia, New Zealand, Burma, and Morocco. In consequence, when they first came, they were treated like gypsies: disreputable and dirty and corrupting. I loved them.

Before they arrived in our valley, they slept the night among the wild sunflowers that carpeted the basalt hills at the Kaleden Junction. The next day, they lined up under the bristling hot pines. The men were dressed mostly in cast-off clothes from the American Army. The women dressed like their great-grandmothers might have done in prairie schooners squeaking across the continent to Oregon. They were largely on the road to protest the US Army's program of slaughter and poison in South Vietnam, which they saw as nothing of their own lives, and to protest history, to renounce it, to start all over again and get it right.

The day I first saw hippies, cicadas were screeching from the dry roadside as we drove up to a line of them and my mother told us in a clenched voice, "Quick! Lock the doors!" We drove home past them, up the hills in the hot wind. As we cruised through, some of them jumped onto the road in front of us—many of them carrying guitars—

and begged for us to give them a ride. Others ran their fingers over the car as we passed, for a quarter mile, as if we were sitting in Kennedy's limo as it cruised through Dallas before the bullets started to fly. It was 100 degrees Fahrenheit. My mother didn't hesitate. As the hitchhikers surged onto the road in front of her, she clenched her jaw, set her gaze straight ahead, tightened her fingers on the steering wheel, and hit the accelerator. I asked my mother why we hadn't stopped to pick up a hitchhiker.

"There are too many of them," she said, trying to sound reasonable, the fear gone out of her voice. "If we stopped, they'd all try to get a ride, and they'd steal our car and kill us. We can't give a ride to all of them, so we have to just drive on and ignore them." I thought it was pretty dumb. I liked the look of those guitars.

Those kids on the road were like the flotsam fleeing before the front in a war, like the men and women and children with their bullocks and bamboo carts in Vietnam, pushing one way down the roads while the Americans pushed against them in a snarl of jeeps and chickens and crying children. It all looked so pointless on TV, as if they would all be better off if they just stopped where they were.

Twenty years earlier, it was my great grandmother, Auguste Leipe, who was running before the storm, clutching a small, black cardboard suitcase, and maybe, just maybe, even a Bible, evading the Russians on the back roads, hiding in the ditches as American planes strafed the columns. One Sunday a month, it was my father. We'd pull into Customs at Oroville, Washington. As soon as my father opened his mouth and betrayed himself as a German, the air got chilly, and he'd try to warm it up with a few jokes and a lot of deference, a lot of uncharacteristic "Yes, Sir," this and "Yes, Sir," that. Every time we drove through the peach orchards of Osoyoos for a cruise down through the desert to soak in the power at the Grand Coulee Dam, he began to panic that he might have forgotten his ID at home and would be deported to Germany, and would never see Canada, his wife, his farm, or his children again.

—

When the hitchhikers had made it over the pass, they invariably showed up at our door looking for work. A few struggled in every day, with their bright clothes, their packsacks, and their hunger. My father gave them work, for a few days, or a week, among the pear trees, before they moved on, restless, trying to see the world for themselves. A few days, or a week, of standing still was all they could stand. Many of them couldn't even last out a day. My father invited some of them in for dinner, talked politics, and cracked open a beer for them. Our house became a German pub. My mother had grown up in the North: after a few initial questions about where the boys, and sometimes the girls, were from, what their families were like, and some comments about their home countries, designed to show that she, too, was a woman of the world and as knowledgeable about the Empire and history as anyone, my mother never took part in any of these conversations. While she cooked and served and cleared the table and did the dishes and brought out more beer and plunked it down, though, I sat there, and did not understand about the bitter politics of farming, the American draft, the Russian invasion of Czechoslovakia, or the degree to which the state has the right to interfere in our lives, although that talk shaped my life as completely as the meadowlarks outside in the grasslands up against the burnt rock of the mountain. I understood perfectly, though, that my father was a hippie too, which was a shock, I tell you.

One night, the talk was about Jews. The air was suddenly tense, and though I had never heard of a Jew before, when my father said he liked Jews just as much as other men, I sensed there was something that my German father and that young Jewish man circled around and never touched, yet which I needed to understand well and could not, because I did not yet know what a Jew was. The next day, I asked my parents, but all they did was exchange worried glances and say that a Jew was a person, just like any other person. That was just no help. It was obviously not true. I felt pushed aside.

As the years went by, fruit farmers from Washington came up in their big Cadillacs, and talked of money and infrared packing line technology, and the damned EPA that would put them out of business soon, of their thousand-acre orchards, their money, and how good DDT had been to them. I asked my father about the EPA. He told me it was a government agency in the United States that was set up by a bunch of hippies to protect the environment.

"It has more power than it deserves," my mother added, her voice tense, as it always is when she gets defensive. "They are stopping people from farming."

"They are passing laws to force people not to use chemicals," added my father. "They are a bunch of communists." He didn't say it with bile. He said it in a very level, matter-of-fact tone of voice.

My mother had an opinion about this as well, and she was not going to miss the chance to make sure her son understood how the world was being dragged into ruin by people who had never done an honest day's work in their lives. The list of these unsavoury people, these half-citizens, would soon to go on to include Dave Barrett, the premier of British Columbia in 1971, who had started as a social worker. That was beneath contempt to my mother. "He has never worked a day in his life," she said. "And he thinks he can run the province!"

"It's not chemicals that are the problem," she said about the EPA, "but how they are used. The bureaucrats are going to put people out of business." Bureaucrats were sub-citizens to her, because they, too, were not part of the tightly knit culture in which she had been raised. "They have no right."

Not so well anchored in the North, my father tried the scientific approach. "All the chemicals we apply on the farm are organophosphates," he said, in a conciliatory voice as smooth and murmuring as any politician's. "They are organic. That means they are natural chemicals. These people who are fighting against them are criminal. Not only that, they're stupid. They don't know what they're talking about."

After that, I looked on the Washington orchardists with a degree of pity: they were victims of a government that knew nothing about the needs of the people who were keeping the citizens of the country alive by producing food for them.

Otherwise, I hated them. They came in smelling of Listerine and whiskey, with their polyester summer suits and their bald heads with long strands of hair combed over them and their blue stubble chins and their loud politics and harsh judgements. They wanted Goldwater for president. They wanted to "drop the Atomic bomb on the gooks" and put an end to "the problem over there." They were as frustrated as all hell that their Army was not doing that. Their ideas of boyhood—cars, machines, guns, sports—excluded me. All I wanted was trees, water, animals, plants, and independence. They looked at trees as something to farm, to own, to squeeze.

When the Americans were inside our house, the sun outside glinted off the windshields of their big Cadillacs. The orchard mud of our driveway was spattered on the magnetic advertising signs on their doors. The Yanks came with bottles of whiskey and splashed them around in my mother's glasses, or opened the magnums of Canadian Club my father had run down to buy across the line in Oroville, Washington, where it was cheaper than it was back at home—as if we always had rye whiskey in our house. My father spoke earnestly of his desire to farm among them, who understood well what the '60s were all about, which the farmers in our valley of mosquito green light, corn roasts up the Ashnola River, and cooperative packing houses certainly did not. The Americans were mechanizing. They understood that the '60s, and the future, were all about opportunities and turning a back on the past, and not about community. Community, however, was what the farmers of the Similkameen, and my mother's parents, and my mother, and I, were looking for. Ironically, my mother had married my father to ensure the survival of that community.

My father often talked about moving down among the Americans, but he never did: not until the '60s were over and it was too late. He stayed in Canada, because while my brother and I turned brown in the heat, watching fighters from Spokane practice maneuvers in the clear blue air just over the border at the bottom of the reserve, the sons of those American fruit growers were being driven insane, had come back from 'Nam to the big fruit ranches above the Okanogan and Yakima and Columbia rivers unable to do the hard work of taking over those great industrial farms with their three hundred wetback labourers and their tractor crews and packing lines, too drunk and stoned and fucked up to drive around in convertibles hooked up with radio telephones and electric thermometers, and there was no way my father was going to subject his sons to that.

What my mother wanted or thought was private. The same thing went for the American wives. When they visited, stepping into the heat out of their husbands' Cadillacs like Hollywood stars, they first boasted about their husbands' achievements, how many acres had been planted, how many tons of cherries they had picked that year; then they talked about their children, how the boys were beginning to take over; then, when the tea or the iced tea or the lemonade was flowing freely and the apologies about the plain dishes to put the cookies on had been made and accepted, because they were all farm women, after all, and daughters of the Depression, they relaxed and started to tell stories about their husbands: silly, reckless, childish stuff. My mother jumped right in, and they all laughed along, and I sat with them, a little to the side, enjoying the banter, the honesty within their voices, and revelling, like them, in these small moments of freedom.

"That conversation was so stiff," my mother said, years later. "We tried to make polite conversation, but we had absolutely nothing to talk about."

In 1969, my father made his plunge: he bought the Richter Ranch in Upper Keremeos from an American vegetable grower who had been forced out of Los Angeles a decade earlier when his land values—and taxes—had gone through the roof. My father's dream was to plant the four hundred and fifty acres into apples, and pack a million boxes of apples every year. My mother's dream was the old ranch house, a palatial piece of Victorian colonial history. The immigrant's daughter, shoved off into the bush to live or die as God saw fit, was going to get back her Canada—the Canada of the land—with sweet revenge.

At 2:00 AM, my father often took it upon himself to teach young men how to play skat—an old German card game resurrected by the Nazis. When he was riding the swells of the North Atlantic on his way to Canada, he learned the most important component of the game: to roar with rage. Skat is a game of deceptions and ruses, of tricks and partners, and sheer dumb luck. There is plenty to rage about, and lots of room for logic and keeping track of the cards, a task made only more difficult by the vast amount of beer necessary to play the game. In those years, playing skat was the one thing my father did that was just for my brother and me alone.

I always was very happy that there was a war in Vietnam. It kept me from living among those men who talked of packing lines all the time, back then when the hippies picked pears in the nude and my twelve-year-old brother had the job of trying to convince them that to shake all the pears onto the ground and to pick them up from there was not good for the pears.

—

If the pickers made my father angry, they sent my mother into a rage. My mother was already living in a past and a country about which the hippies with their gingham and their long hair full of flowers were only guessing. She knew it as a tough and ruthless place. The rest of us, though, didn't have her knowledge, didn't know what we had. We all longed, in our own way, to get out, to leave, to get onto the road. For my father it was to the United States, the John Birch Society, the billboards, "If the US government took over the Sahara desert, within ten years they would run out of sand," and the five-mile-long caravans of dark green trucks heading for the docks in San Francisco. For my brother, it was to join a bike gang, on the road, with the soundtrack to *Easy Rider* pounding through his blood. For me, it was to join those hippies, to pick fruit on the orchards, among young women with beautiful long hair, and to own nothing, maybe not even any clothes. You can't blame us, I guess: everyone came to our valley of grassy light, the swish of Rainbird sprinklers on the air, for which the rattlers came down, laying themselves out right along the sprinkler pipes—you had to watch where you put your hands—and every one of them left again. *That* was our education in politics. My friends and I talked about it a lot, and grew our hair long. My brother, who had started to stash a Bible in the back pocket of his jeans when he went off on his Norton 500, to make it easier to pick up girls, asked me once, "If you saw a biker broken down beside the road, would you stop and help him?"

"Yes, of course."

"Well, then you are a better person than most people. Most people wouldn't." He roared off with his Bible and the broken foot he had earned from trying to kick-start that old Norton. I too left to follow a girl to Victoria, and soon discovered that I was not a hippie, whatever else I was.

So it went for all of my friends, and there was not one of us who came back from our travels unchanged, who did not wonder where those young people went, what they remembered of their few weeks picking fruit there, at the centre of the world, or if they just remembered nothing. I still wonder what the Irish students—the impossibly beautiful woman with long black hair, the tall, laughing men—made of my lectures on how to pick Red Delicious apples, and my deductions from their wages for sloppy work. I wonder if they remember how they had held back their anger and said, "Whatever you want. Do whatever you want," rather than get into a fight with a skinny kid with a fascist attitude. The hot wind curled over the highway gravel after they were gone, and soon we were gone too, and the orchards curled up, the leaves on the trees like flames in the desert light.

When I came back, I had grown into a stranger and had to start again with nothing, in pickers' shacks, drinking wine, in the late '70s, after the war in Vietnam. By then, my parents had moved at last, to farm cherries in the shadow of the Hanford plutonium processing plant, where the Bomb was birthed, and were screwed by one of their very good friends. It wasn't long before they too came back with nothing at all to show for the '60s except bewilderment, because not one of those young men and women who were on the road picking fruit told us that what takes you away, what gives you the world, is not that which brings you home: what brings you home is the knowledge that you have no other place to go. What they also did not tell us is that you come home again and see the place, for the very first time, as a place well worth leaving, and a place well worth coming back to, all at the same time, and that it did not matter whether you went to Vietnam or not, because we were at the end of the road.

My mother had known it all along.

—

My father was fighting his own demons. One day he took me aside and told me how in the Russian Revolution all the men were lined up; if they did not have the calloused, dirty hands of a labourer, they were stood up against a wall and shot. "Remember that," he said. And I did. Actually, I went right outside and got dirty in the mud puddles on the driveway, where red insect eggs drifted in the wind. When I came back in I was careful not to wash too well. I wore those dirty hands as a badge of honour.

—

One spring afternoon in 1964 when my brother was at school and I was bored to dizziness, my father was burning the whole apricot orchard, where just two years before he had carried me from tree to tree in a picking bag slung over his shoulders and the dappled light had wafted over me in endless afternoons. I was allowed to light the match. I ran back quickly with laughing men as flame licked up, roaring, in defiance to my mother, who stayed inside where wind shook windows. I was a man among men. I lost my eyelashes that day. So did the men. We all came in with little curls of white above our eyes. My mother was appalled. She gave my father a piece of her mind.

"You don't do that with a child," she said. I thought it showed that she was weak.

As the years went by, my father had me crawl down among the trees with an old rubber car tire, a can of diesel fuel and a match, set it all alight, then scurry back up the loose gravel and cactus slope between the web of branches. The trees went up, shadows licked across the grass, ashes fell, the sun darkened, and the wind was given voice, louder than any wind that had roared through the trees when they had stood in their long red rows, with their broad leaves and big, swollen apricots like clamshells. I stared with the men in awe as flame poured forty feet into the air. As I watched, I was fire and smoke and dust and trees going up. Nothing else.

The men ignored me when they started their tractors to push down more trees and to drag them across the trampled earth with chains.

Out on the lawn one day, in the back of the house, not far from where the septic tank bubbled up in a bright green patch of grass against the back wall, I watched my scorpions mate, twining around themselves in an intricate dance, as if they were following the patterns of Irish lace. I thought they were trying to poison each other. I didn't know that they were scorpions—no one except me knew that they were there, so no one could have warned me about them—but I do remember thinking that it looked dangerous.

~The Christmases of Our Defeat~

There are two types of men: those who believe in time and those who believe in space. The men who believe in time believe that Sir John A. MacDonald's imperial inclinations and Marco Polo's first taste of noodles in Beijing permeate the soil of even the smallest mountain valley of British Columbia. The men who believe in space believe in the present, in what they can touch and hold. They believe that trees are wood and stones are rock and there is no history but the history of men who believe in space.

Once there were my grandparents, my great aunt, my second cousin, my parents, my brother, my sister, and me. There was silverware, candlelight, crystal, fine china, and stories filling the dark house. Suddenly someone would shout and we would all rush to the windows. There in the dark it would be snowing. We would watch the crystal flakes drifting down in the few inches of light on the other side of the glass, as the wind swept up off the gravel and saskatoons, Oregon-grape and cactus, slamming into the stucco, pushing hard against the windows. We all laid our hands on the glass and felt it flex in the wind. My mother brought out the crystal glasses she had bought for her hope chest when she was eighteen and working in the railway office up north in Smithers, waiting—praying, actually—to get out of town: lead crystal, with strawflowers cut into the tall, thin glass. In the dim room, the light of the candles caught in the crystal, so that in the wine the candles burned again; all around the table there were tiny yellow candles. The wine was from the Mosel, fruity and pale. The glasses were paper-thin against our lips.

I saw those Christmases on TV in the late '80s, in the German TV miniseries *Heimat*, or Homeland—"Heartland," in American. It was 1933, the first Christmas under the Nazi regime. Everyone sang together in church. Everyone had a job and money and could buy presents for each other that they had been unable to buy for years. As they stepped outside and the Christmas bells echoed over the village, the new snow dusted their faces and they laughed together, "This is the Christmas we have always dreamed of." As my young daughter, Anassa, slept upstairs, I watched in utter fascination and horror. I had thought my Christmases were exactly like everyone else's in Cawston, British Columbia. I had thought there was nothing German about me at all, only a connection with relatives I did not know and would never meet. I was Canadian, and proud of it. But that was my Christmas there, in the Hunsrück, in the high country above Frankfurt, in 1933. There was no evading it.

The country in which these Christmases unfolded was the Okanagan, a land of apple trees and blue mountain ridges falling range on range to the sea, with crickets in the evening and rainbow trout sinking cool in a curve of a creek, a cup of coffee over an Arborite farm table, a pot of pea soup on the stove. In the beginning, Tom Ellis ranched everything from Paradise Ranch sixty miles south to Haynes' place on the border at 'Soyoos. The big pines, the sage and clay benches, the blue creeks running out of the hills in deep arroyos of cottonwoods and dogwood, the lazy oxbows of the Okanagan River, were all his. He could ride his horse for days and never get to the end of it, through deserts of greasewood and creosote-scented antelope brush, past sunbathing rattlers, while red-tailed hawks screamed overhead and blue herons startled out of the lowland scrub. My corner of that country was over the hill in the Similkameen, among the stumps of the first fruit trees in the Interior—sixty acres of pears laid out in a forty-foot grid by Francis (Frank) Xavier Richter, who had come to the American Southwest from

Friedland, Bohemia, in 1863. After being wounded in a skirmish with Indians, he travelled north to the Similkameen the next year. Nestled in a bend of the Keremeos Creek bench at Inglewood, his pear trees lasted for seventy years, the creamy smell of their blossoms wafting through the parlour windows of the California mansion he built to shelter his bride from the Keremeos wind, which my father bought for my mother, and in which she never got to live.

Frank was a restless guy. Inglewood was not his first ranch. His first was on the flats between the big bend of the Similkameen and the hanging valleys of the Barcelo Bluffs. It had been sketched in as an Indian reserve, but Frank got there first and planted thorny black locust trees along his driveway. The reserve wound up in the swamp, tucked out of the way by the border. A portion of that ranch became the townsite of Cawston, when Frank sold out to move on to a bigger spread, the R Ranch, on the Richter Pass, between Chopaka and Spotted Lake. Frank planted locust trees there, and, in 1880, an acre of apple trees from Wm. Clarkson's nursery in New Westminster. In the 1970s, ranchers would pump the lakes of Frank's ranch dry to irrigate their silage fields, but when Frank was there—and when my father arrived there in his Volkswagen seventy years after him—it was pretty well paradise. As my mother explained it to me, Frank's least-known ranch—seemingly a final subdivided parcel of his original one—was on the floodplain at Similkameen Station, on the northern edge of the reserve.

Where the pear trees at Inglewood came from, though, is a matter of local legend: back in 1969, my mother told me they had been packed up the Hudson's Bay Company Brigade Trail from Oregon. My father upped the ante by saying they had come from Johnny Appleseed himself (Well, sure: two generations late and half a continent out of place.) Walla Walla—the only historical contender—is also, sadly, only a rumour. The house, though, was a showpiece. Frank reputedly had the plans and fittings packed up from California, a complete Victorian mansion with a sweeping staircase, a turret, wide, screened verandas (front and back), a formal Victorian parlour, and a dining room that could seat thirty, with a red-painted wooden floor. Mind you, it was still a California house. It had no insulation. Frank did bang on an extra layer of wood all the way around, but that still didn't quite keep out the winter chill. Intriguingly, the Ontario farmer Daniel Freeman left Inglewood, Ontario, to build his own mansion in Inglewood, California in 1888—the intended culmination of a genteel development to turn Los Angeles into the Garden of Eden. What it became, however, was the victim of a real estate slump. Ain't that the way, eh?

Obviously, there were Inglewoods all over the place in those days. There likely was little or no direct connection between Freeman and Richter. Mind you, there certainly was a spiritual connection: Frank's Inglewood had two acres of rose and herb gardens stretched around the parlour and a sweeping driveway lined with honey locust trees. Out front of the house, Frank planted an American Basswood. It looked like one of the lindens of Bohemia. The parlour was a circular room in the bottom of the turret, with a peacock mosaic for a floor. Immediately above it, Frank built a bedroom for his wife, Florence—the turret was her own private sitting room, where she could watch the light rise and fall across the face of K Mountain. A romantic garden, with lilacs and hanging yellow roses, was laid in an island in Keremeos Creek. Years later, Florence's daughter built an artist's studio in the attic, and painted watercolours.

--

When I grew up there, the Okanagan still had an English planter culture—as strong as those of Kenya or Southern Rhodesia. It looked back proudly to 1903, when a visiting American, John Moore Robinson, ate a peach growing in a ranch garden, renamed the area Peachland, and subdivided the old ranches of Louis Riel's Canada into small orchard

Journeys Through a Dark Century - 35

plots. The place was steep. The popular joke of the time was that somebody was going along the road by the lake when a man fell flat on his back in front of him. The man got up and said, "This is a hell of a bloody orchard I've bought; this is the third time this morning I've fallen out of it." We were still telling that joke on the orchards of Naramata in 1977, as if we had just made it up on the spot.

Hot on Robinson's heels, the Kelowna Land and Orchard Company was formed, offering up the East Kelowna benches like petits fours on a silver platter. With a long view over Kelowna and the blue of Okanagan Lake that looked like an extension of the sky, and an even closer view of the McCulloch Hills, dusted with snow or burning with heat haze and the screeches of cicadas in the tinder-dry days of summer, East Kelowna is a rocky deposit left when the glaciers melted eleven thousand years ago and the Okanagan people first moved up the valley. The first European families in East Kelowna arrived from England, lured by real estate brochures printed by the joint London office of the Kelowna Land and Orchard Company, the South Kelowna Land Company, and the Belgo-Canadian Fruit Land Company, back when London was the hub of Empire, and the streets that led like spokes from the wheel of Trafalgar Square—that's to say, from Admiral Nelson standing on his pillar among the pigeons—were crowded with colonial administration offices: British Columbia House, Uganda House, Kenya House, Australia House. British Columbia House now shelters the tourism offices of British Rail. You can go there to buy cheap advance train tickets, as long as you're willing to queue.

There was something about a civilization living for refined tea parties and ideals of the soul that found irresistible the possibility of realizing them on this earth. It was an awful lot like going to Kenya to raise chrysanthemums or pork, though: your markets were a little distant.

Mortgages were typically at ten percent for a three-year term, although you would not get a fruit crop for at least a decade. The money of the British Middle Class was spread throughout the Empire in this way, and dissipated. When the Brits thought of orchards, they thought of pink apple blossoms in the spring, of planters' knives—ivory-handled, silver-bladed, perfectly balanced, and of just the right length to slice an apple in two; they thought of calvados in the evenings, a study lined with books, tea on the veranda, clematis vines, and fruit on the trees in the sun. It was like something out of John Keats or William Morris. In his reply to the address to the Royal Agricultural Society on the occasion of the opening of the New Westminster Exhibition in 1910, Earl Grey, Governor-General of Canada, referred to fruit growing in the Okanagan with the soaring words: "Gentlemen, here is a state of things which appears to offer the opportunity of living under such ideal conditions as struggling humanity has only succeeded in reaching in one or two of the most favoured spots upon the earth."

Much of the scheme was financed from Belgium, which in those days was a darned good place to leave behind: King Leopold II was operating it as a kind of money-laundering operation, to clean up tainted money from the Congo. Wild jungles, Stanley discovering the Nile, the mighty river, gorillas, forest elephants, drumbeats carrying for miles from village to village: such romance! The reality, however, as Conrad wrote in *Heart of Darkness*, as Sven Lindqvist deconstructed in *Exterminate All the Brutes!*, and as Adam Hochschild detailed in all its horror in *King Leopold's Ghost*, was that under the pretence of international humanitarianism, Leopold was actually running a slave camp. Ships left Belgium heavy with ammunition and returned heavy with rubber and ivory. That was the extent of the balance of trade: no foodstuffs, no medicines, no clothing, no machines, no books, nothing. Under Leopold's protective rule, ten million Congolese lost their lives. In its heyday, the Congo made Auschwitz look like small-town America in the

1950s, under the elm trees. It's no wonder Belgian investors put their money into the Okanagan. In a time in which Europe was expanding rapidly into colonies and dominions, Canada was far more palatable than central Africa. Besides, it really wasn't such a stretch: with its feathered trees, long vistas, broken shorelines, ridges, and sloping points, Okanagan Lake itself was similar to Lake Kivu, just over the Rwandan border. For their part, the orchards themselves seemed solidly prosperous. This was definitely a colonialism of a gentler sort, which makes the irony even stronger: the rubber that sheathed the wires that connected the phones between headquarters and the front lines at Vimy Ridge, that had to be repaired every night, that sent the men crawling out of the trenches into machinegun nests from Verdun to Ypres and Passchendaele, bolstered an economy that was able to pay for huge land development schemes in Kelowna, on the rolling hills north and east of the Kokanee and shadow of Mission Creek. It's an area known today as the Belgo—local shorthand for The Belgo-Canadian Fruitlands Company. Airplane tires, truck tires, cables: the Great War would not have been possible without the rubber; the rubber would not have been possible without the Congo; the Okanagan would not have been possible without the insane profits, or the grief. The Belgians must have been damned happy to get their money out. A group of them with foresight invested in the Winnipeg-based Land and Agriculture Company of Canada, known locally in the North Okanagan as the Belgian Syndicate. The syndicate then bought up 15,000 acres northeast of Vernon from Cornelius O'Keefe and developed it as orchard land. "Grow fruit in Vernon," they advertised, "and grow rich." That's for sure.

The English would not have been all that shocked at any hint of money being tainted with genocide, though—however directly or indirectly. It was just business. When the English spoke of going into the army to make a man of a boy, after all—and they did, a lot—one thing they had in mind was teaching young men how to kill blacks and Arabs and Indians, that to have any beauty on this earth—a pretty rose garden, for instance, or pink apple blossoms in the rain, with bees buzzing through the flowers like distilled droplets of the sun—someone has to be a man, someone has to swallow his squeamishness and do the work that needs to be done, the hard practical work that opens up the world to the mind. No wonder the women with their needlepoint were kept in the dark. No wonder the Germans decided to bully their way through Belgium to seize France in 1914. No wonder they were offended that the British were miffed.

For European immigrants and the poorer of the Brits, however, there never was a white planter's suit and an ivory-handled planter's knife. Instead of a country house, with wisteria growing up the pillars, with chilled lemonade and the tinkle of laughter coming out of the parlour, there was a one-room house of weather-faded clapboard, insulated with newspaper, with black widow spiders in the well. Although the tinkle of lemonade certainly was there for the taking in Frank Richter's time—in fact, was the whole point of the enterprise—all that the immigrants who followed him got were long days of sweat in the heat, caked with dust. Instead of long rows of orchards blooming in the spring sun, the petals drifting over the furrows like the edges of a Valentine's Day card on Oscar Wilde's writing table, and the renewal of civilization, there was self-poisoning with the arsenic of lead, lime sulphur, and nicotine sprayed to keep down the bugs. Ironically, those apples were shipped around the world, renowned for their size and sweetness and beauty.

Among the first ranches to abandon cattle for the plantation culture was Greata Ranch—the kind of spread where Rudyard Kipling or Somerset Maugham would have been happy in the evening over a gimlet. The Chinese bunkhouse above the main dock was two stories high and a hundred feet long. For two decades, the second sons of England's greatest houses—the wealth, if not exactly the pride, of an empire—roamed through the hills above the ranch, hunting deer and roasting them on the beach in parties that went on for days. It was the Goa of its time. When one of the young British gentlemen got a remittance, he'd catch the boat to town, where he'd buy a bottle of scotch and celebrate. When that bottle was gone he'd start in on a new one. He'd go on for four or five days, treating everybody in sight, until the money had vanished. Then it was someone else's turn.

Summerland followed, then Naramata, then Kelowna, Oyama, Kaleden, Keremeos, and Osoyoos. The Okanagan and the Similkameen had become the garden of Eden. It was a powerful dream, dreamt by a civilization that still believed in poetry, that had seen William and Dorothy Wordsworth leave the city a century earlier for the countryside, where they could write poems and shell peas. An early Battle Creek Michigan investor in Naramata, quoted in J. M. Robinson's advertisements for the Naramata subdivision, noted: "The good thing in trying to interest people to come to Naramata is that there is no excuse for anyone enlarging on the facts, and the hard thing is to endeavour to conceal one's enthusiasm while telling the truth." Daniel Freeman would have been proud. Very few of the early orchards in the Okanagan showed any kind of a profit before the First World War.

The best land went to the British. The dry, sandy soil of Oliver remained for European immigrants after the war, when it was planted out with a few branchless saplings, and rattlesnakes in nearly-dry irrigation ditches.

It was a different group of people who moved into the ruins after the moaning minnies and whizzbangs, the jam tins and trench foot, the tanks and shock troops cutting wire in no-man's-land. All the remittance men who had come out from England, and who had used

English money to scratch out polo fields in the bunchgrass, had heard the call, had gone back to do their duty and to earn back a place in society, and to a man were cut down by machine guns as they strode in front of their men with a riding crop. What was left in British Columbia was no different than a blasted church spire in Flanders. Anyone lucky enough to be standing among the piles of rubble—not bricks in this case but the rump towns, orchards, and failed irrigation schemes—the dreams reduced from wealth to survival, was the British Empire then. All that was left of it was in their hands. Whether they were German, English, or Doukhobor didn't matter one bit. They had become the only show there was. They moved into the forms of the land the way finches on the Galapagos Islands move into and fill ecological niches. Prairie farmers came, sick of the cold of the plains, where, as a European would see it, one's greatest wealth—land—became one's greatest liability. With their own empire lost, the Germans came to those ruins, too, and stayed. They settled in the Okanagan with the same dreams that had taken their ancestors to the Volga and down the Danube to the Black Sea. The Okanagan was their new South West Africa. They could imagine that the sun on their faces was the sun of Angola. The paddlewheeler on the lake, the S.S. *Sicamous*, was like a steamer on the Sudan. For thirty years, the Germans were cast adrift by history in the Okanagan. They burnt away into the sun and made their own culture, built a pastoral—and peaceful—German country centred in the orchards stretching above the lakes north and south of Penticton. It was a country duplicated only in Paraguay and Argentina, a Germany without modernism, a pure dream only, a black-and-white photograph that had suddenly come into colour.

By the 1950s, the Germans had been living in the valley longer than most everyone else. From palatial Mediterranean villas high up amongst the pines, with flagstone terraces and views down over the lake, year by year they picked fruit from the clay benches, trucked it to the packing houses, and let the Old Country, and all of history, fall away. Ironically, if it weren't for the Germans, the colonial dream and English planter culture would have died out in Canada long before they finally did.

The death knell came in the early 1950s when history came back at last to an Okanagan isolated by the war. It came in the form of a new German generation that had been through bombing and terror, from a country—West Germany—in which communism had been exterminated in the death camps and the fire-bombing of Hamburg. In the Okanagan, though, the communists had come through unscathed, and were there to guide a new generation raised under fascism—my father's generation—and to give them their past. In the Okanagan, Germany's lost provinces and the old Germany portrayed as a romantic dream of brotherhood still existed. These were the people who came to my grandparents' house on the Cawston floodplain and pinched my cheeks—a lost tribe dying out on the far side of the world. I was their hope. They looked to me for the continuation of their dream, for the survival of their culture, which could give their lives meaning. I saw it in their eyes, in the more than usual excitement with which they greeted me, and in how, years later, they tried to sell me their orchards, wished I would marry their granddaughters.

Nazis settled among them, too—rapacious men with glinting blue eyes and booby-trapped attics, with shotguns on trip wires to discourage thieves. They sized us up. In 1975 one of them offered my father a job managing his orchard. This guy had Alsatian guard dogs and a butler with a pistol strapped underneath his jacket, a collection of old tapestries, an elevator leading to a speedboat waiting on the lake. In 1977, when I started working on the orchards myself, I met another one, with clematis vines growing up the walls of his villa. He interrupted me halfway through my late-evening sprinkler change to tell me that I was Martha's grandson, Dorothy's son. I agreed. The light burned from orange to blood red in the clouds above the lake, stretching north to Commando Bay, where in 1944 Special Forces troops had trained for amphibious infiltrations behind enemy lines in Malaya and Borneo. To that thin old man, with my shock of blonde hair, working late, and living on the land like that, I was a dream. Within five minutes, as deep purple tones caught the centres of the clouds and the sprinklers lazily swished beside us through the grass, he told me what a good German boy I was, what a great people the Germans were, and what a shame it was that Hitler had lost the war. I made excuses that I still hadn't finished my work for the day and walked away, my heart pounding. I was shaking. It was 8:00 PM. Mosquitoes were beginning to fill the cooling air.

The old man had low blood pressure. He used to go for long walks into the Gold Hills, to get his heart beating. When his wife drove him into town in his diesel Mercedes, he sat in the back seat. Like a mousy chauffeur, she eased the big machine out through the trees and down the mud driveway in a loud cloud of blue smoke.

There was always something shameful about being a German boy, and it wasn't just the strangeness of Germanness, either—the rooms full of cigar smoke and men talking politics, treating children with a cold formality, cloying women in sweeping dresses sipping lemonade, and even an old woman called Broomhilda, who lived under the pines by the river. Broomhilda! It was the name of a comic-book witch, and there she was in the drug store in Keremeos, an eighty-year-old woman with a hunchback, dressed in a threadbare black coat an old friend of my grandmother's.

When I was in Grade 1, my teacher, Mrs. Farmer, singled me out in music class. We had been learning the German walking song,

> I love to go a wandering,
> along the mountain path,
> and as I go I love to sing,
> my knapsack on my back.
> Fal-de-ri! Fal-de-ra!
> Fal-de-ri! Fal-de-ra-ha-ha-ha-ha-ha-ha!
> My knapsack on my back.

She played the piano. I sang along quietly, almost inaudibly, except for the laughter of the "Fal-de-ra-ha-ha!" The whole class belted that out loudly, competing with each other to see who could laugh the loudest and the longest. One day there in the corner of the gymnasium, Mrs. Farmer stopped playing and asked me to sing the song in German. I was so embarrassed to be singled out that I couldn't speak. The checked logger shirt that my mother had sewn for me suddenly itched at my whole body, all the blood fell from my face, and my throat seized up.

"Do you know it in German?" Mrs. Farmer asked kindly. I couldn't speak. I had been betrayed. Worse yet, I knew no German. I felt a double shame. I felt that my secret was out, and now I would be open to ridicule. I was terrified. I just wanted to be a boy like any other boy there.

"No," I said softly. I had to repeat myself for her to hear.

Mrs. Farmer smiled and said something light to try to make me feel at ease, but it was weeks before I felt at ease again. Isolated on the farm five miles south of Keremeos, I slowly began to be swept away again into the world: goldfinches in the trees, bullsnakes coming to drink from the washbasins in the basement, the creaking of crickets all night as I tried to sleep.

The embarrassment was never far away. There was always something to bring it home again. One year it was seeing a pair of German boys at the Elks' Parade in Keremeos. The parade was an annual affair to celebrate the spring rodeo, with floats decorated with tissue paper flowers, and the rodeo queen and princess waving at the crowds. It was the highlight of the social year. Banners were strung across the highway to catch the bumper-to-bumper traffic streaming to the Okanagan for the May long weekend. For two hours, traffic was detoured on the farm roads around town, and the parade took over. Shriners rode tricycles, threw candy to the children, and honked ridiculous rubber horns. Horses pranced in silver harnesses and dogs sniffed each other with bows around their necks. Children rode their bicycles, the spokes decorated with coloured crepe paper. There were prizes for best-decorated bike and best pet. Main Street was packed for two long blocks, as everyone craned their necks to see the parade come and go. There were the visiting queens and princesses from the Omak Stampede, over the line in Washington. They wore richer costumes than the local girls, and rode on ponies done up with silver and turquoise. The queen and princesses came from the Peach Festival in Penticton, the Regatta in Kelowna, from Vernon, from Princeton, and from Osoyoos. It was the whole world in all its finery.

And there was shame. During the Keremeos Rodeo Parade in 1964, I was eating a special treat—red licorice from the confectionery—when I saw two other German boys, my age, dressed in lederhosen, with green felt straps over their shoulders, their cheeks scrubbed, their hair slicked back, and their father wearing a Bavarian felt hat with a pheasant feather stuck in the band—all of it so German that I could barely watch. I knew those boys. I felt the world fall away below my feet. I felt everyone's eyes boring into the back of my head. I watched furtively, so that no one would see me watching, and when the boys looked my way and our eyes briefly locked, I flushed red and turned away. My heart pounded in fear that someone in the crowd had seen me watching them, that I would be made to share their shame. I didn't want anyone in Keremeos to see that I knew those Germans, nor to link my Germanness with theirs. At the same time, I really pitied the boys, and couldn't understand how a father could subject his children to that degree of humiliation. It was not a multi-ethnic society. Ethnicity was completely out of the question. A folk-singing club would have been like drinking poison.

Twice, my grandmother, Charlotte, sent lederhosen from Germany. She wanted to do something for her grandsons, whom she had never met, so sent the most practical thing, the thing that all boys would need: leather pants. She figured we could use them until we were old enough to wear long pants, at puberty. With their felt-padded suspenders, with the rough leather chaffing our legs and hanging heavily around us, those lederhosen shorts were terrible things.

My father unwrapped them from the package with glee. "When I was a boy," he crooned, "we wore short pants all the time. You only had one pair of pants. They were meant to last you for your whole childhood."

My brother and I wore them a few times around the farm, under duress. There were terrible fights. After that, we just refused to put them on anymore.

Three years later, the long lederhosen arrived: knickers. They cinched up below our knees with leather straps and little metal buckles padded with green felt. They were gorgeous. They were also heavy as hell. We hated them, too. I don't think we wore them publicly even once. I was proud to think that my father had worn things like this all the time when he was a boy. It was the proper German thing to do, I knew, but if I tried to put them on, the shame overwhelmed me.

I told my father about it thirty years later. "Yeah," he said. "They were awfully uncomfortable things, weren't they? I hated them."

On the other hand, there was pride in being German. "You just tell that to your teacher," my father said one day, out of the blue. "Tell him we're related to Karl Marx and Erwin Rommel."

"Who's Karl Marx?" I asked. "Who's Erwin Rommel?"

"Don't worry about that. Your teacher will know. You'll see. He'll be impressed. We're not all a bunch of dumb farmers here."

No, that's for sure. In this corner of the earth that has been bought, sold, traded, logged off, burnt, subdivided, developed, redeveloped, cut with roads, excavated, backfilled, paved, photographed, hyped-up, and finally banished from the imagination, there were also the Brits.

"I remember the young man they brought in from the reserve at Chopaka," says Margaret Mennell, who had left England to nurse the Free French under De Gaulle, then became the Public Health Nurse for the Similkameen Valley. Except on Thursday afternoons between 2:00 and 5:00, when a doctor came over the pass from Penticton, she was the entire medical system, for decades. "They brought him in with terrible wounds and a smashed skull. He had been out on a spirit quest. He sat in the bush for three days and nights with hardly any clothes, in the snow. It was twenty degrees below freezing. He slipped in the dark when he was weak, and fell over a cliff."

Margaret, too, was trying to find a home here—no more or less than I was, who knew it as my first earth, no more or less than the eight-year-old Similkameen boy from my class who slid under the barbed wire behind his house in 1967 with his dad's 30-30 Winchester to do a little grouse hunting, got caught on the wire and shot himself in the chest.

Our education in the loose and easy days of schooling in the 1970s was the education suitable for such a generation. It was designed to foster independence and creativity, individualism but not obedience, wilfulness but not regimented order. In atonement for fascist crimes and a world set in flight by war, we were given the job of transforming the world. We were meant to be an antidote.

I once spent half a May night driving north from Kamloops to 100 Mile House with my friend, the writer Kathy Waldron, on our way home from a day teaching writing to schoolchildren. Up on the Plateau, there was still six inches of ice. Hoarfrost cloaked all the trees. In the headlights they looked like they were made out of twisted Mexican silver. Down in Kamloops, though, in the grey and dusty bed of the Thompson River, apple trees and lilacs were in bloom. As traffic roared past, kicking up the last of the winter dust, I stopped the car on the edge of the city and cut an armful of apple branches from a scrubby little tree growing in the ditch. All around me were the scorched brown grasses of Paul Mountain, the wrecking yards, the four-by-four roads scarred in the sand, and the heavy trucks snorting by on their way to Jasper and Edmonton. I loaded the sweet-smelling boughs into the back seat and drove Kathy north in the scent of apple blossoms, with petals scattered all over the upholstery. The car was perfumed. I felt like Omar Khayyam.

As the dark blew over us like a wind, Kathy and I talked to keep the sleep away. She told me about her childhood in the Jewish community in Denver, how she grew up not knowing about any other kind of life, about her family back in Poland, who had all died in the death camps. I told her about my childhood on the farm in the Similkameen, and talked about my German family—in Kattowitz, in Eastern Germany, then Western Poland, then the Generalgouvernement, then back to Poland. It was the Golan Heights of its day.

"'It was a terrible place,' says my father. 'Papa left in disgust in 1924.

The French were there to keep order. They were whipping people in the streets.'"

"I dream of writing a book together with you some day, Harold," Kathy said, as the Thompson fell back behind us and the first silver wind of the high country aspens rose up in the starlight like calligraphy. "It would be a book about your family, and mine. I have the strongest feeling that we have the same story."

We swung around a corner. The black road spilled through the trees, like a ribbon unwinding from a woman's hair and across her pillow. We had entered a dream. "I'd love to write a book like that, too." I laughed. "I don't think it would sell, though. I don't think people are ready for it." Every sentence was interrupted by minutes of silence that had a physical presence in the night. I spoke into the dark. "There's a lot of pain."

The silence went on and on. "That's exactly why we need to write the book," Kathy said, at last, dreamily, as if she had fallen asleep and only slowly found her way back to the world. As the lakes of the high country spilled out around us, white sheets of snow in a world of starlight and frost, she had become only a voice and a presence in the night.

On nights above the orchards when I was a boy, the sky was not so broad. It was only a narrow ribbon above black mountains. I looked up through the winter branches of the trees to stars so close they were hanging on the twigs like late winter apples. In summer, wind surged up over the hillside of sagebrush and Oregon-grape and tore at the limbs of elms swaying and roaring in the darkness. I lay as close to the ground as I could, a thin sleeping bag and a dog drawn up around me, staring for hours into space. Stars fell those nights, streaking down through the sky with golden tails.

My mother recognized fruit-growing as a career with promise.

As my father put it, "After the war the French decided that they would not be dependent upon imported sugar again, or upon the labour required to till sugar beets. To solve the problem, they planted forests of Golden Delicious apples. Even if all the men were at war, or in prison, or killed, there would still be sugar. The Poles did it, too, planting cold-hardy Antonovka apples in big wild forests in Poland."

All through the starvation of the war, the wild fruit trees of Kuppenheim had sustained my father: cherry trees and zwetschge trees, the dark purple plums of the Black Forest, which the Dowager Duchess of Baden had planted after the Thirty Years' War so the peasants would always be able to make schnapps. The wild children of those plum trees, cast along the avenue in thorny thickets, kept my father alive through the starvation after World War II. In his love for this civil wilderness, the first lines of his 1956 collision course with my mother and her own experience of the land came clear, the reason she would find him irresistible: it was like one of those old arithmetical problems you give to children: "If a train leaves Hamburg at 5:00 pm, at 50 km/h, and another train leaves Berlin at midnight at 70 km/h, how many hours will it be until they meet?" My mother didn't stand a chance.

As he was leaving Germany, my father ran upstairs in his leather riding britches and confided to his stepmother that he couldn't fit everything into his suitcase. "I told her that I didn't have the heart to hurt Papa's feelings, but the *Collected Works of Schiller* that he had given me the night before just had to go. I told her I liked the Goethe he had given me better, anyway—which was true. I didn't lie about that. I asked her to keep the Schiller safe, and not to let Papa know. She did! So I got rid of that one!"

In 1994, Death was staring my step-grandmother in the face and she was staring back, directly into its eyes, and did not flinch.

"I want you to have this," she told me, in her bare apartment, with the light filtering in from lace curtains. I was standing at the window, watching people play tennis on a court made from ground-up bricks: rubble from 1945. I turned. It was the Schiller.

The Goethe barely made it to Canada. The trip on the boat was a two-week party. The hold was crammed with young Germans, twenty or twenty-two years old. As the ship rolled through the Atlantic swells where seven years earlier the Canadian Navy and the German *Kriegsmarine* had slugged it out with depth charges, magnetic torpedoes, and sonar, my father and his new friends spent two weeks drinking beer and hardly sleeping a wink. After the end of the party, two things had happened: my father had fallen in love with a young skat player, and had fallen out of love with her as well. As a farewell token, he gave her his father's Goethe while they were packing up to leave the ship in Montreal. She didn't suspect a thing. She kept that Goethe for forty-five years. Then she gave it back, wrapped with a bow.

"You gave it to me all those years ago," she said, reverently, as one would speak of the Bible. "I would like to return the favour."

"What was I going to do?" my father said to me a week later. "I had to appear grateful! I had been so glad to have gotten rid of it back there on the ship. 'You've really done it!' I thought to myself. I had thought I had been very clever! Now I have this thing back, and I don't want it! I just don't want that book! So I'm giving it to you. You're the one in the family who can make use of it."

It sits on my shelf, next to Schiller, half asleep in the afternoon.

My grandfather had hoped Schiller and Goethe would carry the strength of the *Volk,* the German people who had sprung from the land—the farmers and charcoal burners who lived in the forests, who remained true to their language despite all the wars that had been thrown at them. For an aristocrat, this was a great temptation—to find a stratum of the population immune to the vicissitudes of society, inoculated against French occupation, powdered wigs, doctors poisoning women in childbirth, the pomp of the French Court, and the vanity of Napoleon's Grand Armée. On the surface, this patronizing attitude appears to demonstrate how human goodness springs not from social etiquette, nor from philosophy or religion, but from people themselves, but it doesn't. It is a profoundly aristocratic doctrine. It speaks not to the worth of individual human life, but to the worth of the masses, not to the human intellect, but to the foundation of the rights of kingship. My grandfather must have had some of that in mind, all messed up with what Nazism made of its face, when it was no longer the aristocracy that derived its power from the *Volk* but Party members with their red armbands. Instead of wearing sables and velvet and eating off of silver plate, each piece engraved with their coats of arms, the new princes wore suits, worked out of offices and answered telephones. As an antidote, my father brought with him to Canada a loathing for the nobility and all its pursuits, including a profound anti-intellectualism and a complete distrust of all bureaucracies, universities, and any other form of organized human activity short of grass-roots organizations of producers—farmers, for instance. Those he joined with a zeal no greater or lesser than that with which his father had joined the Nazi Party.

"Stuff is worthless," he told me. "It means nothing. I have seen so much stuff just smashed up and lying in the street. I have seen so many old ladies die in the bombings because they did not want to leave their china tea sets. Store something you can trade. Fill your basement with honey. When the economy collapses, it will be worth more than gold."

When the English came to British Columbia they had been isolated from a life on the land for so long that instead of founding functional settlements they set up idealistic orcharding communities, with picnics in the hills among the balsam roots, with chilled raspberry vinegar and wine in wicker baskets. There were white lace parasols and pink peach petals. Men rode the hounds across the cactus and sagebrush benches, chasing coyotes. Equally caught up with a romance in direct contrast to the harsh work of survival, Methodist, Presbyterian, and Catholic missionaries washed across the high plateaus, forced their way into deep river valleys, set up shop along blue mountain lakes, and planted gardens among the grizzly bears in Kelowna. They stumped around in Kamloops, kicking rattlers out of the way with their thick black leather boots, and heard the railways come, thundering along the river shore, shattering the valley forever, and they smelled progress. They took the natives aside in Metlakatla and taught them to blow trumpets and tubas and French horns, and they made a marching band. They taught the women how to be Irish peasants, setting them up with spinning wheels in rows in front of their new clapboard houses, to replace the iron machines of the Industrial Revolution. In the age that gave us The Great War, that was what the churches could imagine, as they washed over the land like a flock of crows. They could imagine the Middle Ages.

Meanwhile, in what passed for intellectual rigour, the American poet Hilda Doolittle was dreaming of nymphs and fairies, Robert Browning was dreaming of Rome, Tennyson was dreaming of the Lady of Shallot, Yeats was dreaming of old Ireland, while the English colonial army marched bloodily across Africa in the name of law, and Old King Leopold was sending shiploads of automatic ammunition to the Congo. In the Congo, local administrators chopped the heads off of black men, as a warning, and used them to rim their gardens.

We decorate gardens here in British Columbia, too, with whitewashed stones in front of a singlewide in an old trailer court across from a wrecking yard in the sagebrush. Pick your town; it's everywhere. It's how people like to spruce things up. The aluminum siding peels off and bangs in the wind and some old lilac bush flares up every spring, and you know you are in civilization at last. The only touch some woman could make to soften a hard life was a few irises, traded with friends, a lilac or two, some white stones marking her own Eden. She knew how things were, well enough. The rest of them, though, the men, the missionaries, the good people, the educated, the people with money, the people who sent back reports on how they were converting the heathens to civilization, were all dreaming, while the colonial government sent its gunboat, the *Beaver*, up into the inlets, with its big steam boiler amidships like Fat Boy primed for Hiroshima. They anchored the *Beaver* off the villages, just to let the natives know it would be best not to interfere with the surveyors laying out the new—and ridiculously tiny—boundaries of the reserves.

In 1945, when my mother was ten years old, living in a clearcut in that country, picking raspberries and chasing the family goat among the rotten red stumps of the first giant trees, my great grandmother, Auguste Leipe, was fleeing before the Russians. She had good reason: the Russians were bayoneting the Germans they found on the roads. It was a shock to everyone—far to the east there, in that Silesian countryside, the land had still been untouched by the war. There were no nightly bombing raids over the farms. Silesia still looked like an eighteenth-century etching: geese still swam on the village ponds; children played in the rushes and willows; in an intricate web of deceit farmers planted potatoes and sold pigs on the black market, while the police tried to ferret them out; slave labourers tilled the larger fields. The slaves were Poles, French, Jews, British, Canadians. They were dressed in rags, and they were starving. They often collapsed with hunger, were beaten and shot—not always, but often enough to keep them in fear.

"It was a great adventure," says my father's cousin Sybille, who fled along that road with her mother and her grandparents in 1946. "I was four years old. We walked all day. At night, we slept in a barn, if a farmer let us. It must have been terrible for my mother, but for us, as small children, who didn't know what was going on, it was like camping. I remember my mother crying, and wondering why. My mother tried to keep up a happy face. We walked for six weeks. For us it was like being in the circus." She lives on Hoover Street, in an old Red Cross camp outside of Karlsruhe. In retirement, she escaped at last from the East to grow tomatoes on her patio above the Rhine.

Auguste didn't leave it so long before she got out. She had a healthy fear of pretty well everything. It was a damned good thing, too: when Berlin fell, far to the north and west, two and a half million German girls and women who lived in the cellars of that landscape of ruins and smoke were raped by the men and boys of the Russian army. Age was not a factor: whether you were eight years old or sixty-five, you were forced into sex. It was like a storm that comes a hundred miles across the plateau, so dark and quick you cannot avoid it. You only have time to bring in the garden hoses and dig the last carrots before the big flakes are driven like ash against the windows. It was like everything and nothing. In 1945 Berlin, a woman's best chance for survival from the worst of the violence was to find a protector, a strong Russian, to be gentle toward him, and to let him fight off the others.

It is unlikely that Auguste Leipe was in any danger of being raped. She was less than five feet tall and close to three feet wide. She had started off much taller, by almost six inches, but over the years her height slipped off and moved horizontally. Her face was long and flat, as if the protruding features—eyebrows, nose, lips, and cheekbones—had been pressed back into it with a heavy weight. It looked like a mask carved out of a flat piece of wood. Mountain people hang masks like that over doorways in Austria, to scare away demons. Auguste's skin was grey. She didn't look like a woman at all, but like something that haunts your dreams. She looked like one of the witches who danced around Satan on the Devil's Pulpit, a rough granite outcropping on the Werra River north of Eisenach. She looked like one of the Fates snipping the threads of life from all the young German men sent off to their deaths in Finland and Odessa and Smolensk. She looked like one of those stuffed straw targets that soldiers are given in boot camp, and on which they practice their skills with the bayonet. She had reason to run.

— —

The war tore Auguste Leipe out of her life: two small rooms lit by oil lamps in a big old house in Leipe-Petersdorf, a suburb of Breslau, the teeming, industrial capital of Silesia. Auguste had been married to Paul Leipe, a stationmaster on the German railroad, until he died of a heart attack in 1933. To be a stationmaster meant that Paul had clawed his way out of the potato soup of the working class—but just barely. And don't even think of family solidarity: the Leipes were at war with themselves. The Leipes from the one side of the river Oder that cut through Breslau like a coiled grey snake, with slow currents and the stink of waterweeds rotting on the sandbars, did not talk with the Leipes from the other side of the river. That was that. It was a world of twisted silence and the struggle to keep just ahead of grinding poverty.

Let me tell you about twisted. It couldn't have all been the fault of those other-side-of-the-Oder Leipes, whatever insanities they suffered from, whatever the closed, Byzantine world they lived in, however the suppression of the working class had affected them, however the mechanized butchery of the Great War had broken them, however much they dreamed, as the right-side-of-the-Oder Leipes dreamed, of when the family was rich, lived in a country house, kept serfs, banqueted with the King of Prussia. It couldn't have been all their fault, because even Auguste's son, Alfred, who definitely lived on the right side of the Oder, was nuts. Yes, the shrapnel that had torn out a chunk of his skull on the Chemin des Dames might have had a lot to do with it, granted, and the piercing headaches he lived with for the rest of his life, certainly, but the one surviving letter we have from Alfred shows him cursing the German postal system and the German character and culture that lay behind it, because it improperly forwarded his mail in the collapse of all civil authority in Germany, the loss of whole provinces, and the scattering of his family to the four winds. Later, in Sweden, he had his own wife committed to an insane asylum for five years. When she got out, she immediately turned the tables and had him locked up for five years himself.

Auguste's son Bruno, my grandfather, was just as difficult, quoting Marx around the dinner table and fighting with Alfred every night, while their sister, Martha, looked on. "He hated his brother," says Frank, Bruno's son. "He had no use for him at all." The feud went on far too long. When Bruno married his sweetheart Martha Marsel, at the age of twenty-eight, the new couple moved into Auguste's living room, which they roped off from the rest of the apartment with a sheet. "They were at each other's throats," my mother said. "Mom spent nearly every day in tears." This would, sadly, become a family refrain.

Auguste stumbled down the road on her arthritic legs, hiding in the ditches when the Russians and Americans strafed the columns of net shopping bags, wheelbarrows, threadbare wool coats and stumbling children clutching dolls. She begged at farms for food, and was turned away time and time again. Through a combination of fear, rumour, and trial and error, though, she found a path between the German and Russian lines and moved ever further north and west.

A dozen years earlier, millions of German women had thrown themselves in adoration on Hitler and his boys. Now they spat on German soldiers, laughed at them openly as they shuffled by in retreat, and taunted them to come and save German womanhood. Better than anyone, except perhaps those women, the men knew they could not. Jokes were made about manhood. The men didn't even lift their heads.

One of those men was Auguste's grandson, Walther—Alfred's son. Walther was in Italy, on Lake Como, where the Roman Emperors used to go to get away from the intrigues of the city by lying in indolence for a few days, drinking Swiss wine and toying with dark African and pale German slaves and, like any good tourist, watching the sun set on pastel water. Walther was a pilot in the Luftwaffe—without a plane. To make him useful, the army gave him an anti-tank battalion instead. When the time came for him and his men to sacrifice themselves and hold back the Americans, they gave up on discipline and agreed to a man to bolt for the hills. Covered in scrub, the hills around Lake Como offered very little protection, but Walther figured they had a chance. It was all in the timing.

Many Germans were stranded in Italy that night. As the novelist Erich Kästner describes in his journal *Notabene 1945*, their officers took the last cans of diesel and drove north, abandoning whole divisions in the dark. Tens of thousands of men were captured. Tens of thousands made it over the Alps on foot, to arrive in Mayrhofen, Austria, in rags. As soon as they were back within the borders of the Reich, they stripped the insignia off their tattered uniforms and left their army greatcoats lying in the alpine pastures for the goats to nuzzle. When they offered Reichsmarks for food or shelter, they were sent on by stony-faced mountain farmers, who had been watching armies and governments fall in ruin for a thousand years, and refused to share a single loaf of bread.

Tourists come to Mayrhofen by the hundred thousands now, for a bit of quaint Austrian Tyrolean life. They come on the Zillertal train or on big glass buses. They stay for three hours or for three weeks, to enjoy the discotheques. Walther was caught by the Americans and imprisoned. Walther's brother, Heinz, was in prison as well. Alfred's sister, Martha, all four-foot-ten and 250 pounds of her, was with her skinny, sick, joke-a-minute husband, Joe Schreiber, in Reinerz, a mountain resort town up in the Mountains of the Giants on the Czechoslovakian frontier, with palm trees in planters on the streets and winds scented with pine and fir and snow. It wasn't her turn to run. That would come.

The other guests that spring in Mayrhofen were Kästner and the members of his film crew from Berlin. As Kästner puts it, in the disorder of the collapse of civil and military authority and the destruction of every city in the country, the one ministry of the government of the Third Reich that functioned right to the bitter end was the Ministry of Culture. The filmmakers had planned their escape months in advance, when they knew that the situation was irretrievable: every night a thousand British and Canadian planes bombed the city into bricks and the bricks into gravel and the gravel into sand; the Russians were rolling across Poland like a bunch of combine drivers working day and night to get the crop in with the thunderclouds behind them. The film was to be a rousing propaganda film, with innocent German peasant girls and terrible invading Russian soldiers and the bittersweet romance of unblemished German peasant boys sacrificing themselves to protect the homeland—and the girls—from the Asian hordes. There was a big budget. All the cameras and materials were packed up and shipped ahead to the Tyrol. The crew followed, in the last cars out between the German and the

Russian lines, weaving a crazy all-night trip in the dark, at high speed, down the back roads of a Germany strangely quiet. It was as if they were driving to the end of the earth.

Kästner had remained in Berlin during the entire war, opposed to the regime but too well known and well loved to be imprisoned, tortured, or shot. His plan was to hide out with his crew and their Reichsmarks until Germany surrendered, then to come down, confess his dissident status to the Americans, and regain his life. When the German army struggled back over the high passes, their faces hollow and ashen, Kästner watched them pass by, as if they were souls marching out of Hell. By that point, he was starving in the mountains himself, in the most beautiful scenery in the world, reduced to eating grass and the first shoots of flowers. He lay on the slopes with the world falling out below him, soaking in the mountain sun, watching farmers refuse the soldiers food, just as they had refused it to him. The soldiers threw out their Reichsmarks among the flowers, where they mingled with the Reichsmarks Kästner had thrown out the week before.

My father watched Kästner's films. The women wore dirndls and white blouses and the men wore grey uniforms and a sense of duty. They fell deeply, passionately in love, with the love that comes from a love that has only a weekend before it is torn apart by shared duty and that damned Eastern Front.

Bruno, his wife Martha, and his children, Frank and Dorothy, didn't see any of those movies, but they didn't need to—the movies were already screened in their heads: Frank was named for Martha's uncle, Frank Marsel, who had set himself up on a ranch in western North America right after the turn of the century; Dorothy was named for Dorothy in the Land of Oz. She had long golden braids and freckles across her nose and cheeks. Boys used to dip her braids in the inkwells on their desks. Blouses were ruined. It was murder on the family finances.

"Being a German child in Canada during the war was so shameful. I would come home every day from school in tears. It didn't matter that my parents had been away from Germany for fifteen years, were Canadian citizens, spoke only English, renounced Germany, and were never a part of the Nazi system and in fact had originally opposed it. Children were very cruel."

Although she was growing quite used to being called a Nazi, it still filled her with a sense of injustice and helpless rage. Her only weapon was silence and a kind of tight-lipped pride and an iron will. Auguste would have recognized that.

One day, without any warning at all, Bruno led Dorothy, Frank, and Martha deep inside the landscape of one of those propaganda films. It was May. Martha was weeding her garden and picking strawberries. In the fields, the red wood of cedar stumps bled into the grass. The rainforest was closing in from the road allowances. It wasn't raining, but it had rained a half hour earlier and would rain again that afternoon. The goat needed milking. There in the bush of the Fraser Valley, in the stump farms up against the mountain, Bruno and his little family weren't living in a community as communities are recognized anymore. It was more like a shanty town, more like a collection of hobos out under the trees, more like all the English would allow them. But it was home.

Ryszard Kapuscinski, the Polish journalist who spent the '50s to the '80s in Africa and the Third World, watching revolution after revolution unfold, and fail, and reporting all of it back to his audience in Warsaw as if he was reporting on the Polish revolution itself—either one in the past or one yet to come—says of Africa that it is best characterized by the huge crowds of idle young men standing around in the streets of cities.

"They are," he says, "the future. They have nothing to eat and nothing to do, which means at the same time that they will pick up any sort of work if it gives them something to eat for the day; if they do not get any sort of work, they will pick up anything else, however corrupting or destructive."

This is the world that Bruno lived in back in Breslau—now the Polish city of Wrocław—in the 1920s, and the one Martha's father, the bricklayer Josef Marsel, lived in before that, and it is why there was a war. Kapuscinski's books are only thinly coded.

Bruno grew up on the streets, with stories of the British Empire and the Dutch Indies, of sailing ships and Tahiti, coconuts on the beaches, and the life of a sailor in Surabaya, in Valparaiso, in Cape Town, in San Francisco, in Shanghai. Drunk on the cynical, romantic songs of the German revolutionary playwright Bertolt Brecht, he dreamed of a life tramping the world, shipping to and from German West Africa with a cargo of diamonds or gold or ivory, or carting cinnamon or sandalwood or rubber in the South China Sea. What Bruno got instead was a pipe like a wily old sea captain's and a military cruiser in the Baltic, doing exercises for the last two years of the war. Deep in the hold of the ship, he was trained as a machinist, oiling camshafts. After the war, he worked for a half year in a machine shop. After firm after firm went broke in the collapse of Germany's economy, after an apprenticeship as a carpenter with an uncle collapsed because in the chaos and resulting uncertainty his uncle took on his own son instead, Bruno wound up hanging around at streetcorners early in the chilly mornings, with other men dressed in unwashed, brown wool suits, with cloth caps pulled down low over their brows, waiting for someone to drive up and offer work: digging a ditch, lifting rails, shovelling coal, lugging bricks up a scaffolding to build a wall, mucking out a slaughterhouse—anything for a few pennies. By 1922, family connections got him on part-time with the railroad, where he eventually rose to the dizzying heights of train dispatcher. My grandmother fell in love with his Bohemian roots. After the tight control of the Catholic Church, it was a great relief and promised a radiant future. Bruno made her laugh. When Bruno and Martha were married, they had to receive a special dispensation from the bishop, for marrying across the faith. It was scandalous.

The one Leipe family picture we have from that time shows a perfect middle-class family: Bruno's sister, Martha, in a white lace gown; Alfred in his Imperial Army uniform; Bruno in his *Kriegsmarine* blues; Paul with a peaked Prussian helmet; and Auguste, back when a Russian might have looked twice at her as more than a lodging for his bayonet—all sitting and standing in a spacious and elegant parlour, with paintings on the walls and, behind them, a table draped with damask. Life was good in those days. Or the dreams were good. Because, except for those military uniforms, it was all fake. You can tell by the wrinkle in the table that continues up the wall behind it, like an earthquake, and the way the room folds up at the bottom left corner, revealing the wooden legs holding up the set. The room was a cloth backdrop, like the ones photographers pull down these days for kids at high school: a wall of books, or a blue backdrop with stars. For $34.49, Package A or B, you, too, can be a Hollywood star. They give you a list of suggestions about what to wear, how to do your makeup, how not to cut your hair. Every starlet should move to Hollywood with such good advice. The spiked Prussian helmet? A stage prop.

It was a good time to be a member of the working class, though. After a century of unbridled romanticism, after a hundred thousand paintings of peasants under trees, peasants in carts under a setting sun, peasants leading cattle into fields, feeding chickens, unloading ships—the mainstay of any gallery of Old Masters in Northern Europe—there were so many people trying to help. One helping hand was the *Wandervögel* movement, the apolitical, romantic, folk-cultural precursor of a rash of German youth movements, all designed to give young people some escape from a rapidly urbanizing society, and which eventually transformed the original impulse into the regimentation of the Hitler Youth. Luckily, Bruno and Martha's years of wanderlust came before all that.

Wandervögel can be translated as "migrating birds" or even "free as a feather." The movement was set up in 1901 by ten romantic men, including four writers and one doctor, dreaming of chivalry in a Berlin suburb. A *Wandervögel* lived neither in the past nor in the future—his or her flight out of the adult world was a flight into the present, without worldly goals, and with no program, except to remain flexible, fresh, and free from judgement—and from the distinctions of class.

The Germans weren't the only ones dreaming of knights. In England, Lord Baden-Powell turned his upper-class childhood fascination with medieval chivalry and his lengthy education in hunting, theatre, sport, and war into a youth movement of his own: the Boy Scouts. As a military officer in charge of training troops, he had often been impressed with the beneficial effect of woodsmanship upon the usefulness of urbanized recruits. The year was 1908. When war was declared in 1914, many of the first scouts went out to the trenches, in fine shape to fight and die in mud.

The *Wandervögel* did it even one better. They hiked across Germany from hostel to hostel, along the old medieval trading routes and networks of castles that once guarded them. The most famous of these roads was the Via Regia, which originated in Spain and eventually followed the low valleys east from Frankfurt to Leipzig and on to Minsk, and bound the West to the East for a thousand years. It passes right through Eisenach, where in 1817, on the fourth anniversary of Leipzig's popular uprising against the Napoleonic occupation, five hundred students gathered in the ruins of Wartburg Castle and agitated for the creation of a unified German state as protection from any future repetition of Napoleon's adventurism. Those students would certainly have read their Goethe. They would have read the lightly disguised nationalism of the romantic lyrics and the proud, damnedly devilish *Faust*. Some of them would likely even had spent a night partying upon the Devil's Pulpit, with an imagined Faust and the imagined Devil who had bought his soul for all the knowledge in the world. It was a popular party place, like running up the Ashnola River in my own childhood, with a few cases of bootleg beer in the trunk and skinny-dipping in the river.

Year after year, the students continued to meet in the Wartburg, prolonging their youthful dreams and transferring them to a new generation. In 1838, the Wartburg was rebuilt, not to the original plans—no one knew what they were—but to a few old sketches, and with lots of gold leaf, brightly-coloured paint, and lush tapestries. Only a couple of the original rooms remained. In the twelfth century, the medieval love poet Walther von der Vogelweide had written most of his love songs there. That was good luck. Luther translated the Bible in the Wartburg, too, with a vertebra of a blue whale for a footstool, ha ha ha.

To his own wanderings in the soul-nourishing forest, Bruno brought a guitar, much like von der Vogelweide himself. When he sat around the campfire late at night, his transformation into a painting was complete, maybe even with gold leaf on the frame. Bruno and Martha and their friends sang as the sparks rose up into the darkness among the pine trees. Just like the hippie women of 1960s America, who dressed in gingham in honour of their grandmothers who had crossed the Autumn passes of the Tetons with covered wagons, Martha dressed in a peasant costume, half gypsy, half Polish, with a kerchief over her bobbed, black hair, and a big smile on her cheeks.

Each hostel had a library of important books: the essentials of civilization, as the Socialist Party saw it. In those libraries, Bruno sank his teeth into Confucius, Marx, Engels, Brecht. The revolution was taking place in Russia. Talk of communes and freedom was in the air. It was the best of times.

It was the worst of times. There was nothing to eat. Silesia might have been a German province for seven hundred years, but its population was still largely Polish. Families, like mine, had intermarried, and had hushed it up. My father's mother, Charlotte Koernig, born into a family of privilege, learned Polish from her nurse, in a nursery with a big rocking horse and coloured blocks. Only later did she learn German, the family tongue. In 1920, the League of Nations stood back while Polish soldiers seized a few key points in Silesia. Eventually, a loose mob—the *Freikorps,* or "Volunteers," took the train up from Bavaria as tourists. Flush with the victory of having not so secretly suppressed the communist government in Munich, they came one at a time, their guns disassembled, packed in separate pieces of freight and luggage. The Freikorps saw Germany as a body, and the armistice of 1919 as a pillow held tightly over its face. They brought a mortar with them in their luggage, and drove the Poles back over the border.

To escape his own degradation and the anger that flooded through the sheet that separated Auguste's living room and dining room and made an apartment for the newlyweds, Bruno spent two years kayaking with Martha. They paddled right up the length of the Canal Grande among the gondolas, and slipped past the canal boats carrying coal and tourists through the Rhineland, with the vineyards on the steep slopes and the shattered castles on the hills. In 1929, Bruno decided to embark on the greatest adventure of all: travel to Canada. He was helped along in his decision by the fact that he had taken part in street protests, big orgies of blood and brotherhood, as a member of the Communist Party, when the communist army of millions, in mimicry of the pre-war, independent German army, fought it out on the streets. Its fighters identified each other by red sashes tied to their arms. Their opposition, also an army of millions, was dressed in brown shirts, the SA, Hitler's private army. Their red sash held a crooked black cross. Night after night in Breslau and across Germany, the gangs roughed each other up. The police sided with the SA. Bruno was put on a black list. A spot of adventure in Canada seemed prudent. The writing was on the wall.

—

They left just in time. Those were the years when German intellectuals smoked pipes and called each other "gentlemen," in English: the years just before the National Socialists sent them to construct Buchenwald as their own mass grave. On the day after Hitler came to power, long lines of men grovelled on their knees, scouring asphalt roads with bars of bath soap and scrub brushes. Storm troopers stood over them. Nazi officers strutted past to make sure they erased the white letters of their Social Democrat and Communist election slogans painted on the road. The scrubbers included newspaper editors and the mayor of Dresden. Postmen crossed and recrossed between them as if they did not exist. Milkmen threaded their carts through and rang their bells merrily.

—

The East Prussian *Heimat* writer Ernst Wiechert was there. He was one of the first literary heroes of the generation that had come through the Great War. The son of a forest warden in East Prussia, his childhood was spent with the trees and lakes of Masuria. As a young man, he trained to be a teacher. War drew him away from that. After the war, he found his way back to his lakes, swamps, and forests, but only emotionally—by writing of them out of a combined sense of longing and loss. His political tendencies were towards order and duty. He spoke for a generation.

At first, literary fame drew Wiechert to Berlin. He quickly wearied of that swollen city of four million, though, and by 1925, as right wing political rhetoric became ever more violent, he began to lose faith in it as well. In 1930, when the violence continued to escalate, he broke away altogether and retired to a tranquil life far to the south, in Hof Gagert, near Wolfratshausen, in Upper Bavaria. In 1933, he travelled to Munich, where in a speech called *The Poet and Youth,* he publicly warned university students about soul-destroying tendencies in the new Nazi regime. In 1935, he returned. This time his speech was titled *The Poet and His Time,* and this time his criticism was much sharper. Authorities suppressed the speech. Certain students, however, made secret copies, and passed them from hand to hand. Copies were still circulating at the end of the war in 1945.

After a 1938 letter in which Wiechert refused payment of a tax levy to support winter relief work—"as long as Pastor Niemöller remains in custody and his wife is herself in need"—Reich Minister for Propaganda Josef Goebbels himself signed the orders to have Wiechert taken into custody. Niemöller was a special case: he had publicly rejected the Nazi system on moral grounds, had set up a support network for persecuted protestant ministers, and, just prior to the 1936 Berlin Olympics, had signed a declaration smuggled out of Germany and printed in the July 27, 1936 edition of *Time* magazine: "We must warn the Führer, that the adoration frequently bestowed on him is only due to God."

Because of Hitler's personal interest, support for Niemöller was not tolerated, even by a writer whose writings on land and home meshed perfectly with the Nazis' own propaganda needs. Influential friends protected Niemöller for a time, but in 1937 he was arrested for treason, released on a suspended sentence, immediately re-arrested on Hitler's own orders, and held in the Sachsenhausen and Dachau concentration camps until the end of the war. Wiechert's arrest followed similar lines.

He was seized by three Gestapo officers in plain clothes, spent two months in a Munich jail, then on July 4, 1938 was shackled to another prisoner and sent off in a mass transport to Buchenwald. He spent six weeks there, felling trees and hauling rock. He was one of the lucky ones: at the end of August, on the verge of death, he was released, transported to Berlin, and brought before Goebbels, who told him that if he renewed his criticisms of the regime he would be sent back to the camp until his "complete physical destruction." Wiechert spent the war under house arrest on an estate on the sprawling blue shores of the Starnbergersee. He wrote furiously for all the war years, but showed his manuscripts to no one, choosing instead to bury all of them in his garden including his most famous work, *The Forest of the Dead*, his witness to the cruelty of Buchenwald. It was Buchenwald that clinched it for Wiechert: if Nazism considered itself a cure to the displacement of rural community and a connection to the soil, there Wiechert came to consider it as a symptom of that loss. Buchenwald, *beech forest* in translation, was a horrific irony: the sheltering forest of the *Wandervögel* had been turned against this forest warden's son like a mocking laugh.

When it was clear that the Nazi regime would soon fall, and that it would leave behind a vacuum of violence and abuse, Wiechert wrote another book, called *Fairytales*—little known even in Germany—to give his people hope. Wiechert populated it with scarcely disguised Nazis under the thrall of creatures from a remorseless fairy world, who could only be defeated by those few remaining people—most often children—who still followed the inclinations of their own hearts: although starving and beaten, these pure children were unharmed by a nature to which they gave themselves without reserve. Typical of these stories is "The Moorman," in which a crippled girl ignores her family's fear of the swamp that borders their land, and begins to spend all of her time out in its beauty, hoping to find the Moorman, so he can heal her.

That's not all Wiechert was writing at that time. "There is a people," he wrote in a song for Christmas in 1944, "lost in darkness, a people alone as no other, and yet children are still born to them tonight, and every one of them will have a heart as white as snow." In "Grandfather's Stories," he wrote, "Soon after the people started for home, and as they slowly walked through the snow, it was as if the old stories went with them, the stories of the old, gloomy houses, where so much happened, but where men could still be changed, if a voice could touch their hearts." He was still the poet, telling the fairytales of the northern forest.

In 1945 Wiechert returned to Munich and once again addressed students at the university: "We had a fatherland once, that was called Germany. It is easy to break a staff across an entire people. You should dig up truth, justice and freedom again, and out of the dust of the hard road that our children must now walk, uncover the pictures for them again, to which the best minds of every age have looked up." Just as it had been with Goethe, just as it had been with the *Wandervögel* of Wiechert's youth, the writers and teachers were still looking for social change from the young, under the direction of the old. Metaphorically at least, they were still sending them out to the trees, just as Hitler had sent them out to forests of barbed wire and anti-tank ditches.

"If you want to understand the Germans," said my cousin David in 1995, laying down his viola in Zurich as his mother's forsythias flooded in through the window like drops of yellow rain, "read this book. Any other country fills its fairytales with princesses and magic music boxes. Germany fills its with people wondering where they are going to get their next piece of bread."

―

Bruno never asked Martha if she wanted to go to Canada. It wasn't that kind of a marriage. She didn't want to, actually: eleven years after the end of the war, she had finally landed a job with some prospects. She was a secretary, did filing, typed letters, kept books of accounts, answered the phone, was deferential, smiled and laughed the infectious laugh that stayed with her through all hardship. That laughter rose from deep inside her until it shook her whole body, trying to get out, and then it did get out and she wiped the tears from her eyes. She was bureaucracy's human face. This wasn't her favourite job, but it was a good one. Her favourite job had been as secretary of a theatre group. She loved working with artistic people—not as an artist herself, but as a part of their circle. Unfortunately, that position had only lasted two months: the troupe folded; audiences didn't have any money. Martha wasn't even paid for her last month's work. I have her file of recommendations from employers. To the last one, those letters, typed on thin brown paper with elaborate steel-engraved letterheads promising hope and respectability, tell what a good employee Fräulein Martha Marsel (and then Frau Martha Leipe) was, how good she was with people, how dutiful and punctual she was (important German qualities!), and how, unfortunately, the employer had gone bankrupt and was closing up shop. They wished her every success. The tone was always resigned.

Martha adored Bruno, though. She would have followed him to the end of the earth.

She did.

The end of the earth was the Okanagan. An entire group of *Wandervögel* from Breslau and Magdeburg had hopped on board the good ship *Montcalm* for a two-week wallow across the Atlantic, past the pack ice and whales of the Gulf of St. Laurence, and into the docks stretching along the river in Montreal. They disembarked in that maze of steel track and decayed red brick and took the train across the continent, off to start a commune in the Okanagan Valley. Day after day they clattered and swayed deeper into a vast and ever increasing, ever more terrifying, ever-emptier wilderness. The track, spilling out behind them in its chill tongue of cold iron, was all that connected them with their lives—with the whole world they knew. Every hour, it grew ever more tenuous. After a week, they had left even Canada almost completely behind and had landed deep in the heart of the British Empire, in Penticton, British Columbia. They might as well have taken a train from Mombassa, up to Nairobi, and then west to Lake Victoria, passing through the savannah and the flame trees, past Masai villages and derelict train stations and mad Englishmen who had hitched zebras to their carts and careened wildly through the bush while their polo horses died of sleeping sickness and their coffee plants withered and shrivelled with blight and locusts stripped their corn fields down from spring to autumn in five minutes. That is how far they had gone. Nothing they knew meant anything anymore. Suddenly, their dream had become very, very real. Their train hissed away, leaving empty, spent rails behind it. Smoke rose from the Indian reserve, on the dry land up against Kruger Mountain. Orchards stretched out around them in the distance, across the fields of gravel, rabbitbush, and sand surrounding the station and behind the wall of cottonwoods rising out of the bed of Penticton Creek as it trickled into the mosquito-riddled oxbows of the river. The hills were blue.

Bruno and Martha did not have eyes to see what was actually in front of them, though. Standing on the station platform as a hot wind blew off the prickly pear cactus and ruffled their unwashed hair, Bruno and Martha thought they saw a wild earth, full of Indians with bows and arrows and proud princesses and turquoise beads. Actually, the Indians were only a mile away, and if Bruno and Martha had bothered to go out to the old Green Mountain stagecoach road to Inglewood they would have seen them. They wouldn't have liked what they saw, though. No one did. Even the Okanagan people were put out by it. To tell the truth, it had been forty-nine years since anyone had seen any good in the place. That was in 1880, when Charles Hill-Tout, an amateur anthropologist and stump farmer from Abbotsford, rode into Penticton to record the bones of the

Okanagan language before they were only a tagged display in a museum case. The Indians complained to him that the ranchers had secured all the water rights, that without water they could not farm. Knowing well the English they were pitted against, Hill-Tout tried to calm tensions by divining for water on the reserve's bunchgrass hills. He walked up through prickly pear and wild onions, the iridescent green beetles, the loose gravel of the old creekbed, the anemones and sage, with a forked stick pointed at the grass and the wind tearing at his cloak.

Soon after Hill-Tout left, the reserve was reduced from ten acres for every adult male to three acres. Always the cool rationalists, the ranchers considered the Indians incapable of making proper use of even that much. In time, the ranchers sold out to English farmers, who used the stolen water to grow peaches and apricots and to process them into jam in competition with Robertson's marmalade—an echo of English country houses, exotic gardens sheltered behind tall brick walls, and espaliered trees raised behind glass. In other words, by the time Bruno and Martha arrived, the Okanagan people had been living without water for two generations, squatting in log cabins no better or worse than the cabin our two *Wandervögel* were going to be living in later that week: cheap, thrown up to keep off the sun and to keep out the wind and the rain. There was little rain. Nothing kept out the wind.

Instead of economics, Bruno and Martha thought they saw the Gold Hills to the east and Giant's Head above Summerland to the north, the farms on the clay slopes above the lake, and the wild land behind, untouched by any hand. They saw their hands touching that land. (They did not imagine they saw God; they had already renounced *Him* when they had married three years before.) They stayed the night at the Incola Hotel, on the shore of Okanagan Lake.

In the 1960s, in their future and my past, the Incola had deteriorated into a beer parlour, with old, mildewed rooms upstairs, framed by sun-rotted white curtains, peeling paint, and black glass. Spiders lived there on a diet of echoes. When I walked by with my mother on the way to the beach, the sweet smell of old beer wafted across our faces. Beer was twenty-five cents a glass. Every May long weekend, bikers came over the switchbacks of the Hope–Princeton Highway from Vancouver, roaring through the streets of Keremeos in a parade a mile long, their throats dry from the hour-long ride from the bar at the Princeton Hotel. Their bikes filled the entire street in front of the Keremeos Motor Inn and the barber shop where everyone got the same military crewcut and read the same hunting magazines and spat into the same spittoon. Deafened and bowlegged like bronc riders, the bikers strode in to the small black tables and the dollar bills nailed to the wall behind the bar. A few hours later, and after a few fights with busted chairs and a few men bursting on their backs through the big padded doors onto the street, they were at the Incola, to celebrate Queen Victoria's birthday in style. They pulled in with their chrome-plated hogs and their hand-painted choppers with custom gas tanks and long front forks, some painted with psychedelic colours, others with pictures of nude women twining over the moulded steel, others with the welding burns still showing and the engines running rough. Many of them didn't have mufflers. People stood stony-faced on the streets and watched them pass. As I carried my brightly coloured beach towel, my snorkel and my mask, my mother told me that they were murderers. She told me not to watch. She grabbed my hand and hustled me away.

In the 1970s, the Incola was torn down into a pile of old slats and plaster, then graded into a level plain of gravel and wireweed. With nowhere to go, the bikers started to tear up the whole town, from the square dance arena's patio bricks, to the willow-shaded family campgrounds by Skaha Lake Beach. Every May long weekend, Penticton became a fortress of police. If Bruno hadn't been dead by then, he might have felt at home.

With its Tudor fascia and covered veranda, though, the Incola had been one of the great colonial hotels, where you could drink your gin and tonic waiting for the ship to come in from the plantations stretching north into the Interior. "Penticton," advertised the Kettle Valley Railway, "with its mild even climate, never excessively hot or cold, beckons one to forget care and become a child again among its fruits and flowers." The Incola served fresh eggs, butter, cream, vegetables and fruit from the railway's experimental farm, and sat across from the bathing beach and the Aquatic Club building. Back when Bruno and Martha stopped in for an afternoon and wound up staying the night, it was the main transit point for the valley. Docks stretched out into the lake. The steamer, the S.S. *Sicamous*, was roped to the creosoted pilings, and men were loading fruit and coal on board, and lumber, barbed wire, and all the freight bound for Kelowna, Okanagan Landing, Okanagan Centre, Greata Ranch, Fintry, Peachland, Naramata, Paradise Ranch, Trout Creek, Carr's Landing, and all the other points up and down the ninety miles of cold glacial water.

Bruno and Martha saw a lake. What they did not see were the people, just like them, new immigrants from Europe, who had come a decade earlier, had stood where they were standing, looking north over the waves, and knew in the pits of their guts that they had been cheated and had nothing and were ruined. Tired of a rough life in the cold of the prairies, those were people neither rich enough to buy a quarter section in the black earth of Southern Ontario nor poor enough to have to stay in their sod huts, picking up buffalo bones. They all had one thing in common, though: they had all answered a particularly lavish advertisement for fruit land in the Okanagan. The comfort, and the dreams, were seductive: the fruit simply grew on the trees; you did not need to plough the sod; there were no blizzards. A surviving advertisement from the H. P. Lee Real Estate company of Vernon sums up the excitement of the times: "RU Coming to Buy A Home B 4 It is Too Late???" The card is divided in two: on one side of the Rocky

Mountains a tall, square-jawed Englishman in white cricket flannels stands under his juvenile fruit trees in the spring sun; on the other side an immigrant wrapped up in heavy coats and a fur cap stands in the snow, staring longingly west and clutching a suitcase spilling over with money. When you were scrabbling in a gully for saskatoon berries and wild onions in a high rage of mosquitoes, such advertisements must have sounded delicious. They would have promised a way out. They would have seemed too good to be true, so good that no time could be wasted. You had to seize your chance immediately, or forever regret it.

Our particular advertisement, however, was wilder than most. Across the prairies, couples must have counted the last of their money, and one by one, over dinner, perhaps, made the low-voiced, trembling, hand-in-hand decision to take the plunge, to cut their losses, to write their alkaline prairie land off as a mistake. They pooled their last savings to buy fruit land on the strength of that ad. The land was offered sight unseen, good bottom land in the basin of the valley, with the promise of a train trip to the Okanagan to view it, and the offer of a refund should it not prove satisfactory. People felt secure. The catch—there is always a catch—was that when they came to the front verandah of the Incola Hotel and walked forward to see their land (the country road stretching through newly surveyed fields, men riding out, white-flannelled, with a horse and carriage into town, women strolling with parasols), they saw only water, lapping gently at the pilings. It smelled of fish. An enterprising American realtor had surveyed the lake bottom, on paper, had drawn the whole thing up into lots, and had sold every last one. By the time the buyers got there, he had fled back to Montana. Not one of those buyers ever collected a single cent.

When Bruno and Martha saw the blue water stretching north, stirred by a light wind into low, white, breaking waves which hushed on the gravel, they must have thought they saw the Reichenau, the island of pansies and fruit trees in the *Untersee,* the shallow west arm of Lake Constance separating Germany and Switzerland. The abbot Pirmin came in 724 and promptly drove out all the snakes. Pirmin was Irish, so he had a thing about snakes. The serpents fled in fear into the lake, in all directions, and drowned returning to the Devil, who had spat them forth. His goal was to recreate Eden in the wilderness created when Adam and Eve abandoned the Word of God. You can still see the faint outline of the story in the frescoes of St. Peter's church—the oldest church in Germany—on a hill above the rushes, where the vineyards tumble down to the shore.

The Reichenau is the rich *Au*—an old German word signifying a place of exceptional fruitfulness, a refuge in a wild world. The abbot Ermenrich von Ellwangen wrote in the 9th Century,

> Reichenau, green island, you are blessed above all others, rich in the protection of knowledge and in the holiness of your inhabitants, rich in tree fruits and the plump grapes of your vineyards: there are always lilies blooming on your soil and mirroring in the waves, and your fame calls out far, even into the foggy country of the Britons.

Today the Au is covered with fields of pansies, glass greenhouses, churches, three small villages, and a luxury beach hotel, the *Strandhotel Löchnerhaus,* where my father's father, Dr. Hans Rhenisch, came to dine every weekend and to watch the sun set like red gold on the water, broken only by the long trails of a pair of slowly swimming swans.

I went to the Reichenau for coffee and raspberries with my daughter,

Anassa, and my cousin Thomas. Napoleon had kept a villa on the far, Swiss, shore, facing east; no doubt he used to sit on his terrace in the mornings, over coffee, while Josephine called out inside, wearing a gauzy something. I stared at the pink silhouettes of the villas in the haze and wondered which one had been his. Thomas was lost in his memories of our grandfather sitting unsmiling over that table and staring into the glare of light where the six-year-old Thomas was coaxing the swans to the shore with a few crumbs of bread. Anassa was licking the cool of ice cream off a spoon and watching a Turkish man with an old kitchen knife slowly scraping the grass from between the flagstones of the terrace in front of us. He scraped a couple stones clean, stood up, stretched his back, stared around, took a drink of water, moved a couple chairs, then bent back down. It wasn't work so much as a stage act. The hotel's private beach was empty, although just a few feet away the public beach was so crowded people could hardly move.

The idea of *Heimat*—the homeland from which men and women spring like stalks of wheat—draws Germans like flies to flypaper. That day in the summer of 2003, Anassa and Thomas and I met a thousand of them at Unteruhldingen, where they decorated a hundred metres of Lake Constance beach and its seven shops selling souvenirs, beach toys, mass-produced skinhead T-shirts, Tyrolean felt mountain hats, tie-died rayon skirts from Bali, coloured glass jewellery from Venice, and pottery to lay out on the kitchen table. The holidayers were served by two pubs, two sausage stands, and a little train with rubber tires and an engine the size of a Sears garden tractor, which shuttled people back and forth from the parking lot. If you walked, you'd beat the train every time. Up the hill from Unteruhldingen is the white plaster and gold leaf pilgrimage church of Birnau. That's why we were there. Anassa and I had been touring Baroque churches. In so many of them, the cherubs were uninspired, as if picked up by the case in a craft shop selling porcelain moulds for the Christmas craft fair market. Not so at Birnau: framed outside by tall pear trees and vineyards falling down the almost perpendicular fields to the lake, the cupids in Birnau surround the twelve stations of the Cross, shocked and worried, but in *mock* panic and *mock* concern, because they are laughing, barely able to contain their joy. They know a secret, that all the suffering of Jesus, as the soldiers spear him in the side, throw dice, make him drag his cross through the streets of Jerusalem, jam a crown of thorns onto his head and goad him with their laughter, is going to end in a story of great happiness. Delighting in their joke, the cherubs can hardly hold back from giving away the last few pages of the Book. They sprout out of the walls One of them is even dipping a finger into a honeypot and licking it off—"a metaphor for the Holy Spirit," reads the guidebook. It looks more like a metaphor for sweet sex. In the vineyards and orchards above the church, a plane carrying three hundred Russian school students crashed a few years back. It fell out of that blue Baroque sky into the *Heimat*. No one survived.

Standing on the verandah of the Incola Hotel under the clear blue Okanagan sky, with the white clay cliffs falling into a narrow shoreline of willows to the northeast, Bruno and Martha and their friends would have seen a farming country. In fact, I even have the album of that country. It belonged to one of their communal friends in Naramata, and chronicles a nudist colony in the marshes outside Magdeburg, where women played in the mud, smearing it all over themselves before walking through the reeds into the cold water of the river, and young girls walked around nude with their middle-aged fathers, to have their pictures posted in glossy magazines distributed throughout Germany; where young men posed like sculptures by Rodin, throwing a javelin or casting a discus, where young women posed in Midsummer dances, prancing around a man dressed as Pan; where everyone gathered naked in a meadow in the morning, to sit in a series of concentric circles, welcoming the sun.

In the morning, Bruno and Martha packed their bags and took the steamer north to Kelowna. I have a photograph of them on their first day there, among the rudiments of their commune, on the stony soil of the South Kelowna Bench: a low log cabin, knocked together out of six-inch jackpine, Martha's five-foot frame filling the doorway, Bruno leaning on one leg against a pile of firewood, with his beret and his pipe, a few other Germans chopping wood, a thin blue column of smoke rising from a tiny, scrubby fire, one woman dressed in a flour-sack dress. A week after that, the commune that had brought them all across the Atlantic to Canada broke up. Its members went their own ways, sharecropping for Old Man John Casorso, Kelowna's onion king, who had first come out to the Okanagan in 1881 to farm for the Oblate priests. That summer, Bruno and Martha grew tomatoes in the moraines and lived on credit from Casorso's store. It was the end of April, 1929. They had thought they had found Rudyard Kipling or W. Somerset Maugham, in the peace of colonial isolation. They had found *The Grapes of Wrath*.

At the end of a summer of weeding, irrigating, and the back-breaking labour of picking tomatoes into wooden cases and loading them onto wagons to be hauled down to the cannery, Bruno and Martha had made less money from the tomatoes than they needed to cover their bill with Casorso for flour and milk and cooking oil. To add insult to injury, the stock market collapsed. Feeling guilty about his promises of easy wealth, and how it had broken up the commune that looked by then like the only thing that could save them, Casorso took pity on Bruno and Martha and called the debt even. The word in the German community was that things were better at the Coast. Digging deep into his savings, Bruno bought his first car, a Model T, and got his driver's license on the same day. They were ready to roll.

"The test for the driver's license was quick and to the point," says my mother. "Dad got into the car on the driver's side; the examiner got in on the other side. Dad drove the car around the block, stopped it, and was awarded his license. All he needed to know how to do was to start and stop."

"In 1929, Kelowna was serviced only by a few narrow dirt roads, which snaked around the contours of the hillsides. The washboards were so rough they shook every thought from your head. A trip from Kelowna to Kamloops—which now takes two hours—took the whole day. You were basically just driving across the fields."

My mother tells the story.

"Mom and Dad had troubles with the car, and got a late start. They didn't get through Kamloops until it was far too late to make it through the Canyon before dark, but they tried anyway. That was really stupid, if you ask me. They didn't have a clue about the road, about how far it was, or what condition it was in, and wound up in the middle of the Fraser Canyon at night in the rain, and you know how bad that is. You can't see your hand in front of your face. The Model T's lights weren't working well, and Dad couldn't see where they were going. Mom was scared half to death—not so much of the road, but of the isolation. She absolutely refused to stop for the night. She didn't trust the people who would live in such a place.

"Suddenly Dad stopped the car. He always said he didn't have a clue why he did it. Something just didn't feel right, so he stopped in the middle of the road. Mom asked him what was wrong. He told her he didn't know. She told him to stay in the car and keep driving. He shook his head. Then he stepped out into the pouring rain. It was a real Fraser

Canyon downpour. You know the headlights they had on cars in those days: you might as well have held a candle out in front of yourself, that's how little they lit up. Mom says she saw Dad stop ten feet in front of the car, stand there for a moment, then slowly walk back. When he had the door closed again, he told her. 'The bridge is washed out.' They sat in the car shivering until the morning, when a crew came and repaired the bridge. Someone was looking after them that night. If they had driven another ten feet, they would have died right then and there. That would have been the end of us all." My mother laughed.

Bruno didn't find a job. There weren't any jobs. Mind you, in the entire history of British Columbia, there have hardly ever been any jobs. When the Fraser Valley was cleared in 1880, when the Chilcotin and the Cariboo were settled, when the orchards were sold in Keremeos, Winlaw, and Proctor in 1909, there was no work. Only in the last forty years has there been any work in British Columbia, and that has been off and on, too—mostly off. Much of British Columbian history has been the history of people camping out in the bush, like the immigrant community pressed up into the sodden cedars away from the river in Mission and trying to make them into something humanly recognizable. It works for a few years, then peters out, because you just can't keep that kind of energy up forever. Eventually, someone tries something new, either in the same old place or, more likely, somewhere else down the road, and the young people drift away from all they've known to some other impossible dream of stability. In the meantime, people get by. Mission was as good a place to try as any.

Bruno and Martha barely got by. For four years, they lived off of the remnants of the eight hundred dollars they had brought from Germany, plus the pennies Martha made in the one summer before she was pregnant, working alongside the Sto:lo and Chinese women in a salmon cannery on the Fraser River as the seagulls rose and fell outside, screeching, and tugs shunted up and down the current. In their poverty, Bruno and Martha had good company, though: all the Finns and Norwegians and Germans out there in the woods lived without money either. They lived off of salmon from the Fraser, and blackberries, and whatever they could grow in their gardens. If they had chickens, they got eggs. If they had a goat, they milked it. That was Martha's world, and she grew to love it. My mother loved it, too. She does not remember the Norwegians as dreamers. To her, busy with Martha in the kitchen, canning their year's supply of food (eight hundred quarts) over a woodstove, the Norwegians, along with Finns and other Germans, were their friends. They played cards and drank homemade whiskey and rhubarb wine that could tear the lining out of your throat. They danced the schoolhouse roof off. They stood in solidarity against the English—except for Bruno and Martha's New Year's parties, with beer and pickled herrings: everyone made a special point of coming to those. "In Stave Falls it was the custom to have a Christmas party complete with Santa Claus and gifts for all the children. All the adults donated a couple of dollars for the gifts.

"The Norwegians always had a pot of coffee on the back of the stove," my mother told me another time. "They dropped cold water into it to settle the grounds. When you came in they always gave you a cup. They were dirt poor, but they were the most generous people. They looked out for us, and we looked out for them. When Mom and Dad first arrived, they made sure they got properly settled, not like it was later in Smithers. Smithers was such a shock compared to that."

Out in the Chilcotin, the Cariboo, the Bulkley, the Peace and the Nazko, the Babine, the Similkameen and the Stikine, the Finns and Swedes came, as Frank Ayres puts it, pointing out the hand-adzed logs of the branding corral on his farm on the Dean River, "to be alone. As soon as someone else moved in within a day's ride of where they had cleared the bush into a farm, they felt hemmed in and moved even farther out, and started over. They repeated the process again and again."

The mindset is recorded in the Norwegian novelist Knut Hamsun's masterpiece, *Growth of the Soil,* in which Hamsun writes about Isak, a man who moves out into the wilderness, turns it into a farm, and makes a life there. The book is steeped with resourcefulness and loneliness, with "The long, long road over the moors and up into the forest." As a first step for his Isak, his Adam in the bosom of God, Hamsun has him stripping birch bark in the woods, carrying the strips on his back miles into town, and trading them for flour, bacon, a metal pot, a shovel, "as if life without a load upon one's shoulders were a miserable thing." Another Norwegian, Trygve Gulbranssen, wrote almost the same story in his novel, *And the Forests Will Sing Forever*: a single man leaves the towns behind, strikes out into the bush, and through brutal hard work builds there a new, pure country, unblemished by human fault, sustained by honest faith in God. The copy I have was published in German in 1953—noteworthy for that alone: after eight years of occupation, Germany had just become an independent country again. It was still largely in ruins; the Russians were pressing from the east; for eight years, the publishing industry had been cranking out books approved by the censors of the American Army and still did not have the resources to publish indiscriminately. They did, at last, however, have the ability to publish what people wanted. They wanted this:

> But there was still the North. And north of the cleared land the forest had survived as it always had been. It sang its old song of cliff and high land with a dark, powerful voice towards the North without end.

Still, not having a job didn't mean you gave up trying. A year into his poverty in Mission, Bruno tried to make a little money cutting shinglebolts. As a new immigrant, penniless, not yet a citizen, with a wife to feed and a son on the way, he had few options. Together with an equally desperate friend, he floated a raft onto the hydro reservoir at Stave Lake, above Mission. Down in the Fraser, salmon were still fighting their way up into the canyon at Yale and from there into the high country. Along the river, English canning factories were putting up cases of raspberry jam, blueberry jam, and blackberry preserves, but in the mountains it was a different world. High above the dam, between granite shoulders muscling down towards the Fraser, dead cedars thrust out of the water—killed where they stood when the water level was brought up over them. It was a land of grey and ragged ghosts.

Bruno and his friend poled their raft from tree to tree. The only sound was the slap of the water, the thunk of their poles, and their breath. Occasionally a raven knocked one of its wooden bells overhead, then glided on into the fog. The sound carried for a little while after it passed, sending ripples in the fog; then it vanished as well. The men felt as if they had left the earth. Fog condensed on the trees and dripped off of the fine branch tips when they brushed against them. The two men cut those trees into lengths with a crosscut saw, split them, and floated them down the lake to the access road above the dam. It was a staggering amount of work, considering the rain, considering that they were working from a raft and that the trees, when they fell, smashed heavily into the water, throwing up huge waves that soaked the men and nearly upset the raft each time. They must have been working in slow motion. The water must have splashed up over them like liquid hydrogen.

They were cutting shinglebolts because a businessman in Vancouver had agreed to buy the bolts from them for a dollar a cord, that's to say for a pile eight feet long, four feet wide, and four feet high. Now, *businessman* is a term that needs some translating. It is a discredited term these days, a thing like *poet*—not something you're likely to mention in conversation. You might as well say *mobster*. It sounds unclean. Back in the immigrant British Columbia of 1931, though, when everyone had to hustle to set anything aside, not for retirement but for next week, it was a genuine occupation. It was right up there with *banker* and *salesman* and *plumber*. Most people couldn't give themselves such a noble title back then. Most people didn't have a career. The whole province was a small town plunked down in the scrub; people had just come over from Europe—from a whole bunch of Europes, really—all of them hopeless and turned on their heads, and they were all trying to work things out, to find some way to turn trees and rocks and water into food and into civilization. A man had to have some pride. It was desperate. It was pretty damn near hopeless. Everyone was trying to be a magician. Everyone was trying to pull a rabbit out of a hat, or a brace of pigeons, or a crust of bread. Everyone was trying to invent on their own what had taken the collective strength of Europe a thousand years to build. You can't do it, but there's nothing else for it, so you have to try.

—

Even today, there aren't too many people in Needles or Port Renfrew or Buffalo Creek who have an actual occupation you could nail down on a census form. You do a little of this, a little of that. Should any actual money ever be unlucky enough to make its way into town, it gets passed around and around until it is exhausted and makes its way back out to the world on its last gasp, shredded and torn. Living in a small town is like sitting around a hole in the ice at thirty below, fishing. The wind blows across the lake, raising a cloud of snow a foot deep above the ice. It moves like a fast river around you; if you stand still for a minute it begins to settle around your boots. Since you're ice fishing, though, you *have* to stand still. You stare down and wait for a fish as you drift in; you have all the time in the world to stare down and wait: if a fish doesn't come, nothing else will, and there is nothing more pressing than this confrontation with nothingness to pull you away.

There was a businessman. That was enough. In Germany, a businessman, a *Geschäftsmann,* would be successful, if not, perhaps, a little disreputable. He would wear a suit: a little too loud, a little too flashy, a little too cheap and shiny. He would talk like Duddy Kravitz. He would schmooze. He would have his shoes polished and would flick a coin to the shoeshine boy when he slid off the seat. A small coin. Just the term, *Geschäftsmann,* was an indication that he had climbed out of the unwashed masses who hung out with Bruno on the streetcorners, hoping to be picked up (by a *Geschäftsmann,* of course) for a day's labour. It was a hell of a life. In a world that could produce a *Geschäftsmann,* no one had a job, unless some rich woman wanted her house painted, or her husband wanted a spike or two pounded into his railway, which was used to transport goods from another rich man's factory to some place where it could be used to extract more money from the masses. Work was something over which other people held the monopoly. In that world, a man as a body was nothing.

For my grandfather to do a deal with a businessman would be like uncovering three Ford Explorers in a row on a scratch-and-win lottery ticket. Anything was possible if you had suddenly found yourself that close to money and power. You would feel very clever to have had swung a deal with a man like that. Luck was everything: either you followed a man who had it, or you made it yourself, or you didn't have it. That day, Bruno had it.

A shinglebolt is an eighteen-inch-long length of clear-grained red cedar that can be split by an axe into shingles and used to side and roof a house. Shinglebolts are made out of old-growth trees, eight hundred years old, because it is only trees like that which have no knots. A younger tree will not split along the long, straight grains of the wood. If you try to split it, your axe will either curl around the branches to give you useless bent shingles that a squirrel could crawl through, or will jam at the knots. If that happens, you won't even be able to make kindling. When you have a piece of old-growth cedar, though, and split the wood, the resins spark in the air like the sun. The scent stays in your lungs. You breathe sweetly.

Men who regularly split shinglebolts get blood infections from the splinters that flake off of the wood. These splinters are finer than the needles that come in those dollar packs, twenty-four needles pushed down into folded blue paper by ten-year-old girls in Bangladesh. Shingle-cutters usually get a bonus to do this dangerous work.

Bruno and his friend loaded their raft down until it sat heavily in the water, but the businessman never showed. In the two weeks they spent drifting in the lake, poling and lining themselves from snag to snag, in that ghostly dead landscape trapped by fog, the businessman went broke. When they telephoned him, he wasn't there. That was that. They had come up against emptiness once again. You couldn't rely on anything, but you could rely on that. Unwilling to throw away their work, Bruno and his partner divided their load in the rain, and hauled it home in the rain. They stacked it behind their houses. It sat out there in the rain.

A few months later, a son was on the way. To celebrate the event, Bruno split some of the shinglebolts to sheet and roof a small house—quite literally, as my mother puts it, half a house—for the new family. A few years later, when half a house was just not enough, they moved to a bigger stump farm, and Bruno used some more of the shinglebolts, this time to sheathe a barn and even to fence a one-and-a-half acre field. Rain splashed out of the wood when he pounded in the nails.

Bruno and Martha took out Canadian citizenship in 1935, as soon as regulations allowed them to do so. Of all the Germans who had built themselves houses out of shinglebolts and driftwood and scrap tin up in the dark cedar forests of Stave Lake and Mission, they were almost the only ones who had become Canadians.

"There was another family we were close to," says my mother. "Most of the families wondered why Mom and Dad had taken out Canadian citizenship, when they could have stayed in Canada on an immigrant visa. Dad said it was important, but they laughed at him. This one family had two boys, Frank's age. They went back to Germany to visit in 1937, but couldn't get permission from the Nazi government to leave the country again. The government wanted the boys to go into the Hitler Youth. For two years the family tried to get back out, then they were trapped by the war. The mother used to write to Mom in tears. She was terrified. She had come to hate Germany, and wrote that she wished that she had never gone there, and that she had taken out Canadian citizenship. They weren't able to come back until 1947.

"During the war, it was hard for the Germans. Those who hadn't taken out citizenship suffered. The men, and that included any boys sixteen years old or older, were sent to the copper mine in Princeton, away from the Coast. They were only allowed to come home for two weeks every year, at Christmas. As soon as any other sons turned sixteen, they were sent to Princeton to join their fathers. The government paid the men a decent wage, though, and let them send it down to support their wives and children. If a man was a Canadian citizen, the government didn't bother with this detention. They let Dad stay at the Coast with us. By that time, he had been working for three years with BC Electric at the hydroelectric dam at Stave Falls. His wages were frozen, as were all wages in the country, and would remain frozen for the duration of the war.

"On September 1, 1939, Dad came home and said that from then on we would only speak English in our house. From then on we would only speak German if there was no one present who was not German."

The Penticton photographer Hugo Redivo recalls that he was very fortunate when he came to the Okanagan in 1949. Remembering Bruno and Martha's communist friends, who took him and his wife Dorothy under their wing, he writes: "We were fortunate to meet this particular group of Germans, because the Canadian authorities knew them as the "good" Germans, who were not Nazi sympathizers. There were others in the valley who were sympathizers. During the war, those Germans had had to report regularly to the authorities, whereas the ones we had met had only reported once a year for the duration of the war."

For my mother, growing up on a stump farm behind Mission, in an ostensibly English country, there were very few English, and what few there were were resented highly.

"They thought so much of themselves. An Englishman who knew nothing of the country could come and vote in any election after three months in the country and would get one of the best jobs, while a German or anyone else would have to wait years to vote. The immigrants had all the tough jobs. The English were the managers. During the war it was different. With the young men gone, some of the immigrants, like Dad, moved up the ladder into good jobs, but after the war, when the men returned, *they* got all the management jobs. Once again Dad thought that his chances for advancement had been reduced to zero. You can't imagine the frustration."

Back in Germany, things were even worse. In British Columbia there might have been a Depression, but in Germany there was a Depression *and* another Freikorps—of sorts. This time the Germans called it the government. Knowing from personal experience how things get started, it had made it illegal for anyone outside of the army to own a gun. And once again, the Freikorps was on the front line in Silesia.

Walther, Alfred's oldest son, was there for the entire summer before the war—a thin, iron-bodied member of the Hitler Youth. At the same time, the six-year-old boy who would become my father was hiding Dr. Rhenisch's blunderbusses and rifles in the attic of the villa and swearing an oath of secrecy. The blunderbusses were used to shoot ducks in the *Altrhein,* the reedy oxbows left when the Rhine was straightened out into a canal for commercial traffic. The rifles were for shooting boars in the woods. The boars were as uncontrollable as rats, and threatened all the crops. In fact, the house was decorated as a hunting lodge, with boars' heads and stag antlers, dark floor-to-ceiling oak panelling, gun racks formed from rows of symmetrical boars' tusks and the short antlers of European red deer.

Walther and his Hitler Youth buddies had not sworn themselves to secrecy. They were hiking and training along the Polish border. To provoke the Poles into border raids, they kept themselves as visible as possible at all times. The Poles did not bite, but it must have made them squirm, especially when Walther and his squad laughed at how the Poles were imprisoned by political necessity. Walther was free of that, at least: Hitler saw the Poles as a gaggle of weak old women ready to be drummed out of the kitchen by a group of soldiers full of testosterone, so while Walther and his goose-stepping, shovel-carrying troupe were staring at the Polish border guards over the striped wooden barrier that formed the frontier at Beuthen, just as they had been doing for week after week, month after month, Hitler was speaking in the Reichstag, assuring the world of his peaceful intentions in Poland, as he did on April 28, 1939, for instance,

> I have regretted dearly this incomprehensible attitude of the Polish Government, but that alone is not the decisive

fact; the worst is that now Poland, like Czechoslovakia a year ago, believes, under pressure of a lying international campaign, that it must call up troops although Germany on her part has not called up a single man and had not thought of proceeding in any way against Poland.

Walther and his comrades told the Poles how their days were numbered. They told them how they should be pissing themselves with fear. Walther told me he had known damn well what he was talking about, that only the French and British hadn't yet clued in: the Poles sure had. After all, the region had been fought over, back and forth, for seven hundred years. Everybody in the whole area knew that there was going to be a war. Even Shakespeare knew about it: in Hamlet, Poland and Prussia are being torn one way and another in a long series of pointless wars. The East is a battleground. Everyone knew that. There are even children's rhymes about it, "Fly little ladybug fly, your mother's in the war, your father is in Pomerania, but Pomerania is burnt to the ground!" People knew a lot about this subject in the East. They didn't have to be told twice. Their knowledge was a special knowledge, however. The whole area was labelled a special security zone. News did not get out.

News never seems to get out. Silesia seems to be the Bermuda triangle of European history. Just pull out a map, an old one from before the war. There, at the easternmost corner of Germany, three countries—Poland, Germany, and Czechoslovakia—converge on the huge coal mines at Beuthen. Contrary to anything Hitler was trying to suggest with a revolution aimed at subverting the communist impulses of the workers to the needs of industry, in the society that surrounded those mines, right and legitimacy did not come from the people but from God himself: church, Kaiser, the nobility, and, at the end of the line, my great-grandfather Rudolf Rhenisch. He managed the mine. His chief engineer was Georg Koernig—my grandmother Charlotte's father. Below them were the Poles. They went down into the deepest coal mine in Europe, following the anthracite seams a mile and a half underground. They were crippled and broken and died young. It was so hot they felt that they were knocking a hole into Satan's parlour room. It was as if the coal was going to flame up around them in that dark that was darker than dark. It made men black. It turned them to coal. You could set them alight with a match. Above ground, their strikes were crushed. There's too much bad history there for it all to be a coincidence. As my uncle Michael puts it, "My grandfather was the most hated and the most loved man in all of Upper Silesia." It was a hell of a place. British POWs who made a career of escape were sent there during World War II—because the mine at Beuthen was considered such a bad place it would kill them before they could ever think of escaping again.

Seventy kilometres to the north, in the town of Linden, Charlotte grew into adulthood. Twenty kilometres to the west of Beuthen, lay the border town of Gleiwitz. Because both of these towns lie within a wedge of Germany thrusting into Polish territory to the west of the 1921 demarcation line that saw Kattowitz and the bulk of the mining district given to the Poles, it has the dubious distinction of being the town in which the Second World War began—a piece of theatre if there ever was one. The Nazi boys who had crashed Brecht's plays in Berlin to give standing ovations to Brecht's capitalist villains had learned their lessons well. The war was sculpted for the media, a kind of dinner theatre that had worked excellently for the British in the Sudan and which Hitler had studiously copied. There was no reason to think that opening night wasn't going to be a gala splash. After all, aggression as propaganda had worked for Hitler before. It worked when he had the Reichstag, the German parliament, torched, and the blame thrown onto a planted communist—

a ruse that allowed him to eliminate democracy. It worked again when he dismissed generals unsympathetic to his consolidation of power by blackmailing them with charges of consorting with prostitutes—that time he gained control of the army. It worked in 1936 when he marched an under-equipped and under-trained army into Germany west of the Rhine, to wrest it from the French Occupation Forces. When the French did not hold their ground, Hitler gained his freedom from the armistice designed to prevent a second world war. When he unbalanced Austria by sending in spies to agitate against the Austrian government, then trapped the chancellor in Bavaria and gave him an impossible ultimatum, he gained Austria without firing a shot. In Czechoslovakia, which had a heavily defended border and was prepared to defend it, he manufactured attacks against Germans living in the Sudetenland, to which he played the role of the reasonable conciliator and bluffed the French and British governments into reneging on their treaties. Poland was supposed to be next. This was theatre on a world scale. Truth was irrelevant. In fact, in this poker game, truth was a weakness.

To bring the theatre off at Gleiwitz, the SS dressed up a dozen political prisoners in Polish army uniforms, shot them in a scattered pattern around the Gleiwitz radio tower, then blew up the tower. Germany immediately rushed into Poland to restore order and to protect its borders from the aggressors. This time it wasn't a few hundred Freikorps adventurers from Munich coming up on the night train with disassembled rifles in their cardboard suitcases and straw boaters on their heads, but seven tank divisions, four mechanized divisions, and forty-three divisions of infantry, including 231,000 horses dragging artillery pieces, all headed by dive bombers that howled and screamed like the dead come to life.

To complete the triangle, twenty kilometres southeast of Beuthen lies Kattowitz, and another thirty kilometres southeast of that lies Auschwitz. Members of a Silesian Homeland association still meet annually in Stuttgart, singing sentimental songs, eating sausages, and working out the details of the eventual reclamation of their homeland. In 2004, old Silesians petitioned the German government for the return of their properties in Silesia, as a precondition for Poland's upcoming entry into the EU. In this game of poker, Poland retorted by explaining how Silesia, which was seized from Germany in 1945, was a payoff for ceding Eastern territories to Russia, and any claim on Silesia would be answered with a forty-billion dollar bill for war damages.

There on the border, my family passed their days. It was like living as a guard family out on the Great Wall, looking across to the central Asian steppes and wondering when Genghis and his drinking buddies were going to ride up without passports. Life at the court is so brief, and then you are banished to a sandpile or a swamp where no one speaks your language, and there, in exile, in the colonies, you make a life, but the life you live is no longer the life anyone makes at home. Back home, people move on. In the colonies, you get frozen in time, until you begin to feel you contain the true seed of your culture, pure of the corrupting influence of a centre gone to self-indulgence.

When the mines were given to Poland after the Great War, Rudolf Rhenisch gave up the whole idea of honour and knowledge that comes from living on a border like that—an idea only really valued by those who live there—and moved back to the centre, to the heart, to the source of his values, even to his name, actually, Rhenisch, "of the Rhine." He became a city man, and lived off of his investments, in reduced circumstances, like the head of a once-landed family in Atlanta, Georgia, embittered by the American Civil War. Even with the ten cents on the dollar he was paid, even with the three hours he was given in the middle of the night to accept or reject a buyout, he had enough money to make that move from the land to the core of the idea of the land. A short hour north on the train from Kattowitz, however, and without any money at all, working-class

Bruno and Martha could only make weekend trips out along the Oder or long trips between youth hostels with their folding kayak. There was no push within history helping them along, as there was for Dr. Rhenisch. For them, a move within Germany, if it were even possible, would have led only to a different, dirty industrial city. Canada, and the promise it held of land not yet soiled by failure, was their only way out.

My father should know about that: he followed the Allied Army to North America, to escape the degradation of a Germany bombed back to the Stone Age. He joined his colonizers with nothing but the shirt on his back, a naked man, a nothing, a Robinson Crusoe ready to do anyone's service. He had thrown Rudolf's whole world away—and his father's: the damask, the crystal, the four kinds of wine glasses, the glasses for Riesling and Sekt and Claret and Burgundy, the water glasses, the heavy monogrammed silver; he threw it all away for oilcloth-covered tables and a bowl of cream and some pigs behind the barn. Dr. Hans Rhenisch should have known that, too, the darling of the family, the spoiled, tender and brooding son, with his Beethoven and his Chopin to steady his nerves, always such a sensitive man, such a deep soul. My God, he played sonatas and nocturnes as the nightingales hooted and the slow yellow German mosquitoes rose up from the mercury-poisoned water of the canal. He gave up the whole past, gave up his power as a nobleman, set his life to serve the people and the land they came from, debasing his privilege to ensure the health of the state, breaking the last bonds of democratic Germany so that the people could rise up again from the earth like a new crop in the spring; he bandaged the SA, the Brownshirts, the Nazis' private thugs, after their fist fights and knife fights in the streets, and some poor communist bastard lying dead in the gutter and no one ready to bandage *him* up, and the great Red activist Rosa Luxemburg tossed into a canal like a cigarette butt. The rest is history: the rose garden and the espaliered peach trees of my father's childhood, the willow by the canal, hanging its long weeping branches over the water like a Japanese *tanka*, the French doors open to the evening and the big flagstones of the terrace. This is what the aristocratic life of minuets and courtiers and Meissen china had come to: Dr. Rhenisch hunting boars in the Black Forest like the rat catcher of Hamelin and slicing open the people in town to lift out their gall bladders. My cousin Rainier should know that. He spent years in a corporate headquarters in Hamburg. He had a hundred and eighty engineers working for him and a budget of 175 million Deutschmarks—real money, not the monopoly money we play with here in Canada.

"When I had my department running efficiently, I'd get about twenty-five percent slack in my operations," he said to me once years back. "Then I looked around the organization, saw what Sep was doing, and thought, hey, I could fit Sep's department into mine."

He told me how he arranged a meeting with management and laid it all out, how he could do Sep's thing with his twenty-five percent slack. Everyone shook hands, and the next day Sep and Sep's people were out on their ear. Sep had been looking around, too, of course, but he had been too slow. "Six months later," Rainier continued, "I had the department coasting along again, and had found another twenty-five percent efficiency. So I started looking around the firm again, thinking, "Hmmm . . . Peter's department . . ."

You can bet that before you can say Rumpelstiltskin, Peter was maybe taking that posting to Qatar his wife had previously refused to let him consider. God, Rainer should have seen the end coming. How long can you keep it up? A decade? Two decades? A lifetime? Well, a decade, actually. Finally they asked him to cut his own job. My father and I should have seen that the gig was up, too: the jam factories were shutting down, the tomato factories were pulling out for Ontario, the canning plants had moved to Australia. But we didn't see it coming. We woke up and our Canada was here no longer and we did not want to live in the new country we found ourselves in, with its designer colours and its California condos and its strip malls, but there was no other country in the world for us, because this was our last chance and if we couldn't get it right here, we couldn't get it right.

"I don't have a clue what my father did during the war," says Eberhard, over a glass of Okanagan wine, on a casino terrace of plastic tables and moulded plastic chairs made out of recycled pop bottles overlooking the old Incola Wharf. People walk along the embarrassingly narrow public sidewalk between the water and the Corona umbrellas, carrying wakeboards, jostling them carefully to get them past. In Penticton, this is called public access now. A mile down the beach of imported sandstone ground back to sand and lined with elms the S.S. *Sicamous* has been beached for fifty years, its black prow jutting into the water. The wind is sharp. So is the wine. Eberhard makes a face.

"I was always ashamed. My father never talked about the war. He came back a broken man. His life was effectively over. Never again would he apply any energy to life—and he had enormous energy at one time. He had worked like a man possessed. After the war, he would have been happy to have spent the rest of his life lying in bed, and he was not an old man, only forty-five years old, but his life was over. In those years, I was always afraid to turn on the radio. Some days you turned it on and heard about how some war criminal, some Eichmann, had been arrested. There would be a litany of his crimes, and your heart would sink at the horror of it. I was always afraid that I would turn on the radio one day, and the announcement would be: 'Doctor of Medicine Hans Rhenisch of Konstanz am Bodensee was arrested today on charges of such and such terrible things that he had done in the East.' There was something about him that always left me in doubt, something about the way he looked. I never trusted him. I was always afraid of the worst. I had no evidence, but I was always afraid.

"My uncle Paul," Eberhard continued, "was one of those men who always spoke about how the problem with modern Germany was its lack of Order. He was always longing for the days under Hitler. He had a loud voice and was always very embarrassing to us at gatherings. There were many times when he explained to me the right way of running the world. His friends would sit around and agree. They spoke in low voices, and paused when I came in, waiting for me to say what I had to say and then leave. Once when I came in, Uncle Paul told the men in his group that my father was of the same opinion as he was, and held me forward as if my presence could somehow justify it. His friends nodded and agreed. I was scared by that."

Bruno kept his Marx and his Confucius to the end, but when the Russians turned against the Americans he concluded that the Boeing Plant in Seattle, and his own hydroelectric dam up the Fraser Valley, would be prime targets for his former communist heroes. His solution was to start flipping through the want ads in the *Province* newspaper. In that time, with his background, that would have been a sophisticated activity, like dumping a complex online database onto your hard drive would be today. Bruno's attention was soon caught by a goat farm under the Hudson's Bay Glacier west of Smithers. The ad offered the farm and the goats, on reasonable terms, financed by the seller—nothing unusual, really: in those days, no one wanted real estate and no one had money to put down; most deals were conducted over kitchen tables or in hay barns and ran for decades. Martha nixed the idea in the bud—there was no way she wanted to leave the Fraser Valley.

Martha thought she had made her wishes clear. She hadn't. After the goat farm idea had fallen through, and after making a cursory survey of farmland elsewhere in the valley to keep her happy, Bruno sold out and dragged her up north with Dorothy and Frank, without so much as a roof over their heads waiting for them at the other end. Once they arrived in Smithers, all that was up for grabs was a rotting Norwegian homestead in Evelyn. It wasn't exactly *Better Homes and Gardens,* but when the Russians flew overhead, Bruno would be able to hunker down in his flock of tumble-down cabins and kiss the modern world goodbye: enough was enough. This time he was going to get it right. Martha was bitterly angry, but she had stepped onto the treadmill; there was no getting off. Once again she had followed her guitar player to the end of the world.

You can find Norwegian farms scattered throughout all the remote valleys of the Interior. They tend to be located in the most intractable land, on which any attempt at farming is bound to show little success—but then again it was not meant to: this kind of work, of clearing the bush by hand, isolated from civilization, was intended to be a private conversation between man and earth. As Bruno put it, "trust no one, follow no one, believe no one, whether they are poets, scholars, or politicians, but cling to one thing only, the small amount of will which is yours, the will to defy the world until it is time to surrender it back to God, the totality of will in the world, to whom it rightly belongs." At the core he always maintained the will to try again, always with nothing, always shucking off whatever supports there were around him as being inadequate, as being dishonest, as not working for the ideal.

"My father did not believe in taxes," says Frank, now an old man himself, speaking in the slurred, native-influenced dialect of Northern British Columbia. "That's how you can tell he was a real communist. The real communists did not believe in a welfare state."

Indeed. The idea was to make the state unnecessary.

In British Columbia, it was largely so already. In 1856, the Cariboo Wagon

Road had been chopped out of the bush with axes and shovels by the swearing, iron-disciplined, red-jacketed Royal Engineers of the British Army, to bring the independent-as-a mule American miners within the orbit of the British crown. The road was a three-hundred-and-fifty-mile-long ribbon of mud. The men heading north to the goldfields made the trip on foot, stumbling along for weeks among mud-smeared freight wagons and red stagecoaches. Their destination, Barkerville, was also mud. Storekeepers built their sidewalks high above the ground to keep their stores out of the damn stuff. When Dorothy hit the road ninety years later, British Columbia, the country the road had been designed to foster, was a ruin, with no economy whatsoever, but the mud still hadn't dried out. Bruno drove Dorothy up through it with her dog on her lap, like Toto on Judy Garland's lap in Kansas.

For my mother, the week-long trip north and west through the pines and spruce and aspen was a great adventure: 750 miles of trees brushing both sides of the Model T Creekbeds were filled with cribs of logs and rocks; in many places, the road was a wooden track lashed to beams, "jammed," as my mother puts it, "into cracks in the cliff." It was single-lane traffic the whole way. They had left the twentieth century behind and had gone back to the previous one, and even to the end of the eighteenth century. The towns were collections of one or two log cabins, usually in low, boggy land. Frank, who had begun to make his own life with friends in Mission, was furious. The trip was like driving across Siberia. Frank ended up speaking West Talk. He ended up speaking Chinook. By the time the North was finished with him, he no longer lived within the state at all. He would have been at home sitting down with Louis Riel over tea.

It didn't matter how infused it was with the wild spirit of God, reality just stared Martha in the face in Evelyn. Where Bruno saw a garden, Martha saw a hell of a lot of work. What other farmers in the Bulkley Valley saw was a greenhorn from the south, and a German to boot, a

Jerry, a stupid Kraut. They fleeced him for every cent he had. In the evenings, there were regular gatherings in homes. People played cards, danced, and told stories around their kitchen tables.

"We also had community picnics in Evelyn, Driftwood, and Glentanna in the spring, between seeding and haying times. Everyone came from up and down the valley, bringing food and having a great time with games and softball and real ice cream. Someone would bring heavy cream, someone else would bring sugar and salt and a hand-cranked ice cream machine. It took a long time but was it ever good!"

Maybe it wasn't the world he would confront years later, the palace of Inglewood at Upper Keremeos, or Herb Clarke's old house below the Rod & Gun Club firing range three kilometres along the side of Kobau Mountain, with a formal ballroom in the basement, with panelled ceilings and a sprung maple floor, but it was a pale mirror of it and it kept the community alive. In return, in keeping with northern etiquette, which holds that neighbours help each other to get through the winter, folks came over, all helpful and full of ideas to get Bruno on his feet.

"They convinced him to get into dairy farming," my mother said. "They told him he could make a good living selling cream. The bastards didn't tell him that the wartime subsidy was about to be discontinued and that the price was soon to drop through the floor. They didn't tell him that before the war the Bulkley Valley had shone with wheat fields, fields of oats and cattle, and mixed farming. They told Dad that the cream would be picked up at the railroad siding every two days, and shipped two hundred and fifty miles to the Coast at Prince Rupert. 'You can't fail,' they told him. 'The government is giving its money away.'

"Immigrants were resented terribly in those years. Every new group of immigrants was hated anew. In the '20s, when there were a lot of German immigrants, people said they were scabs, who worked for nothing and made it so that a decent man couldn't support his family. In the '40s it was the Dutch. People hated them even more than they had hated the Germans. When the Doukhobors came, when the Hungarians came, when a new generation of Germans came, it was always the same thing. People blamed everything on the immigrants. They were quite vicious.

"Before the war, everyone had a few animals, a few fields of grain, and maybe some vegetables. During the war the Ministry of Agriculture sent so-called experts up to each town, to tell people what they should grow for the war effort. Some bureaucrat sitting in an office in Ottawa had decided in his infinite wisdom to rearrange agriculture to maximize yields, and to make sure that there was enough of each product to ship overseas to the troops. For Smithers, it was milk. Why anyone would decide on milk in that climate is beyond belief. They'd obviously never been there when it was sixty below, but they gave wheat to the prairies and gave us milk. Other places had to give up their wheat for cattle, or their cattle for wheat.

"When Mom and Dad arrived, the other farmers had been slowly starving to death on a milk and cream economy for seven years. When they met Dad, they were very friendly, as people are in the North. Friendliness and neighbourliness were forms of self-preservation in those remote days. If you didn't look after your neighbours, they couldn't look after you, and you *couldn't* live alone in that country. You needed each other. For one thing, the transportation was hard, if not non-existent, and you could be snowed in for weeks. For another thing, if there was an emergency, you had to take care of it yourselves. There just weren't enough people. Our neighbours were the picture of helpfulness, but they were really cold people. No one trusted anyone. It was all for show. If you hadn't been there for two generations you were treated the way they treated outsiders: as someone they could rip off in order to survive.

"Sure, life was hard, but what they did to Dad was cruel. The neighbours all agreed to sell Dad cows, at reasonable prices, too, to help him get going. Unfortunately, they sold him all of their cows with mastitis, and he was too proud or stupid to notice. All of his savings were used up paying for penicillin to cure them. Whatever milk they gave, he had to throw away. I can still remember him pouring it into the ground. It was a bitter time. Dad had his first heart attack.

"By the time his six sick cows were cured, cream was bringing in only seventy-five cents a can. He stored the cream in the dairy room. It was a cool log building with three-foot thick walls. It wasn't very sanitary. Dad wasn't cut out to be a farmer. He knew the train schedule days ahead, but he was always in a rush at the last minute, swearing at the Model T as he tried to start it, then racing down to the Evelyn Siding three times a week. That train with seventy freight cars which had come across the continent from Montreal would stop in the brush of the Evelyn Siding, without a house in sight, pick up the two or three big cans of cream from the gravel, and leave the same number of empties in their place, just the way a milk delivery van would leave glass bottles of milk on a doorstep in Point Grey. It would do this at siding after siding, every ten miles down the line, then pull out for the 250-mile ride down the Skeena River to Prince Rupert. We very nearly all starved to death up there from the generosity of our neighbours. It was worse than Stave Falls, where we had the Finns. Mom was furious about being wrenched out of her raspberry patch for that sour, thin grass."

Fortunately, they didn't haul all their belongings with them. Those went by train. Since the CPR was looking for settlers in the North to build up business along the rail line, it lit on the idea of enticing them with free shipping for all their belongings. The scheme had worked on the prairies two generations earlier, so the railroad was happy to haul a freight car full of shinglebolts up the Fraser Canyon to Kamloops, to Tete Jaune Cache, between the Cariboo Range and the Rocky Mountains, north along the Rockies again to Prince George, and, finally, two hundred and fifty miles west, to Evelyn. The car was shunted and recoupled, set aside at the back of rail yards or in the middle of the bush, pulled forward again, left on sidings, and picked up by the next train, until months later it was finally parked amidst the salmonberries, horsetails, and mosquitoes of the Evelyn Siding. For a week, as the wind fell off of the glacier and moved through the lanky grass as if it were a spirit itself, Bruno and his fifteen-year-old son, Frank, unloaded that car, hauling up to the farm the shinglebolts, tools, chicken wire, eight hundred canning jars, bent scraps of metal, and everything else Bruno and Martha (but mostly Bruno) had collected during the Depression and the war. The shinglebolts were stored in the attic of the barn. During the summer and the early winter they were covered with hay. It smelled sweet. It skittered with mice. Swallows nested on the rafters, chirring. The cats came hunting. There were dozens of cats. When you walked underneath, straw settled in your hair. Martha was reduced once again to wearing flour sacks. It was worse than the Depression. Bruno was forty-six years old, too old for this kind of nonsense—but, unfortunately, too young to know it yet. Eight years later he had already had four heart attacks, clearing four hundred and fifty acres with a prybar, an axe, and a horse.

— —

Civilization is a disease. Opium, heroin, cocaine, the Cariboo Gold grown in hydroponic installations under haystacks in Forest Grove and Buffalo Creek and powered by stolen propane trucks, even the bud grown in rental houses throughout Burnaby and Chilliwack or tended in clearings in the cedar forests of Nelson and Sorrento and False Bay, are cheap substitutes for the real thing. The real drug is land. It is the primary bacillus, the Ebola virus, so to speak, of the epidemic of civilization. Bruno was not immune to it. He could not have been immune to it. There is no vaccine.

─The Hudson's Bay Company Blanket─

At the beginning of history, Captain James Cook cruised from Port Renfrew to Victoria, his sails flapping like a nun's habit. He was searching for the Northwest Passage—a fabled piece of geography, like something from *The Seven Voyages of Sinbad the Sailor*. He didn't find it. Instead, he saw winter village after winter village lining the Strait of Juan de Fuca, all abandoned, with scrub alder and fireweed growing up through the wooden sidewalks. He sailed past fortified cities terraced above West Vancouver and Point Grey—empty. He saw sick and destitute people. He thought he was sailing into the wilderness, but as Cole Harris documents in his book *The Resettlement of British Columbia,* he was looking into the blank, staring eye sockets of over two million dead—a population British Columbia would not reach again for two hundred years. Cook was sailing into a plague. Smallpox, the first colonist, had come up the Columbia, beating him by four years, and had already wiped almost everybody out.

Imagine a grey Hudson's Bay Company blanket, woven from cheap Australian wool, maybe with a red stripe along one end, maybe with two white stripes. Millions of them were made. A hundred years after Cook, the blankets were stacked up on the docks at Port Hardy and Port Moresby and Prince Rupert, along with sewing machines and blue willow bowls, buckets of beads and pallets of flour in hundred-pound sacks. The natives who were left after the second ravages of smallpox in 1862 would trade anything for a Hudson's Bay Company blanket. Like cigarettes in the camps of World War II, these things were the only currency going. A beaver pelt, a gun—everything was given a value not in dollars but in blankets.

After ten thousand years of civilization received its coup de grâce on the coast, immigrants moved into the wilderness that followed it. They lived in a world of devil's club and salal, float camps, stump farms, logging shows, rain, and mud. They all had a Hudson's Bay Company blanket. For forty years immigrants stepped bleary-eyed off the trains pouring west from Montreal. When the smoke had cleared and the train had crashed and creaked and squealed off into the trees and mountains and prairie, immigrants saw the wind skipping along through the gravel and realized that they had made a terrible mistake. They found what Bruno found that first summer in Kelowna: even if you left civilization because it really stuck in your craw, by the simple act of coming here to escape it you defined this place as wilderness and yourself as civilization, and you were lost. Hans Rhenisch looked at his first Canadian breakfast, a glass of tapwater and a bowl of cornflakes in the immigrant processing centre in Montreal, and thought he had been reduced to drinking ditchwater and eating chicken feed. In Ottawa, when instead of a damask tablecloth there was only a piece of oilcloth, and there was no china, no silver, and no crystal, he thought he would die. A generation earlier, Martha Leipe wept into her handkerchief. She bit her bottom lip. Home for them, and for other immigrants like them, had become a Hudson's Bay Company blanket. There was no garden of Eden. There was no adventure. There were millions of blankets. Business had never been so good.

My parents had a whole collection of Hudson's Bay Company blankets. They burned my skin like a nettle shirt on wash day, when I had my weekly outdoor bath in a zinc laundry tub my mother set down with a clang in front of our house then filled with a garden hose and one bucket of hot water she carried up from the basement. When I was four years old and the sun was as thin as light through a curtain, the laundry tub was my swimming pool. Dust skipped around the corner of the house and snatched my breath out of my lungs. That water felt as cold as steel. I lay in it and was a seal. I was a polar bear. There was no water more pure than that water. The name *water* was invented for that stuff. I stepped into it and it took over my life. It tasted like zinc. Everything around me, from the wind in the trees to the fires rising from the spring burning piles, went silent and still. As a robin prowled around the edge of the lawn, my mother sudsed me down out there, while she was hanging the laundry on the line. She used those tubs to carry out the wash, then she used them to rinse me off. Even today, a chilly summer morning smells like those laundry tubs, like zinc and a water so cold it was like syrup. The drops flowed off of my fingers when I lifted my hands. The wind prickled along my skin, and my skin flamed up like a white sheet wrapped tightly around my body. My pale white skin, my shroud skin, erupted into goose bumps, and my mother laughed, and said I looked like a little goose.

I really thought that I had become a goose, or that in the past I had been a goose and now I was a boy. It seemed entirely possible to me on those cold mornings. I thought about *Swan Lake,* which my mother read to me at night while the wind slid along the window like a river.

Once my grandmother was there on washday, and she laughed, too, in her paisley dress. Her whole body shook with her laughter. Her breasts and thighs and her fat arms and her cheeks shook. She became laughter. When she wasn't laughing, when she was working, she hummed Strauss lieder under her breath: long swelling romantic tunes, all broken up, that never really began or ended. She never knew any of the words, but she had the tunes down pat. She had a little long-running comic opera going on in her head.

I thought I was magic. "It's not everyone who can turn into a goose," I thought. I imagined myself strutting around the farmyard. I imagined myself flying north with the spring flocks that passed over the house, long vees in the thin blue of the March air. For years, I imagined that. I didn't fly off, though, which was very disappointing, really. Instead, I got so cold I started to shake. The wind dried me off. My skin turned blue.

One washday morning as grit blew around the yard, my grandmother taught me how to whistle—how to whistle up a song, how to whistle up a dog, how to whistle up a happy moment in a featureless day, how to whistle my boredom away. I was sure happy to learn that, I tell you; those days were all featureless. They were so flat it was as if they had been hung out to dry and whipped on a line and ironed out and folded and put into a drawer. After my bath, my mother wrapped me up in a Hudson's Bay Company Blanket that she had taken north to Smithers and had brought back down south. It itched and burned and scratched at my skin. It was like wearing a cloth of fire.

I bet every child in Canada from 1880 until 1970 had a blanket like that. Every immigrant to Canada spent nights in a blanket like that as the cold ate away at the walls. Millions of children were conceived in blankets like that. The blankets are all lost now. They are a hole eaten by moths. They are what you can't hold in your hands. For those of us whose parents had been driven out of Germany by the war, we weren't German and we weren't Canadian. We were the invisible children, the ones denied family, history, and our language, and taught English instead, hidden as deep as it was possible to hide within the enemy. That is why my brother and I were there. Those blankets were like the air raid shelters built out of concrete in backyards from Vancouver to Halifax, built to withstand a nuclear assault by bombers coming in waves over the North Pole. They weren't put up by any military, but by simple people who had learned that a nation cannot protect its citizens, that it was all up to them alone, that the only way to survive the twentieth century was to be invisible. We weren't children. We were a wail of grief. For us, the Cold War was not the politics of using Germany as the dividing line between the Russians

Journeys Through a Dark Century - 109

and the Americans, or posting signs on German freeways, giving one speed for tanks and one for automobiles, one for one-way tank traffic, another for two-way military traffic. For my brother and me, it was still World War II. We were hidden from terror and kept distant from the corrupting influences of art and culture, history and philosophy. For our parents, those were the killers. It was the artists who had betrayed the people, the artists whose desire to dismantle culture had led to war. To keep us safe, we were hidden among working people in a mountain valley two hundred miles from the ocean, hidden on a farm in the midst of a settlement of Canadian soldiers, hidden in work and the folds of the land, wrapped up in a Hudson's Bay Company trade blanket, washed in a wash tub, learning to whistle for birds by a woman who could still remember operas, without the words, if that was possible. It was possible. A new world would come from us. We would be a people of the earth, and only of the earth. We would know nothing, and, knowing nothing, would make a free civilization, if that is possible.

I still live in that land neither Canada nor Germany. The snag in the program is that there never really was a 'land' in Canada. There was only an idea, which used people's confrontation with earth to build a country—another idea. What people actually did out there on the earth was invisible. It had absolutely no consequence to the country that was being created, although when I was a boy, I would look up at the mountains and believe that what I saw was eternal: mountains, trees, wind. I felt that what I saw was really there, and that it was a part of the farm, that it was the land, that everything we did fit together.

My father thought so, too. He comes from Kuppenheim, in the German state of Baden, sandwiched between the Black Forest and the Rhine floodplain east of Strasbourg. In Kuppenheim, the decimation happened three centuries ago, in the Thirty Years' War. For an entire generation, competing Catholic and Protestant armies had plundered the area to support themselves. By the early eighteenth century, the rampage had been gong on for so long that society had pretty much ground to a complete halt: peace had come, but there was no longer an economy of any kind—two-thirds of the population of Baden was either killed or driven away and the fields had gone to weeds. In Wimsheim, a day's hike north of Kuppenheim, only twelve out of eighty-four people survived the bloodbath: pretty typical.

The solution was a government construction project, like the British Columbian government building dams on the Columbia River in the 1960s, with premier W. A. C. Bennett cutting ribbons, and streamers flying: a photo op. Even still, it took a hundred years for Germany to become anything more than a battlefield. In the case of Baden, the way to recovery was Schloss Favourite: a summer house in the country for the Dowager Duchess—a big sprawling palace built outside Kuppenheim, with a dozen formal rooms, each decorated in a different style, all of them as tasteless and opulent as the next. To help stave off starvation amongst the peasants, the Duchess hired the men from Kuppenheim and the surrounding villages to build and decorate the palace—admitting openly to her friends that it was really a big china cabinet to house her priceless Bohemian porcelain, which she had brought with her into marriage. While the peasants cut precious stones and laid them in mosaics, their children carried baskets of pebbles from the Rhine. For each basket they carried those eight long kilometres, the children were paid a penny. With those pebbles, their fathers decorated the palace, setting each one individually into the wet plaster of the outer walls. They are still there. The palace looks as if the river has lifted up and become the sky, giving its power to the building, and through it to the Duchess and her son. The land and the aristocracy are one, you see. For their part, *peasants* didn't talk about 'the land.' It was meaningless to them—except, perhaps, as something which brought war down upon them like the plague.

Schloss Favourite was not a place to live, though. It was like parliament. Even though it was a celebration of the age of reason, it was as effervescent as angel food cake. Every room was for public display, linked one to the next in an unbroken ring: the Chinese room, the Duke's public bedroom, the mirror room, the flower room, the tea room, the Dutch tile room, each more impossible than the one that came before. The mirror room, for instance, is decorated with three hundred mirrors, rimmed with crusty gold frames. In an age in which even one mirror was ridiculously expensive, the people who passed through the mirror room were part of the walls, and the walls were made out of the images of passing people. The *earth,* where the peasants lived, was uncivilized, like the lust of a stallion for a mare. I mean, *really.*

This old model of peasant workmanship, however, this lack of civilized sophistication, lies at the heart of my family. My great great-great-great-great-great-great-grandfather, Martin Kornchen, was working as a gardener and a weaver in 1720. His great-great-grandson, Johann Koernig, was working as a teacher in 1860. On the other side of my father's family, Georg Rhenisch's son, Rudy, was working as an engineer in 1890. Rudy's grandson, Hans Rhenisch, was working again as a farmer in Canada in 1953—at last. What goes around comes around.

In some places, though, it didn't come around so fast: whole families of Germans in the Sudetenland, for instance, in western Czechoslovakia, turned their houses into death chambers, silvering Victorian blown glass Christmas ornaments of angels, pine cones, stars, and St. Nicholases right up into the Second World War. Most popular in Victorian times were balls with faceted sides, designed to reflect evil spirits—like the native dream catchers you can buy these days in gift shops in Banff and Jasper and Quebec City. Life expectancy was very low. The medieval methods of filling the balls with vaporized mercury, originally an alchemist's trick, often led to death from mercury poisoning. Thankfully, it gave way to the improved but still dangerous processes of silvering with silver oxide and death from the rare disease of argyria, which turned the body blue, like a witch. As the people struggled to put themselves back on their feet after the war, they took up the old work again, like coal miners' sons in Cape Breton leaving school and taking the bitter plunge into the pit so they could marry their high-school sweethearts, knowing that it would kill them. In whole areas of Czechoslovakia, every house was like a sweatshop in Bangladesh. Unable to afford expensive silver processes in a time of low returns brought on by the competition of mechanized manufacturing in what was by then the modern world, the families resorted to mercury, to keep their costs down, knowing full well the price they were paying. Breathing it twenty-four hours a day, children died in droves. We hung the pretty baubles on our Christmas tree in Cawston, British Columbia. Everybody did.

In Schloss Favourite even the Prince's bedroom was for show. His private bedchamber, where he actually slept, didn't even have windows. The *public* bedroom was for receiving petitioners while he dressed. They got to see that he was virile and strong. Like a daily press scrimmage outside a minister's office in Ottawa, his audience hour leant political stability to the state. For the same reason, to people of his class, the consummation of a marriage was a public ceremony, too. It had to be: paternity suits could rip a state apart. As for the birth of a son—or, God forbid, a daughter—everybody got to watch. For the same reason, the whole palace, right from the power of the river god brought into it through the stones on the walls, to the conch shells above the doors and the Prince dressing in public, was a Viagra pill. When it rained—and it rains a lot on the emerald green fields of Baden—the guests' coachmen drove their carriages right inside the building. The guests dismounted in comfort, out of the randy rain. Similarly, behind the palace, the Duchess had the peasants build a covered promenade two hundred metres long. Between its stone pillars she got some fresh air—again, without getting wet.

The Duchess never came to the conclusion that the people might rather have had the kind of world that is Kuppenheim now: paved roads, comfortable houses, a main street choked with traffic, geraniums on the window ledges, kitschy tiles decorated with pink roses above the stove, a well-known soccer team that competes with teams from other villages in the Murg Valley, a supermarket where the storks used to hunt for frogs, a town fountain that no longer runs, and a black-slate church with copper doors turned green with age; that, in other words, they wanted their own kitsch.

—

We sure did. In our pressboard house in the Similkameen, where the mosquitoes rose in huge clouds in the evenings and green light washed down off the slopes, my father had hung the dark, hand-carved wood of a Black Forest cuckoo clock. A potent memory of Dr. Rhenisch's hunting villa, it hung just to the left of the television's maplewood altar. Where golden eagles rose on the hot updrafts over purple basalt cliffs and their cries echoed across the span of the valley, where coyotes yipped from dens among the tumbled basalt blocks a hundred metres up above the fruit trees, luring the farm dogs out at night to kill them, our definitions of forests were German and our definition of German was beer, accordions, and peasants snowed in, high up in the Black Forest, carving clocks in the winter—and our father, who played oom-pah-pah on the accordion, of course.

We had to wind the clock once a week. It was eighteen inches high—the perfect size for a birdhouse—and decorated with dead stags, rifles, and a brace of pheasants. The weights were two lead fir cones. The bird popped out of its house regularly and chirped the time. For me, it was the picture of German sophistication. You couldn't have told me that there were factories and cities in Germany. I wouldn't have believed it. You could have told me about the Brothers Grimm. Germany was a kind of ghost story. It was a Disney theme park.

—

Kitsch, homesickness, *Heimat,* Home Sweet Home, *Heimweh,* that Silesian plague, is the immigrant's curse. Living in her three-room house below the hill in Keremeos, with the big trucks gearing down above her backyard and the cacti in her window, my great-aunt Martha—Bruno's sister—subscribed to *Die Hausfrau,* "The Housewife," a cheap newsprint magazine distributed across North America from its offices in Chicago, which featured sugar-sweet, sad stories and a few romanticized landscape photos of the Old Country; and to its twin, *Die Heimat,* a homesickness magazine featuring a few romantic poems, an excerpt from a serialized novel, a few photographs of a village scene, and ads for vacations in Florida, mail-order Bratwurst, and flights to Frankfurt. She had it bad.

I found the real *Heimat* in Garmisch, tucked in at the Bavarian border with Austria, just under the Zugspitze—the tallest peak in the German Alps. Well, barely: a hundred paces from the peak, and twenty metres below the summit, any climber coming up from Austria is subject to passport control. There's a customs booth and everything. In Garmisch, Hitler and Goering cheered Germany's athletes in the 1936 Winter Olympics—in a stadium designed to make the audience stand, not sit, so it would be more imposing. In Garmisch, the waiters at my hotel were officious, while the younger bartenders at the sport hotel were young and hopped up on a gentrified German version of rock and roll. When I went with my cousins and aunts and uncles to lunch at a restaurant outside of town, the waiters were positively cynical. These guys were fifty years old. They had seen it all. The food was cheap, about ten dollars a plate—but what a plate. The waiters brought each one of us a folding trestle table, upon which a platter, with enough food to feed four people, was laid. We were then given a plate for the table, and the waiters went from one to the other of us, serving us from our platters. As soon as a plate was finished, a waiter would be there again to fill it up. I'm not exaggerating—the lightest of those dishes, an omelette, was made out of what looked pretty much to be about ten eggs. Those platters were like a magic pot in an Irish fairytale told during the famine: it seemed that there was absolutely no end to the amount of food on any of them. We finished none. The waiters snickered.

"What?" they asked, with mock innocence. "Aren't you able to eat that?" Then they laughed and said, "A real man could eat that." We left in a cloud of derision.

My aunt Margot lives in the *Heimat*. She owns Dr. Rhenisch's hunting villa now: Home Sweet Home. All is not well, though: the roof has been replaced; the sandstone blocks that make up the foundation are sitting in wet soil, without drainage, and are reverting to sand; it costs Margot three thousand dollars a winter to heat with oil, and the mortgage has put such pressure on her that she has sold most of her furniture to make ends meet. The built-in gun racks with their boars' tusks are gone. The ceilings are cracked. If anyone visits now, they have to stay in a hotel: most of the rooms are empty. It is like one of the grand houses of Moscow overtaken by the Bolsheviks after the Revolution, or one of the grand Georgian houses of London, taken over by squatters.

Margot did start out her life as a revolutionary, too—in the wild world of 1960s Germany. Drugs, sex, rock and roll, a life in student communes: she lived it all with poverty and passion. She now works as a tour guide for Schloss Favorite. For her, all of Germany is a ruin. Born in 1945, she has never known any other world. It's not just Margot: the Duchess lived in a ruin, too, and tried to make it into an image of *Heimat*—she was a post-war child, too. I have a photograph of Margot, dressed in a Baroque dress, waving a handkerchief from an open window on the top floor of Schloss Favourite: the new Baroness.

—

Oh, great. Set in a five-hundred-year-old Black Forest farmhouse in Gutach, northeast of Freiburg, there's a museum display about rats—a pretty common bit of country life, sure. The display even features an eight-foot-high plywood cheese propped up against old sleighs and hay rakes in the hayloft. White plastic mice, like you can pick up for a few bucks in a toy shop, are tucked in here and there to make the children laugh—in the country there's always a mouse tail slipping around a corner, see. The mice are even poking their heads out among the remnants of last year's feature exhibition on folk costumes. The display is fairly extensive, too: in a third-floor hallway smelling of hay and smoke, Black Forest hats with black brims topped with three balls of red wool like cherries topping the whipped cream and chocolate of a cake are set next to sugary-sweet dirndl-clad maids and matrons from Bavaria; in the next case, men in lederhosen, flower-embroidered suspenders, and felt hats with pheasant feathers stand in a world of preserved dust. On little cardboard cards beside the metre-high dolls I read that the Industrial Revolution killed off the traditional clothing of the peasantry in the middle of the nineteenth century. Yeah, right. More like: isolated in their mountains for centuries, scraping out a living however they could, they finally had enough cash to buy something more stylish, something befitting their rising status in a Germany increasingly defined by urbanism and industry instead of by the practicalities of isolation and poverty. They would have dressed up for much the same reasons a Haida chief in 1880 didn't dress in a cedar bark cape but in a tux and a beaverskin hat—as if he was on his way to his club in London: they were identifying with a culture from a long way away, and they weren't quite getting it right. Up in the Black Forest, the process of self-colonization manifested itself in a typically European kind of nostalgia: anti-Napoleonic nationalism and the clarification of social classes in an industrialized world in which the nobility could no longer tell themselves apart from the working class. That will never do, will it? I mean, maybe in the sixteenth century it was possible for urban and rural people to wear the same clothing—a legally mandated extension of the Spanish style, actually—but in the nineteenth century, with the rise of both the middle and the working classes, you just could no longer tell. The German solution was to create laws stipulating the wearing of folk costume for national holidays. Like the nationalistic demands of students at the Wartburg, it was a complex reaction to the breakdown of the medieval world, which Napoleon left in his wake.

The first folk costumes were imitations of the costumes of the court. In Bavaria, they were even introduced by the new royal couple, who led sixteen pairs of children in sixteen separate costumes representing the sixteen districts of the state into the Oktoberfest. Homesick for their simple life on the land, the people who had given up their own peasant clothing just a generation before, or even more recently than that, leapt at this refinement: you could have your cake and eat it too. This was the drug of *Heimat*. It spread through the country like an epidemic. When in the latter half of the nineteenth century the whole idea devolved to women wearing fancy dresses from the city, folk costume clubs sprang up to self-regulate the situation. Things were brought back into control. People knew their duty. One thing is for certain, though: there is no base in peasantry or the land for the costumes of the peasants. Everybody was playing dolls, and they were doing so to control social change.

Frank also grew up in Disneyland—the northern British Columbian version. To found it, the German anthropologist and ethnographer Franz Boas cruised up and down the British Columbia Coast in the 1880s, paying old men and women a few coins to tell him stories before they died. Boas was the heir of Jacob and Wilhelm Grimm, who had started to collect fairytales throughout Hessen in 1806, to demonstrate that since the German people—although scattered across a number of small principalities, did indeed share a common culture, one rooted in forest and land, and could make common cause—had, indeed, a precedent for their own national state. It's like negotiating an Indian land claim in British Columbia today, with its roots tangled deep in aboriginal title. In fact, Jacob Grimm supported a theory that fairy tales had sprung up in the forest at the same time as a hypothetical ancestral German language. Boas applied this romantic principle of a people and a language rising together from the earth to his study of the peoples of the Canadian North Pacific, who shared similar beliefs about their own origin. A steam-powered paddlewheeler carried Boas up the grey-green eddies of the Skeena River and deposited him in Adventureland. On a trip like that in those days, you had to be ready for anything. After all, the Skeena was the scene of one of British Columbia's two known incidents of naval warfare: when a sternwheeler pulled in against the current to dock at Gitsegukla, the Gitksan fired on it from the cliff, to keep it away. They wanted no part of it.

Boas did. Two generations before, the Brothers Grimm had travelled with their rucksacks and their walking sticks. They had listened to peasant stories on wooden benches in dark farmhouse kitchens, carefully writing the stories down while children sat on green-tiled stoves and men went into the back rooms to bed down their cows. The smell of pig manure blew through the walls. When it was his turn, Boas set out to record the story-telling traditions of the Tsimshian, Heiltsuk, Salish, Nuxalk, Nuu-chah-nulth, Kwakwaka'wakw, Tlingit, and Haida peoples before they vanished completely under the weight of new political and social pressures. This was the great age of museums, and these peoples were set to become Nefertiti's head on display in a glass case in Berlin or folk costumes in a barn attic. It was the age of the European colonization of East Africa, the laying of a railroad across the plains between Canada and the Pacific coast, and the planting of Frank Richter's pear orchard at Inglewood. The Haida were carving ashtrays out of argillite; industry was married to romance; and Boas sailed up the snaking fjords and big rivers to record stories of Raven and D'Sonoqua, of Blue Jay and Killer Whale, stories of the founding of the world and the invention of humanity. Indian Commissioner Israel Powell was travelling from village to village, with his cane, his white suit and his wide-brimmed white hat, his steamship and servants, with the unenviable task of settling the "Indian Question" by laying out Indian reserves—unenviable because it meant forcing people into abject poverty; it meant constraining their human needs into civilization's needs—for land.

—

The stories Boas collected are the land itself. They are records of legal title, but unlike the scrolls of paper you receive from a land title office when you sign your name on mortgage papers, they could not be bought or sold: they could only be spoken and heard.

Expecting hats like Black Forest cakes, Boas walked into a story. Literally. After the nineteenth and twentieth centuries had their way with that story of the creation and continuation of the world, filling it with crates of Blue Willow china, rifles, and sacks of flour, European culture had planted fields and cut down trees in it, had blasted highways and railways through the story's deep canyons, translating it into a language of tectonic plates, upthrust ridges and fault lines, translating it into European land—but not quite. A drive today along the Fraser River north of Yale as the river foams far below—a couple hours up past rapids and falls and deep channels through Boston Bar to Lytton, then up the Thompson to Cook's Ferry and Cache Creek—is still a drive through the old Salish story of Coyote racing up the river to turn monsters into stone, making the land safe for humans. Despite the efforts of missionaries, land surveyors and Franz Boas, the monsters are still there. Some cut across the skyline. Others lie in the bed of the river, where the current breaks over them in an endless cresting wave. People race up from Vancouver for the weekend to ride their bright red and yellow kayaks like bucking broncos in the rapids at Nikomen as the traffic roars north and the trains squeal by on their way to Moose Jaw and Sault Ste. Marie. The story surrounds them. They never leave it.

Unless they read Boas. Boas' stories are not artifacts of native cultures, not artifacts of the earth and of how people have learned to live on it by creating an earth-bound sense of humanity, but artifacts of the streetcars of Hamburg, the oom-pah-pah bands of Bavaria, the National Gallery in Berlin, the Brothers Grimm. Even the great Romanian anthropologist Mircea Eliade's explanation that native stories tell of circular time rising from and descending back daily into dream is a European construct— how you subvert your will to a conductor dressed in black, and boom on your bassoon through the village wedding scene in Beethoven's Sixth, not how you get along in a world of spirits in the sagebrush.

— —

The *Heimat* comes into focus in Eastern Germany, which a century ago was pretty far to the west, really. I have a postcard of it: an old woman in a long-sleeved black dress standing in the middle of a coarsely cobbled road. This is the *Elbtor*, the Elbe gate, in the old Hanseatic city of Werben on the Elbe. The Kaiser on the stamp is cancelled out: 1917. Centuries of passing wagons have worn shallow grooves into the cobbles. The woman wears a black hat. A white apron hangs to her ankles. It pretty well looks like Werben, the city where Bismarck was born, a taxation centre for trade moving East from Hamburg into Brandenburg and Saxony, in which the Knights Templar maintained a church that figured in the Thirty Years' War, had become a small town at the end of a road rarely used, where people kept pigs. The *Elbtor* is made of dark bricks, once seriously blown up by cannonshot and hastily repaired. A fence lines the road, as if there to keep chickens in a yard. Or to keep people and pigs out.

    I found this postcard in an abandoned orchard house in Naramata, not facing Okanagan Lake in true villa style but away from it to a quiet gully of pines and wildflowers. The walls were full of bats, rustling as I walked through the rooms. The farmer, who had come to Canada with Bruno and Martha, had kept this postcard, which he had sent to his mother from a military posting in 1917, writing, "It is undescribable here," meaning "beautiful beyond words." At her death, the card had come back to him, and then to me. This too is the *Heimat*. So was the bank of grapes gone wild spilling off of the farmer's front porch, among the pork-and-bean tins he had thrown out there for fifty years and the half-century of needles that had fallen off of the Ponderosa pines.

Travelling even farther east, the *Heimat* is a calendar now: a different *Heimat* for each month of the year. It's made out of a small sample of the huge collection of postcards in the Grünes Gewolbe Museum in Dresden, carefully collected and preserved by a communist government that preferred to let all its old houses fall down, because they were deemed too big for single families, and, at 80,000 Marks per apartment, too costly to divide into apartments (60,000 Marks more than to build a new cubby in a twenty-storey Stalinesque block of utilitarian concrete.)

- An eighteenth-century hand-coloured etching of birch trees over the Liebe river, outside of Dresden—shading red cattle and blue-grey goats, in the last days of summer. It is inscribed in French.
- Towering clouds over the Lohm River bridge: late

evening, mid-July. Up on the cliffs, the village church catches the light. A man is leading cattle to a half-timbered mill in the shadows.

- Two women in pale blue dresses and hats stroll towards a temple made of larch trees decorated with garlands. The year is 1800. The temple was built in 1781—a birthday present to the son of the Saxon prime minister. Wind streams through poplars.
- The ruins of Castle Tharand above Dresden. A boy watches sheep which watch a cow which stares at the water which runs over a low fall into quick rapids. The castle is draped with ivy. This picture is set in a pink frame decorated with flowers, like a piece of china.

Postcards: what society women used to make at tea parties for their friends, sitting down one at a time to the side of the chatter and decorating a page in an album with a poem, a greeting, a watercolour, or drawings of flowers, and which for the price of a few pennies industrialization had made universal: a whole people at leisure in the shelter of the land, a whole civilization that had entered a landscape painting yearning for the past. Not one of the cards represented city life—Kattowitz, for example, where the trees came right down from the hills and among the houses, but which was dominated by the smell of coal from the line of mines running through the centre of the valley. Kattowitz was famed for its brown air and its individual, peculiar smell, like cigar smoke, or peat moss tamped into a pipe, which came from burning the famous Kattowitz coal. Kattowitz didn't need sepia photographs. It *was* a sepia photograph.

In 1968, a new generation left the cities to renew civilization on the land. They came with bags of nails and rolls of plastic, with rusty old school busses that smelled of carbon monoxide and dust, with Volkswagen vans powered by chipmunk engines, in 1952 pickups with dented fenders, with whatever was thrown aside by a civilization that was looking beyond them to the Moon. They came in any way they could, but they came, with sacks of soybeans and bags of marijuana, with dried mushrooms and bags of whole-wheat flour and loose white cotton shirts from India. Like Bruno and Martha, they dragged it all out onto old logging shows and abandoned homesteads. They came with images of communes in the mountains of California and recipes for granola. They dreamed of the end of civilization and their own survival, of how they were living with the land, of how they were living like the first people—and they watched the earth's fate become their own.

In the 1970s and 1980s, bitten by this dream, I walked the gravel bars of the Similkameen River in the moonlight, when each of the million stones beneath my feet was a weightless, grey globe of light. It felt as if I was walking through surf. On weekends, I skittered up cliffs and draws onto high meadows of sunflowers, stretching like clouds for mile on mile across the mountains. I looked from Cathedral Ridge a hundred miles across the Coast Range to the line of volcanoes running down the western shore of the continent. I had the continent under my feet. I felt it buckle and sway across thousands of miles in its slow, timeless folding and infolding. I felt the prairies stretch out beneath me like wind, and coyotes run free from one end of the continent to the other. I sat among aspens, with their trunks full of mountain bluebird nests and their branches humming with paper wasps. I stilled myself to the slow breathing of the trees and the rightness of the mathematical, even the musical, placement of wood and water across the soil. History went on.

One of the painters of the *Heimat* was Adolf Hitler. During the 1920s, when he was living in a shelter for homeless men in Vienna, he eked together a bit of cash by painting the linen backs of sofas with polite landscapes in the naïve German romantic style. Grubby, angry, and threatening, he went from table to table under the umbrellas of streetside cafés, selling small paintings of Nature and the city. In one of his watercolours (available from a Hitler-worshipping site on the Internet), a harsh mountain rises three thousand metres in a vertical thunder of ice. There are mossy boulders in the water, and yellow birch trees on a headland of wildly fallen trees. Coarse shrubs grow angrily out of grass. The painting gives the impression that whatever cold is looming like the wall of Heaven over the world is withering the trees and grass up front. It is a painting of stillness, simultaneously lethargic with resignation and tense with pent-up violence. Likely out of fear and charity and just to salvage something of their day, people sipping coffee and eating apricot-scented sachertorte in the cafés of fashionable Vienna bought paintings like that from the bum standing in front of them. The paintings are technically competent, as you would expect from a talented schoolboy, in a style which would find a broad appeal in British Columbia today. The style hearkens back to the German romantic paintings of the nineteenth century, like Oswald Achenbach's *A Mountain,* in which a towering peak dominates the painting so completely that its expected subject, a group of shepherds and their flock, almost vanishes from sight, or the black mountain pool in Adrian Ludwig Richter's *Pool*, brooding like the chilling depths of the human heart, around which travellers carefully pick their way, or the symbolic and nationalistic paintings of Caspar David Friedrich: broken oak trees in the snow, damaged but still living; two young men looking out to an empty sea; a landscape of broken ice; ancient ruins with a new house built among them, so bittersweet. In all of these paintings, the land is either God or a reflection of humanity which rises from it, in a way hauntingly similar to the stories of the Haida. These are paintings full of peasants in situations of deep emotion, drama, hardship, and humour (not always all at once). The National Gallery in Berlin is full of the things, in a collection that also includes technically perfect but otherwise dead paintings by such masters of technical style as Franz Theodor Aerni and Gustav Bauernfeind ("Gustav Farmers' Enemy"!) and stops abruptly with *The Thinker* by Rodin. After that perfection of the art form, nothing more could be done, or added.

Or maybe it could. You can find *Heimat* painting, or landscape painting, in any church in Germany—a traditional form of folk art like crocheting bedspreads or firing pottery. In his villa, Dr. Rhenisch even had one—a mural of the sweeping curve of a lake, lined with Lombardy poplars settling into fall. Tall beds of rushes catch the wind on the shore, their abandon balancing the still curve of the water. This fresco was painted in the entrance hall by the local engraver Erwin Rose. Rose became a family friend. My father passed the fresco every morning when he went to school, and every afternoon when he came back.

Actually, you can find *Heimat* painting in any small-town art gallery in British Columbia. In 1981, I bought a three-colour Haida print of a salmon from a young man standing shyly in front of Victoria's Empress Hotel. He had a bundle of prints under his arm, and his left leg was badly injured—as if it had got caught in a net as a load of salmon was winched on board a trawler in Hecate Strait. He swung it around by the hip as he walked: the knee was no longer doing its job. For thirty bucks he handed me a print. It was nondescript, really, distinguished only by the spirit of the salmon, living in a salmon egg in the hinge between the salmon's tail and its body, out of which the whole rest of the salmon rose—like a dream or a mask. The artist who made it wasn't looking for a *Heimat*—I was. The artist was looking for thirty bucks.

You'll even find the *Heimat* in the fresh air where art really strips down to its Fruit of the Looms. For instance, if you were to drive north from

Vancouver, looking for my house here among the firs and aspens of the Plateau, you'd first pass through the sagebrush and bunchgrass benches of the Thompson, with their abandoned orchards and their desiccated Indian reserves. Framed by some river gravel and some shrubby pines at the intersection of Highway 1 and Highway 97 in Cache Creek, you'd be greeted by a metre-high wooden goldminer, made out to look a lot like the Looney Tunes' Yosemite Sam. He is the town mascot, a relic of British Columbia's Centennial in 1958. Farther south in the Interior, such gnome-figures disappeared when civic councils became eager to embrace more sophisticated images of progress, like pulp mills, drive-ins, and supermarkets. Pretty soon, Canadian postal carriers were bowed down with mass-produced glossy postcards depicting dams, shopping malls, pulp mills, log dumps, and logging trucks filling the roads. In Cache Creek, though, people are so damned proud of the little guy that they have immortalized him out of a chunk of wood knocked into shape with a chainsaw. Similarly, air travellers to Vancouver today are greeted not by the city or by anything that settler culture has created but by a few pieces of middle-class native art, set in glass cases, and by Bill Reid's *Jade Canoe*. The last time I saw that nod to Caspar David Friedrich, travellers were sitting on the tiered benches in front of it, like the audience at a performance of Oedipus in Athens in the age of Tragedy. With time to kill, I walked around that piece of the dreamtime—it is, after all, a three-dimensional piece. I peered around corners at figures peering around corners at me. The piece filled the space around itself, not as a completed work of art, or a record of an integration of native and western styles, but as a promise, held within an image of history. From there to Friedrich's ships in mist just off a rocky shore is not very far. That's what counts for art out this way. A culture that never shucked off its medieval village sense of art when it modernized wants to throw off the whole project of modernization and go home again. It is homesick.

Politically charged terms like *Heimat* are not just about homesickness. People who live in the *Heimat* are like schools of minnows flashing through a beam of sunlight, or starlings gathering in the thin fall heat above a hayfield to suddenly settle along the powerlines for miles, then just as suddenly lift off again: they actually live there, and are dwarfed by it. It becomes both land and country to them. For instance, to celebrate his victory in the Seven Years' War and his solidification of his hold on Silesia, Frederick the Great, King of Prussia, built his New Palace in Potsdam, and had it decorated with paintings of rape and seduction, too, set next to some really big, gold-framed sea battles. The mythical world represented by those paintings—a world of battles and inheritance, of classical myths and military fantasies, was as real to him as the earth on which he stood. It was not an accident that the roofline of his palace was dominated by two hundred statues out of mythology—one to every room. The world they represented was as much the source of his power as the earth he dominated in their name, and for him, stability was about power—especially watching how other people were shaped by it, and manipulating them through their responses. Himself, he had gout. To bring his guests into the maze of his mind, he had his two thousand acres of gardens decorated with marble statues of Satyrs carrying away naked women, in little clearings and squares among rose bushes and palm trees strategically arrayed for moonlit romantic trysts. The rose arbour by the orangerie alone could accommodate a good half dozen couples in its nips and tucks. The garden was designed to shock, to titillate, to be public and yet hidden, like breasts turned into a bust, powdered and half covered with lace. This kind of thing is what made the aristocracy tick, as it was back in Rome with Virgil and Catullus writing of adultery and oral sex and long nights and days, weeks and months and years of seduction. An emperor's relationship to his country was sexual.

By the time Bruno and Martha came along, seduction so artfully and coyly expressed, so contained and civilized, had boiled down to its raw bones: the aristocratic soul had been separated from the working-class body, kept there by new structures of obedience: government, law, poetry about angels, the idea of the immortal soul itself. The entire project made you sigh with tenderness and want to run off to rummage through your papers for that nocturne by Chopin—which is precisely what Dr. Rhenisch did. Well, he could. Bruno couldn't. Denied a soul, he spent long hours, days, and weeks standing on street corners in Breslau, waiting for a creature with a soul to hire him to carry bricks, to build some other edifice to utility, some other transformation of mythicized people and landscape into technical ingenuity and titillation.

What is a landscape, after all, but a painting, one of those works by a Dutch master, with trees along a lane, a country house in the distance, or maybe low blue clouds on the horizon. Before that, there was the Mona Lisa, with a background of mills and a holy mountain and God knows what else—trick fountains in a Baroque garden. In Mirabelle, the Prince Archbishop of Salzburg sat his guests on chairs to admire his fountains, then laughed when hidden nozzles beneath them soaked their dresses and took the curls right out of their wigs.

In British Columbia the landscape has no frame. Don't get me wrong: history books are widely distributed here, even *The Illustrated History of British Columbia* and *The Encyclopedia of British Columbia,* just to name two that ushered in the new millennium. These are very specialized narratives, though, not histories of a people rising from the clash between land and earth. They represent an idea: "British Columbia"—in other words, the old colony as it still lives among us, without the landscape it created. They represent the city of New Westminster, made rich by the trees of Haida Gwaii shipped down the coast to Fraser Mills in long booms and on self-dumping barges, but not the clearcuts back in Port Clements and Copper Bay. When former premier Glen Clarke said that environmental activists intent on shutting down the logging of old growth trees in the few remaining pristine watersheds of the Coast Mountains were enemies of British Columbia, he never said a truer word in his life. They *were* enemies of British Columbia. When Pirmin went out to live in the bush around Lake Constance, he played Clarke's game, too. He built himself a hut on the Reichenau, where he set up a Utopian community, combining education with industry—cheese-making, agriculture, grafting, fruit-growing, and wine-making—to turn wilderness into civilization. The incredible thing is that it worked: there are cheese-making natives all over the Black Forest, and natives making schnapps in little copper and clay stills. Where there is no fruit, high up in the mountains, they make the damn stuff out of flowers, the little dancing meadows of God—oh, let's go out for a quadrille with Heidi while the goats skip around our feet. Pirmin's church is now nestled among fruit trees, flowers, and vines—closely planted, staked, harshly pruned, stretching down from massive, black war memorials, with eagles with rapacious, outstretched wings, and long, long lists of the dead.

The project of civilization succeeded in British Columbia, too—native children across the colony were taught to grow apples and berries right up into the 1960s. Even though all that's left are a few unpruned apple trees full of tent caterpillars in a few unpainted villages as lumber trucks press deep ruts into the asphalt, they could not return to their earth. Zealous Bible thumpers and sky pilots with their New Testaments folded under their arms won the war for civilization with Gatling guns of good works and bullets of the Psalms, with their heads in the clouds and their feet of lead. Assuming that the source of native weakness lay in the Indians' refusal to give up their heathen ways, avert your eyes, Good

Christian Women, the missionaries' government outlawed potlatches along the length and breadth of the Coast; the religious paraphernalia of entire peoples were shipped off to museums for the price of a bottle of cheap whiskey. It's what you might expect if the Crown Jewels of England, or all the gold statuary of the Cologne Cathedral in its walk-in safe, including, as it does, the putative remnants of St. Peter's walking stick, were set up for display way up north among the salmonberries at Babine Lake, and maybe someone used them for target practice, eh?

Hey, it could happen yet. The Canadian novelist Margaret Atwood, for one, smiled her way right through two books about images of the land in Canadian literature: *Survival* and *Strange Things*. These books detail fear of the land as the foundation of the social, literary, and cultural life of her country of stone houses, maple trees, and mill races of incandescent blue water. It is a beautiful country, worth the praise of her art, but here in the Cordillera where mountain caribou walk ghostly through subalpine trees draped in long veils of black lichen as the snow falls around them like starlight, Atwood's Baedekers of the corner restaurants and hidden pensions of Canadian literary life might as well be books about the Byzantine layers of protocol in the Vatican See. To those of us prying the woodpeckers off our windowframes among the black poplars, or crowbarring our carrots out of the Cariboo clay, *Survival* looks like a White Paper, a federal government report prepared for a select parliamentary committee by a writer sitting at a desk passing laws about the snow-drenched land on which my mother and I have lived our lives: *The Foundations of Power among the Canadian Elites,* a kind of literary *Who's Who* for the people who continue to manipulate the agencies of colonial power among us, with their banks and their mutual funds, their parliaments and their flags, their Canada Post, their universities and their customs officials in white shirts.

It's damned frightening. My mother is the daughter of immigrants. I'm the son of an immigrant. What we really want is to have our own experience with the birch trees, the joy of winter snow, and the long blue evenings of mosquitoes recognized, because even after three generations, we still haven't accepted the terms of Canada's relationship to power, the contract that brought my mother's parents and my father here as citizens, the one in which they promised to become Canadians and learned the words to "God Save the King." They promised, and they did become citizens, but for my mother and I, who were born so deep within the land we confronted the earth instead, the whole project flies in the face of our experience and asks us to colonize ourselves. It demands that we give up our particular sense of land in order to become Canadian. You should see my otherwise stoic mother laugh and sing when winter snows obliterate the social world of highways and traffic, shops and mail, and leave her alone with the earth. She's positively ecstatic.

Well, my mother and I might know how to be alone with the earth, but we sure don't know what to call it. Take the simplest word: *forest*. The word is adequate, but disturbingly generalized. We are surrounded by millions of square miles of it, but don't have any decent words for it, as it exists specifically around us and within us, just a few unlikely candidates from the world of land:

- Forest. Too much Robin Hood and the old oak trees that built the ships that sailed the seas. Too many German peasants with their cows and goats in the meadows.
- Bush. Too much Africa and untouched land where no one lives. Too many Zimbabwean women cutting down forests one stick at a time to carry home tied to their backs, to cook dinner, one dinner, one thin blue

thread of smoke at a time, until the eagles are circling over a desert.

• Timber. Duh. Too many Kenworth trucks hauling into town, spitting up chunks of mud from their tires; too many slash piles; too much smoke. Same for: cutblock, riparian zone, wildlife corridor, old growth, prescribed block, woodlot. Too much sign-here-on-the-dotted-line, sir.

•Stick. This is from Chinook Jargon—or Wawa—British Columbia's own language. *Stick:* a tree. As in, "I'm going out to the sticks." *Whim stick:* a fallen tree. As in, "I'm going out to the clearcut." You can hear the sound of the stick falling: whim. Still, this one has legs, as in: "He really lives out in the sticks." That's usable. Thing is, it's come to mean: "What a hick." If you used this to describe a forest, no one would be quite sure what you meant. Part English, part French, part Chinook Indian, Wawa was the trade language of British Columbia, Washington, and Alaska. Even in the 1930s, every newspaper editor in the province had a Chinook Jargon dictionary at his side. In 1898, the language had its own newspaper in Kamloops: *The Wawa*. In 1898.

• Boreal forest. Give me a break. Can you imagine going out for a walk behind your house, and saying to your kids, "I'm just going out to the boreal forest for a while?" It's like saying, "I think I'll stroll down to the Royal Ontario Museum for the afternoon and look at the plastic moose and the Plexiglas loon." All that really works here is something like, "I'm going out to the aspens, I'm going out to the firs, I'm going out to Green Lake, I'm going out."

You can't say it. In other countries it is the job of poets to make up words for situations like this.

• Trees. "I'm going out to the trees."

Nah.
The trouble is, you're not going out. You're already there.

It's not that I don't know any names for things. I have no trouble naming a copse, a grove, a dell, a dale, a forest, a boll, a glen, a brae—in England, full of the king's deer. I learned all that way back from the book table at the 5 Cents to a Dollar Store, when I used to spend the afternoons hanging out with Robin Hood, stringing up monks by the heels among the gnarly oaks. In that English landscape of poachers and porridge and fog tip-tapping at the windowpane, of bleating sheep and clever collies herding them into pens while cleverer men smoked their pipes and knocked their walking sticks and whistled sweetly, my words are at home. It's just that I'm not. On the other hand, in my own land made out of aspen trees and black spruce, rust-red pines riddled with beetles and woodpeckers hammering insatiably through the month of May, looking for a way in, I have no words, but I am home. For all its brilliance with dealing with Upper and Lower Canada, *Survival* just doesn't describe this never-never land between the mirrors, this land neither Eden nor out of it.

The paradox behind my house, the land across the road, the land stretching for three hundred miles to the Rockies and three hundred miles to the Coast Mountains collapsing into the Pacific, belongs, you see, to Elizabeth Windsor, Queen of England, or, as we like to put it, to the Crown. It is held in trust for all of us. It is ours, in the same way that Friedrich the Great's satyrs gave him the legitimacy to channel, through his wit and his will, a people, a land, and a stretch of earth into an empire. In that conflation of terms lies the problem. The dead logging debris on the ground, the shredded, punky wood, the branches stripped off the lodgepole pines by crab-like feller-bunchers and pressed into the thin soil and the deep clay by skidders, all provide nutrients for new soil. The thin trees left standing in this sandbox are still a forest, of sorts—but one according precisely to the requirements of a scientific worldview. A forest like that ensures the continuance of British Columbian colonial culture, British Columbian colonial land, but the only sanctioned entrance it allows into a spiritual earth is through the gate of the industrial metaphor laid upon it, just as its only culturally sanctioned entrance into land in general and earth specifically is through the metaphor of subdivision and ownership. You would think we would have learned better after a whole century of Indian reserves, which cut first peoples off from themselves by the simple addition of snake fences winding along the hills.

In this context, reading Atwood's other hymn to images of the North, *Strange Things,* made me applaud Lucien Bouchard, founder of the Bloc Quebecois, the federal party devoted to removing Quebec from Confederation. When Bouchard said publicly, "Canada is the problem," I just knew what he was talking about: the railroad punched through the Thompson and the Fraser canyonlands, disenfranchising whole nations which had lived there for nine thousand years by laying the rails through their keekwillie huts. It had to be that. Living in half a continent stitched together with the catgut of a railroad and the mustard plaster of some old portage routes, I find it easy to share in the chill power of the St. Laurence frozen in February, with the green-white ice bunching up below Vieux Québec, cutting off the potato fields and maple trees stripped of their leaves on the Île d'Orléans. I share in the sense of canoes setting forth from Montreal on the eighteen-month journey across Paul Kane's paintings of the Cree, too, to bring back bales of furs to be made into men's top hats in London, Paris, and Berlin, so the Reichstag and the Bourse and Parliament could get on with their bowing and their clipped vowels. If I close my eyes I can feel a current of buckskin-fringed and warpainted Indians and smoke-eyed mountain men flowing down the river like uprooted trees pouring down the Amazon, a great novel decorated in its exotic finery spinning perpetually past the city. In fact, with Lucien, I share the sense of a whole continent draining past the *cabanes à sucre* and the tall churches with spires as sharp as knitting needles, knitting the sky together into a sweater for God, draining down like unwinding wool past the thin farms and their fat pigs. That's easy. It's when he suggests that as what he calls an Anglo I will thrive when Quebec is removed from my country, because then I can have the country I've always wanted, just as he will, that I turn from him. If the problem is a set of power relationships among the business elite, which we call Canada, then being locked in a box with that imposed land sense is no better for me than it is for him. I wish he had talked instead about what really mattered to him—the surrender of power to Ontario, perhaps, the Napoleonic wars, maybe the loss of the Ohio Valley, military bungling and betrayal, the lost territories in Louisiana and Detroit, how we got to this mess and what we're doing to keep ourselves here. If he was honest like that, he would not have dismissed my Canada as if it was identical with the vague set of nationalist ideas that politicians use instead of talking about where they really live. So, Lucien, I'll go first: my Canada is the blue silk handkerchief of the Chilcotin River flowing down to the Fraser and past the lost villages at Lillooet and Yale through pine forests smelling of sap and heat. That is the point we can share. Santé.

    I tell you, though. Lucien is lucky. Unlike this place where right now last night's snow is falling in little blue clumps like birds off of spring trees, Canada, Upper and Lower, Bouchard's country, has already defined its relationship to our shared histories of silence, land, and earth. What a country we could make together!

With deft brushstrokes, Atwood paints a complementary image, the land of our masters: the history of a series of stockades in wilderness, a few garrison houses full of scurvy and loneliness, surrounded by wooden walls and guard posts. This history is framed in rococo gold. In its various versions it hangs on the walls of bank offices in Toronto: the advance of fur trading posts across the Northwest, followed by Confederation, settlers pouring in by train, the wealth of the continent bridging the Rockies, carted back in its clickety-clack across the prairies, crushing pennies boys laid out on the rails between the coulees and the sky, and finally brought home into the watershed of *Alouette* and *Chère Lise*. In this picture, contemplated over a brandy and a good cigar, the wilderness is considered hostile; no attempt is ever made to come to terms with it or, in the imagination, to enter it. If you want to read sex into that, you should.

I don't live in that country, though, just as my friend Kemeny, who lives in the tobacco country south of Brantford and north of Lake Erie, doesn't live in the walled suburbs of Hamilton or London, but in an old house butting up against a corn field, trying to replant the Carolinian forest one black cherry tree at a time.

"I'm going to have to leave here soon," he said to me last spring. "I'm going to have to move to Northern Ontario."

I was surprised. "But this is your land. It would be like ripping out your heart."

"The earth is dying here, Harold. Soon it will be toxic."

Kemeny's a good cook—stews, stir-fries from his garden, and wine that tastes of wild honey from the Reichenau of poor poisoned Pelee Island, as the lake drains from around it and dead fish wash up on the shore. In that old house which he is rebuilding in a process as slow as portaging from watershed to watershed across the prairies, the conversation and laughter go on deep into the night. The next time I'm there, Kemeny and I should call Lucien up. We should invite him over for a nightcap. We could make common cause.

Don't get me wrong. I live in a place called Canada, all right, but it's not the same Canada. I live in the Interior, a place that men in the capital cities of Victoria and New Westminster contemplated from such a sense of hostile wilderness that they named it after the British experience in India and Africa. In Africa, no one went into the Interior, except dogs and mad Englishmen. Everyone else stayed in Zanzibar and whooped it up with the Arabs, in the heat and indolence. The indolence was delicious. They stayed up late playing with their slave girls, or boys, *please,* and they slept late, with their heads in a vise of the sun. The sea was the temperature and consistency of turtle soup. In the Interior of Eastern Africa, disease and hostility, barbarism and the slave trade laid men bare: just six months earlier they might have been school boys parsing Latin verbs in Oxford, but suddenly they were whipping their packers until they died; they were sleeping behind hedges of thorns; they were burning their grass huts so that there was nothing for any other man to use; they were dead men. Richard Burton went in there, as mad or as sane as they came, looking for the source of the Nile, and wandered around in hysteria and malaria for a year and a half, was given up for dead, found water going every which way but never found its source, before he finally made it out again—only to want to plunge right back in. In the end, he got out by joining an Arab slave caravan—the voyageurs of their time and place: 1863, to put a nail into it. In those days, a small-time slaver could count on picking up twenty thousand pounds of ivory, valued at four thousand pounds sterling in Khartoum, and four or five hundred slaves worth five or six pounds each—for a total of sixty-five hundred pounds. It was illegal, but profits like that weren't to be ignored. It was the cocaine trade of its day. That was life in the Interior. In those days, the BX stage was running up the Cariboo Road through 150 Mile House, two miles from my house here among the trees, with a driver and a man riding shotgun and chests full of gold dug out of the ground. Jewish merchants were murdered for their gold on the road between the mines at Barkerville and the river crossing at Quesnelle Forks; miners walked the three hundred and fifty miles north through the sagebrush, the aspens, pines, and the bunchgrass, to dig pits in the gravel, sometimes ninety feet down. The mines were below the water table. They were wells, really. Even so, shafts were punched out of them in to leads of gold, shored up with trees cut down on the slopes above town and wrestled down. Water and gravel were lifted out one bucketful at a time. Men came from the whole world to dig and sluice that gravel, and they died young. That's the truth—rather than the dream—of life in the forest. In Barkerville and Quesnelle Forks, thirty years was a good age to die. When the miners had been fleeced by black-market prices and freight costs, they walked back out down to the Coast, through Likely, and Horsefly, 150 Mile House, Chasm, Pavilion and Lillooet, sleeping in the ditches, up to their ears with adventure, bushed. That was life in the Interior, too: except this time it was all legal.

Toronto street poet and now painter of cats and ecstasy Joe Rosenblatt put Lucien Bouchard's quandary to me succinctly one day in his red house of flowers and cats sitting like a pile of driftwood and ice on the East Coast of Vancouver Island. Outside, the old clambeds of the Qualicum people stretched around the curve of Qualicum Bay like family weeping at a funeral—in a town that places the beginning of time in English country life. At this solemn ceremony of forgetting, there are roses and Waterford crystal; there is heavy linen and there is demon gin. Joe sits in the middle of the mourners, still the cantankerous, surly street kid from Toronto, approaching old age with blended domesticity and cynicism, like a tomcat walking along a railing at midnight. Around Joe, in the clearcut that has become the first age of the world, the air is as quiet and timeless as a painting by Turner—light rising into Jerusalem triumphant over England. This was, after all, the centre of colonialism in British Columbia. Once the big trees of the first age of the world were hauled off by steam donkeys and cables singing from spar trees and men with axes strung from their belts, the money moved there, like salmon finding their way home. The judges and lumber barons retired in Qualicum Beach, where the water rolled the shingle around like ice in a whiskey glass and the fog came over the water like the smell of seduction. Tycoons play golf there in the smell of salt and the shh-shh of sprinklers and the tidy clip and snip of a gardener's clippers. Old stock market men from Vancouver plant gardens among the cedar trees. They build Tudor houses on Kwakwaka'wakw earth.

"Canada no longer exists in the sense of a nation," Joe told me, almost biting the coffee out of his cup. "It is a chain of ten cities, surrounded by wilderness. That is the only place in which there is any Canada any more. Only those cities. The rest of the place has gone back to the bush." He swore a blue streak and rummaged around, looking for sugar, looking for a painting to show me, sidestepping a cat. The cat did not sidestep. Joe just laughed at him. Joe laughs a lot.

Bushed. As in "Gone back to the bush." Now, there's a fine British Columbian expression. You use it to describe a man who has gone up-country (into the Interior!), who has lived for months, or years, outside of the city, and who has ceased to treat his situation rationally. Maybe he has packed into the Stikine and lived in a trapper's cabin through the winter. For company, he has had only the snow, the trees, the damned porcupine trying to eat its way in through his door. Maybe he went off for a year to teach school in Gitsegukla, wound up staying for a decade while the violence drove other new teachers away year by year by year. Maybe he went native. That's the real fear. That's what it's really all about. Maybe he forgot the difference between us and them. To be bushed means you have become Colonel Kurtz, somewhere far upriver. To finish you off, they're going to have to send Martin Sheen in a plastic boat full of kids popping LSD. It means that when you kill dear Colonel Kurtz, you do it for your own reasons, not because you have orders to do so. It means you have ceased to take part in the administration. It means you are not going back.

You cannot *find* the land unless you are bushed. Unless you are bushed, you are still dreaming of the *Heimat*. You are thumbing through postcards.

Now, in *Strange Things*, Atwood delivers a stand-up comedy routine that would make Jay Leno proud. Her shtick is about Canadian culture: the weather (North), the land (North)—both of them devouring presences that eat and nibble and marrow-suck and crunch with crab-pliers and dig at with snail forks and pie forks and slice with steak knives and tear at with sharp teeth and destroy, feminine presences which gobble up men and spit them out before breakfast. It's about men losing their selves in the bodies of these women. If you read sex into this, you should.

Well, I've been bushed for years, and I take issue when young teachers refuse continuing teaching contracts in the Chilcotin, preferring instead a day a week of occasional teacher-on-call work in Surrey, at the Coast. I take issue that the ongoing colonization of such Interior cities as Kelowna by foreign capital and a Vancouver university is termed progress, that the exploded monastery of Mission Hill winery, set up on a mountaintop like a film set, obliterating the views around itself, draws thousands of tourists a day to see its Italian bell tower and its French bell, its Austrian stone fountain and its family crest, with a stork folded into itself like a chick in an egg. I take issue with the class of Honours English students I met at a Vancouver university, who did not know where the Interior was. I was offended that I had to draw them a map, that although I was a citizen of their city—the focus of my educational, professional, and economic life, and which I have visited many times over a period of thirty years—they were not citizens of my province, although its future, politically speaking, was in their hands, not mine. Their prof took me out for coffee afterwards and told me that while speaking to another class he had developed the nagging sense that he was speaking a different language than the one he was hearing, how he had pointed to the Coast Mountains rising above West Vancouver and had asked his students what mountain range that was. He told me that they had answered, without hesitation, "The Rocky Mountains," effectively compressing the eight-hundred-mile breadth of British Columbia into a postage stamp.

According to Atwood, Canadian literature is a re-telling of the story of Windigo, the spirit of the Great Lakes and the Shield country, whose insatiable appetite is dulled only by his exhaustion after devouring the life of all the world. Stuffed to the gills, outcast, and on the lam, he sleeps it off out in the jackpine. It's a great, wise story that cuts right to the heart, but one that just rings false in the mountains where the rivers flow down to a different sea. These might be the stories and fears of Canada's literary elites, but they're not the ones of the people who actually live out on this earth and have created a unique land out of it—the farmers, the immigrants, the natives, and the poor. Our stories are oral. A literature that steals our stories from us is not helping. We have our own history of cannibalism here, thank you very much. In fact, we have enough different cannibalistic traditions to keep a university ethnology department flush with grad students for a decade. Our self-basting barbecue traditions range from the Hansel and Gretel and Max und Moritz that Atwood's tradition shares with us, to the winter ceremonies of the Nootka and the Tsimshian: the evil stepmother who leaves you to starve in the forest; how an old woman fattens you up in a wooden pen until you're plump enough to roast on a spit like a suckling pig; the whalers' house at Nootka, dismantled and shipped to the Field Museum in Chicago, with its human skulls thrust onto poles, and some of them not all that old-looking either, to calm the sea for the journey to the other world where whales rise out of the dream of the beginning of time and can be caught with a spear and a sealhide bladder; the Hamatsa dances, the metre-long raven beaks of charcoal-stained wood, the wild men leaping out of the dark around the edges of the longhouse, the screams. These are ceremonies that negate the urge to devour. The mad clown, out of control, tearing around the edges of the dreaming fire, slashing people on the arms, even biting tiny chunks out of their biceps and spitting them out onto the dust, humanizes. He literalizes the relationship between society and the individual to release the curse of society's oppression. It has nothing to do with appetite. It is an immunization. If the spells are conducted well, you will never leave the bush again. Your literature will become the land. In that context, *Survival* is just a ghost story. Boo.

When the blizzards started blowing between the high-rise condos on the Lake Ontario shore in January 2004, turning each sheer plate glass wall into a live-action version of a painting by A. Y. Jackson, there were only a few people on the streets. Bundled up in running shoes, even high heels, they stared their frostbite in the face. Taxis were abandoned in the middle of Danforth Avenue, their hoods up, their radiators steaming, all their lights on and the doors locked. The next day, young men splashed through the slush. Dressed in baseball jackets—unzipped—and running shoes, they kicked at the ice, swearing, "I don't do this shit!" That is the world of new immigrants to Canada now, who have no reason to learn the most elementary lesson about living on the earth: Don't kick the ice! It's bigger than you are. They came for the city. When the earth makes itself known within it it is an invasion. This is why they call up the army when it snows in Toronto. They feel the land trying to smother them. It is stealing their identity. They should be mad. It is! That is the country described by *Survival*. It is a book of brilliant fear.

Those of us outside Atwood's covers, though, my mother and I, for example, welcome the storm. Our fear is more chilling. It is the fear of how *people* will manipulate us, how they will prescribe a national or even a provincial vision that silences our experience. It's like living on a reserve, losing your strength to cultural change, silenced by being removed from any conversations of power. We sure as hell don't need Atwood stoking up the fires. This is British Columbia, after all, where we change colonial masters the way our colonial masters change their shirts. What the English began with a starched collar, the Canadians were quick to put on with studs. They look in a mirror and smile.

In the bush, the North is home, security, safety. It is the bear wandering through blueberry meadows and old avalanche trails, the beds of glaciers, a cabin on a trapline, a lake in the shadow of mountains, the light playing on aspen trunks. It is the liberating blue release of snow, a road cut off, a warm bed, a fire, feet stomping off snow just inside the door. The North is a lover's body moving under a thick, warm sweater, mice making crystal cities of light under the drifts. When winter storms come down from the Yukon to the Interior, we have come home. We run outside and laugh. We dash to the basement for a bottle of dandelion wine, some peaches, add ginger and honey, stir.

A decade ago, my editor Angela Addison, a passionate daughter of 1950s Southern Ontario, put the problem to me very succinctly: "Quebec and Ontario will never separate. Even if there is a political separation, they cannot be divided, because at their heart they share a landscape: they both live in fear of the North. They are awed by it. They dream of it. That's where their winter comes from. You don't have that in British Columbia at all. You share none of it."

If we're going to talk about Canada, and I think we should, we need to include my Canada, and all the other silenced Canadas at the table, or we don't have a nation, only a watch fob.

Some names for my country, not all self-chosen:

> Transmontanus
> New Caledonia
> The Interior
> Columbiana
> Heimat
> Cordillera
> The Land
> Eden
> The Heartland
> The Middle of Nowhere
> Beyond Hope

"It was the highways which ruined Kelowna," said my friend Hugh Dendy. Four generations farming the stony East Kelowna bench, the result of one advertisement set in the window of a real-estate office in Georgian London and eighty years of the Kelowna English with their art auctions, their Yacht club, and their Regatta, had come down to Hugh and me sitting on the back of his truck at Brushy Bottom, an old whistle-stop along the Similkameen River, where I had planted twelve thousand peach trees for him, as part of a shared dream of rejuvenating the fruit industry. We were drinking tea out of a thermos as the wind came down out of Paul Creek with a hint of cold.

"When they put the bridge across the lake," Hugh said, "the culture of Kelowna started to decline. Now it has almost completely vanished." That was twenty years ago. The old orchards were still there, the old families, a house here and there, some scraps of memories: how to set your ladder into a Winesap tree, how to spit the apples down off the branches by pinching them between forefinger and thumb, how to talk to the man at the packinghouse about the quality of the crop, the smells of yeast and wax, how much to pay the men who showed up at your door looking for a week pruning in December, how to fall out of a pear tree without breaking your back, and on and on and on, the jokes, the laughter, the rhapsody of sun and wind and rain. I came to my culture two generations late: by the 1990s there wasn't a banker in the country who would touch an orchard anymore. Land prices had gone through the roof.

Hugh's family has been in Kelowna for four generations. Closer to the land than me—only one generation late—five years ago Hugh planted a cherry orchard in New Zealand. When the trees are mature, he's moving there, and cutting his ties.

My grandmother, Martha, saw through the whole charade—the elites never meant the earth to have any value. Their goal all along was to create a working class dependent upon romanticized notions of landscape. It came about, too: conveniently enclosed within a land sense dependent upon the garrison cities, these classes gave their lives to the earth, and so increased the power of the garrison cities without gaining power of their own.

For this, my father called her stupid. On the first night after my parents' honeymoon, my father came home from pear picking to find his new bride crying, with the light from the lake outside the window splashing over her face. It didn't take long to get to the bottom of Dorothy's troubles: her mother had come over, and had told her that now that she was a married woman she deserved more than the collection of ramshackle furniture that filled the house. The house was, after all, a pickers' shack. You bought stuff at church White Elephant sales to fill up places like that, and stuck in your old fridge, maybe the one you had bought in 1938, and let it hum and spit away for your workers and almost keep things cold. That was the rule of the game. My father knew it, and he accepted it. He wasn't too impressed that his mother-in-law wanted something more.

"Grandma and I came to an understanding that night," he said. "I told her that if she ever, ever said anything like that to her daughter again, she would never, ever see Dorothy again in her life. She could have spit, but she understood alright. After that, we got along great." He laughed.

God, they hated each other! In 1977, I was living in a pickers' shack in Naramata, deep inside the dream, so deep I couldn't see my way out. On weekends, Martha made me Silesian pork chops and apple streusel, and sat me down in her living room with all its hand-crocheted blankets and told me, "That Hans was the worst thing that ever happened to my Dorothy," and "I feel betrayed. They lied to me back in 1938. There were experts back then, who told us in ten years none of us would have to wash dishes any longer, and we wouldn't have to clean clothes." She spoke the word *clothes* as "close," clipped off tightly in the accent of what had become her native language, Germlish—widespread in the valley at that time. "They said we'd have paper dishes and paper close. We could use them once and throw them away. Look at me now. I'm seventy-four years old and I'm still washing dishes and close. They lied." She was genuinely hurt. She really had hoped for something better for her daughter. An adventure in the wilderness had never been her idea. She was a city girl.

The wilderness stole her children—and her grandchildren—from her, though. For two generations we have lived in the bush, with a

Canada of our own. Back in the early 1970s, after Bruno got caught in a riptide on a holiday in Mazatlan and died in her arms, Martha asked if she could move in with us. When my parents convinced her that they had no room, she asked if she could have a singlewide trailer planted on our lawn, even two hundred yards away on the sandy edge of our old apricot orchard. She just did not want to be alone, and she wanted to be near her grandchildren. My parents refused. Twenty-five years late I asked why. My mother's answer was, "You just can't do that sort of thing." When I asked further, my mother was firm, "No way! She would have been constantly underfoot, criticizing, interfering, and dictating how we all should live and who we associated with. Nothing we did ever met with her approval. She loved us dearly, and we loved her, but she expected us to drop everything and cater to her, drive her when she wanted to visit in Osoyoos, Summerland, or Westbank. It wouldn't have worked." Martha died of a broken heart. A bout of scarlet fever during the First World War had left her with heart valve problems. The damage was diagnosed in 1976. "She was considered too old and in too poor health to qualify for surgery," my mother put it to me succinctly, "and she was adamant that she did not want any surgery. She was waiting to die and be with Bruno by that time. The final straw with her moving in with us in any form was when she snorted and called your brother's best friend 'a dirty long-haired hippie.' Your brother turned on his heels and stormed out. No way was I going to have a daily repeat of that." Christ.

"Look at the way his trees grow!" my father said about Bruno's orcharding skills. "I planted him the most modern orchard in the valley, showed him how to grow the trees, and he just messed it all up. He let the central leaders have fruit, and they bent over, and his trees lost their shape. Laziness! You don't lose a whole tree just for a couple of extra apples. He couldn't grasp an idea, a practical idea, if you put it right in front of him.

So Martha was always complaining that they had no money, and they couldn't pay their bills. She was always complaining about something. So I took pity on the old man and hired him to rebuild the deck of my truck. You know, I had bought an old truck for hauling my apples, and it didn't have a metal rim around the deck. The new legislation said it had to have a metal rim. I couldn't afford such a thing, so I hired Bruno to make me one. That was the most expensive deck you have seen in your life! I went down there after two days, and I really needed that truck, but it was nowhere near ready. I asked him, 'Why in the hell is my truck not ready?' I mean, it was a one-day job, to cut and fasten the iron rim! It was just a truck deck. It didn't have to be perfect or anything, like a park bench! I found Bruno whistling away in his workshop, sorting through old tins of rusted bolts, soaking them in oil, and slowly working the rust loose so he could use them to fasten on the iron strips. He would spend an hour remaking a bolt that I could have driven down to the hardware store in Keremeos for and bought for two cents! That was when I really hit the roof."

"Just imagine how it is for me," says my mother. "The Canada I grew up in no longer exists. It is a completely different country now, with completely different values. I used to go out and scythe the hayfield by hand, and ride the haywagon in at 10:30 in the evening, sitting way up high there on the load of hay. It was in the far North, so it was light until 11:00. I would be half asleep and the horses would be half asleep, and we would just slowly go back like that. The mosquitoes hummed out of the trees and the bats fed on them around the heads of the horses. The trees were like soft shadows. It is all gone.

"When I was twelve years old, I got one half day off a week from chores to go and visit a friend. I had to arrange it in advance, then I had to walk four miles down the road to visit my friend, who lived on the next farm. We played with dolls or sat in the chicken yard and talked, until it was time for me to come home again. I had to walk the four miles, alone, again, out in the bush. Dad was never keen for me to have a friend over. He did not see the point of it. It was just better not to get him started. Needless to say, I did not do it very often. Friendships were all fine, but you couldn't call that a close friendship, and it was just not worth all the effort.

"That first winter in Evelyn, the cold almost killed us. I remember putting newspaper in my gumboots, for insulation, to keep my feet from freezing. It was terrible. We didn't have any idea what cold was like. We thought an extra pair of socks would be enough. It pretty near killed us. Dad had forced Frank to quit school, to help support the place. 'You'll never be any good at anything, so you might as well go to work,' he said. Frank was choked. I had to walk the two miles from the house, down through the birch forest, to the bus stop, where a taxi picked me up and took me the fourteen miles into town to go to school. There were only five kids for the Evelyn School that year, so it was closed down. The owner of the taxi, Mr. Wall, was a great guy and full of stories. The end of the line was only two miles past my stop. When Mr. Wall got to me there, at 7:30, it was half light. The sun comes up late in the North in the winter, as you know. All the way down to the road, there were wolves walking along with me, a hundred yards out among the trees. They followed me down, the whole distance from the farm. Then I went into school. In the afternoon, I got out of the taxi at 4:30. Once again it was half light, and I had to walk the two miles, uphill through the birch trees, to get back to the farm. There was no one who lived there and I was completely alone. The wolves were waiting for me, and they followed along beside me, a hundred yards away, sometimes closer, the whole way back to the house. They never did anything else, and they never made a noise, but they were there every day, for six weeks that winter. I was never so scared in my life."

Somehow one makes a forest/copse/grove/bush/wood out of sticks like that.

~The Call of the Wild~

The late poet and historian Charles Lillard grew up in the bush during the '40s and '50s, in a logging show in Alaska. There he lived a life hardly different from the one the Norwegians lived who first cleared Bruno's folly of fireweed and cream cans in Evelyn. It was a West Coast version of Paul Theroux's *Mosquito Coast*: to protect his family from society's corrupting influence a tinkerer and crackpot drags it away from society to the middle of nowhere; there he demonstrates what can be achieved without society's lax standards dragging them all down into mediocrity. For Theroux, the refuge from the breakdown of civilization under its own weight was the Central American jungle, but forty years before Theroux, America was still turning its sights north: thousands of men still dreamed of achieving independence in the northern British Columbia Interior and on the slopes of Alaska falling to the Russian islands in the Pacific. Like Bruno, they dragged their families out to the bush and started hacking at the trees and filling up their yards with twisted logging cables, blown machinery, stumps, rust, mouldering railway ties, shinglebolts turning grey with the weather, whiskey bottles, wrecked cars, and mud. A generation before, the Freikorps tried the same thing. A generation before that it was Ludendorff's men in field grey making a pre-emptory stroll through Belgium to capture France, before France—a democracy, god forbid—attacked them.

Even a good year ago, if you packed up your car and drove out to find history in the Interior, and knew which side road to turn onto and to follow down through which trees, with tall grass hissing along the undercarriage; if you stopped and walked through the woodticks, elderberries, and knapweed, you would find a lilac at Brushy Bottom, a few irises still pushing up through the shale, and a few rusty nails in packed gravel; twenty minutes west, you can still open your car door to a few old cider pear trees at Sterling Creek, brought over from Normandy in 1908; twenty minutes south, if you know where to drive, over which washboards through which cattle ranch and where to brush aside the fir branches, you'll step among the foundation logs of a house and barn above a steep ravine high above the valley; on the heights around you you'll make out the trees filling old fields. Mountain range after mountain range, river valley after river valley, watershed after watershed, dry wash after dry wash, a whole country lies underfoot, barely settled before it was abandoned. Scraps are all that is left to mark what in this country was once called a farm, when British Columbia was a farming country and what a man could make from the land by his own sweat was what a man could make. There was some pride in that once.

These scraps formed the country my mother knew when she had long golden braids. It is the country she still sees when she looks out over the trees. For her, and for the rest of us who live between the mountain ranges of a continent folding up against itself, those last traces of bush farms are like the ruins of Mycenae or the shadows of old Roman roads passing as straight as rulers, covered with a carpet of old leaves, through the forests of Schwabia, with the light flowing yellow down through the trees at their edges, tossed about like waves as the branches lift and rise in the afternoon breeze. If you go to find that first moment when we lived in the splendour of the land, though, you will only find other people looking for it, building log houses above newly cleared pastures, where they can watch aspens reclaim fields that my mother, for instance, once helped hay by hand; you will find people driving their motorhomes on an endless pilgrimage along asphalt highways, camping in crowded RV parks lying along the rail-line, with thirty-amp power and city water and full sewer hookup.

The vast modern orchards of the Okanagan were something the world had never seen before. Completely transformed from their prototypes, the small plots tucked in at the corners of sheep farms in the Cotswolds, they were carefully designed to provide images of English country ease to cramped Londoners with no economic prospects in a tightening economy. The images lasted longer than the orchards. Today, realtors are cashing in by selling Tudor houses in the old orchard land of East Kelowna and by selling off the Chilcotin to Germans looking for a time before Rome; with a frequency you can count on the fingers of one hand, they sell orchards to young men and women who want to grow apples together and make love in the evenings. Whoever they are, though—realtors, doctors with 1 x 4 Tudor fascia and paved driveways, young men with dirt under their fingers—they all learn to live in the pre-Raphaelite painting of British Columbia. The earth is invisible.

That's where Lillard started, though, on the western slopes of the Coast Mountains, where the rivers are white with glacial flour and pour down like milk through spruce, hemlock and cedar, past banks of alders and crabapples, spilling into the Pacific in great dragon tails of silt, and it's where my mother started, on the eastern slopes of those mountains. History wasn't written in books in that country; people lived it; there were no books. High above Lillard and Dorothy, mountain goats grazed on slate cliffs reflecting the sky in the rain; salmon spawned among the roots of thousand-year-old trees; their smolts lived there for a year among trickling ferns, overhanging orchids, and frogs, until they followed the rain down to the sea. If Lillard and Dorothy grew up with fathers who had come to escape the world, it was because everyone's father had. It was a multiple-reality version of Theroux. If you were a young buck like Lillard—or a young woman like my mother—you looked past your father, not to society, but to the earth. You knew stuff your father would never know. You knew a lot of stuff Theroux never knew. You didn't know you knew it.

Actually, Theroux had a lot in common with Margaret Atwood: they share an enthusiasm for the pulp novelist's sense of Hollywood catastrophe, the old late-night-around-the-campfire-at-the-children's-camp-at-the-lake-for-two-weeks trick of telling a story to raise the hair on everyone's head by turning the earth into a body—in Atwood's case a woman's body—that will not die. You have to stand outside of the earth to even imagine such a story could be frightening. True to the genre, the family Theroux takes down to Honduras to build Eden is wrecked by the rain forest and Theroux's inability in the end to conceive of his story as a comedy, because a comedy would have meant going bushed. To write a comedy, Theroux would have had to relinquish control. He would have had to become Kurtz, with a rim of skulls set up around his tent. Instead, like Shakespeare's Hamlet, he settled for the gothic sentimentalist's love of the danger of the unexpected and repressed—a little frisson for a bored afternoon.

Lillard didn't tell any ghost stories. He worked at fish canneries, cutting open Coho salmon among the Tlingit. He spoke Wawa. He spoke West Talk, the language of loggers who boated up the Coast in the 1860s and logged just above water line, felling the trees into the surf at high tide, booming them, and towing them to mills down the coast. English was his third language. He spoke it with a heavy accent—Frank Leipe's accent.

When Lillard was eighteen, he stepped out of the bush. It was 1959. Other poets were finding their freedom, laughing it up with the Beats, hanging out on the road. They rolled packs of Players cigarettes in the sleeves of their T-shirts, wrote down the first words that came to their heads and called them sacred—drawing a line between education and authenticity. They dared anyone to cross it.

Full to the gills with freedom already, Lillard collapsed in a seat at the University of Alaska and challenged everything the professors at the front of the room said. He did it the way I did when I came in from the orchards in 1976 and scoffed at the distance at which Socrates lived from the objects of the world. It is the way of young men who have come in from the bush and refuse to let it go. The particular young man that was Red Lillard had his head full of Joseph Conrad, Jack London, Robinson Jeffers, and Robert Service. He didn't last long. He returned to the trees. He had come too far, too deep out of a history that his teachers had completely overlooked. They weren't thinking, as he was, of taking that history and using it to rebuild artistic, philosophical, and ethical traditions. They weren't using those traditions to talk about the confrontation with earth and history that we call the land; they were trying to replace it. Lillard had lived too far off the edge of the map to accept such reductions. He already had a way of living in time, one that stretched across boundaries which traditional histories deemed unbridgeable. He had touched the things of this earth and he was not going to let them go.

"You'll never find a story of a woman who was bushed," he wrote in 1973. "Women don't get bushed. Men do. Women don't fight the land. They bend to it." He was halfway to understanding, still too deep in a culture that said that "men created; women do basketwork," as he put it to my first class at university in 1976, to see that the women *were* bushed, and that it was their strength—only in fighting against it were the men crippled. Lillard fought it all the way down. He packed dynamite into the Stikine, worked on gyppo logging shows up and down the coast and throughout the Interior, and all the time thought that through poetry he had found a better way. The tension ate him alive: he couldn't live in both worlds at the same time. It was a classic tragic trap. When he finally did settle—at the University of British Columbia, halfway south to California—he still spent his summers logging. On his first summer, he took along *A Little Treasury of Modern Poetry,* the all-purpose, red linen-bound anthology of his generation—and of two generations before. It wasn't a portrait of modernism, so much as of anti-modernism. This was the White Russian counter-revolution of its time. Its 843 pages were on every class list across the continent. Lillard said he figured that if he was going to be a poet this *modern* book was the best possible book to take along. It would be his desert-island book—the one that contained the kernel of his entire world; his Bible, his Homer, his Bhagavad-Gita, the words he couldn't be without. "I thought I'd have all the time in the world to read the book," he said, adding that he figured the lack of anything else to read ought to focus his attention. Out there in his bush, though, where even rumours of Canada had not yet come, with the campfire crackling and the surf jabbling as the outflow of the rivers met the incoming tide and rose in a roaring wall a metre high, there with the waters—fresh and salt—foaming and mingling and pushing against each other, Lillard tried to read the anthology, tried to read its Yeats and its Stevens, its Edward Arlington Robinson, its Dylan Thomas, its Auden and Crane, its "O Lord, the whistling sword is beauty/Both to ear and eye," and its "Truth is love and love is truth/Either neither in good sooth." He got nowhere with it. He couldn't do it. "It applied to nothing," he said.

—

Lillard's "something" was a world straight out of an adventure story by Jack London: whiskey traders, whalers, loggers, trappers, prospectors, Imperial Russian officers, Russian Orthodox priests, Indian princesses, shamans walking the road of the dead, cod jiggers, gandy dancers, Hudson's Bay Company men. Lillard's history was the one that gave Canada the Métis McLean Boys holed up in a cabin of cottonwood logs above Nicola Lake while a posse of white ranchers riddled the walls with bullets, the history that saw James Douglas's treaties with the Indians revoked within ten years by Joseph Trutch, the new administrator from Upper Canada, who understood better how the world worked. For example, when the rancher Cornelius O'Keefe set himself up pretty in 1867 on a fancy 184-acre spread southeast of Vernon, the Okanagan people were living on ten thousand acres of grassland at Nkamaplix at the head of Okanagan Lake, whereas by 1893, under Trutch's benevolent administration, things were a little different: O'Keefe was farming ten thousand acres of "unoccupied" grassland at the head of Okanagan Lake; the natives were living on a five-hundred-acre reserve tucked off past his southwestern fence, bleeding off into the bush. O'Keefe was a driven man. On his cattle drives, he once told his men that they would start driving the cattle when the rooster crowed in the morning. When the damn rooster crowed at midnight, they started out then, and had put in half a day's riding before the sun even came up. That rooster didn't crow at many breakfasts after that.

Lillard's contemporaries are the Métis children of the Hudson's Bay Company men, abandoned when history took the great leap forward and their fathers brought new brides over from Scotland. That's where those McLean boys went wrong, thinking that some of their father's land was going to come their way—or that their mother's people would want them back. It is a history that has been swept under the rug. If you go to a bookstore looking for the history of British Columbia, you will likely find only the histories that replaced this one, and the ones that replaced those ones in turn, in the continual story of recurring colonization and recolonization that in this country takes the place of time and growth and wisdom. You will find the monumental *Encyclopedia of British Columbia*. You will find history with an agenda—the history of finding our way out of the bush, the history of turning trees into profit, the ghost stories of a few bankers and their politicians. You will find the Latin names for trees. You will find that we are making Progress.

Imagine a million grey Hudson's Bay Company blankets. Imagine each made from the wool of a single sheep grazing in the Outback. Imagine every single one of those blankets that was ever sold for a dozen beaver pelts or a dozen sea otter pelts. Imagine the kelp beds empty of otters scooping out abalone like Japanese princesses. Imagine the number of mornings a young Haida man set out in a canoe to catch those pelts, the number of cold winter days a young Cree trapper spent chopping holes in the ice of the muskeg to bring home those beavers. Then you will know something about empire. Imagine all the other blankets, the ones sold to immigrants when they stumbled confused off the trains. Imagine every single blanket sold for the whole four hundred years of the Hudson's Bay Company. Imagine the country that they paid for, the buildings in downtown London that they paid for, the English country houses with their lawns studded with swans and sheep and their walled gardens full of limes and figs and cider apples. Then you will know something about empire.

My grandfather Hans Rhenisch had theories about his name. In German, *Rhenisch* is not a far cry from Rhenish, the Rhine wine that Shakespeare used to loosen up Hamlet's tongue back in 1601. It's also a symphony by Schubert, a credit union, and a weekend newspaper supplement. It's a range of shale hills, a coal-mining area along the Rhine, an old noble family from Brandenburg, the name of a secretary to the Kaiser a long time ago. Whichever truth you choose, however, the family doesn't come from the Rhine. It comes from the East. "We have as much to do with the Russians as with the Germans," says Eberhard.

In Sanskrit, *Rhenisch* means "King of Kings." That's what Dr. Rhenisch figured out, while researching for his Aryan passport. There's a family joke about that—that the name has already been taken, by Jesus. You might not have been able to take the Lord's name in vain, but back in Silesia a hundred and fifty years ago, Old Man Rhenisch had an easy out. Let's say he hit his thumb with a hammer and it hurt like hell—instead of yelling, "Oh, Christ!" and having the pastor come over and waste his whole afternoon, he could just call out, "Oh, Rhenisch!" and break down in laughter. The only catch is that you'd have to know Sanskrit. In the occupied territories of Silesia, you'd be pretty much alone in that. Eighty-five percent of the people spoke Polish. Fifteen percent spoke German. The place belonged to Germany because it had belonged to the Empress of Austria, who had traded it to the King of Prussia to clear a debt, the way you might bet the shirt off your back in a poker game. Although not very many of the poker cards up that way spoke Sanskrit, a lot of them spoke Yiddish and Hebrew. They knew the Word of God.

It would be a funny anecdote, except that when Dr. Rhenisch was researching his name he was a member of the Nazi party, with a brown shirt and a red armband and a black doctor's bag in one hand. The Sanskrit shtick was really the ultimate act of Aryan assertion: to hell with going back to the blond-eyed boys; he was going right back to the Himalayas.

You might think at first that a name like Rhenisch came from the Rheinland, with a nod towards Schubert's Rhenish Symphony—perhaps an old noble name denoting an ancient, lost, country seat, the way you might say Windsor, or Exeter. There's no evidence for it, but Dr. Rhenisch sure wished there was, and he did tell his sons that their family could trace its lineage back as far as Queen Elizabeth could trace hers, which makes you wonder about why five generations back on his mother's side the family name was Troll. Nah, other families might have had a few thousand generations to get used to acting human. With only five generations behind us, we're not doing too bad, I guess. Of course, Dr. Rhenisch could have just been bullshitting; his petty little dig at Elizabeth could have been a reflex action for losing the war, the kind of belittling humour that powered the Nazi party for all its years in the political wilderness—except he was awed by royalty. When I was a boy, he regularly sent newspaper clippings to our farm, about visits by the British Royalty to the beach hotel on the Reichenau, where he liked to go for coffee and cake on Sunday afternoons. I can just imagine him following with great interest the route of the Duke of Windsor through Portugal, to Jamaica, as Hitler plotted to have him head up England as a fascist country club.

My father remembers his last years of school, after the few years when there was no school at all. He was studying Goethe, when one day his teacher exclaimed that Shakespeare was sooooo English. He drew the boys' attention to the endings of the great tragedies—*Macbeth*, *Hamlet*, *King Lear*—and exclaimed: "Everybody's dead! He couldn't think of a way to end his play, so he just killed everybody!" Touchy, huh?

No, some Rhenisch, or whoever he was, wandered east. Once he got to the colonies, to settle land or to teach someone else how to dig coal out of it the rhenisch way, people didn't know what to call him at first, so they identified him by what was to them his strongest characteristic—his foreignness, and his damned habit of repeating over and over again how they did it in the rhenisch mines along the rhenisch Rhine. And so, in the same way that a Scotsman living in London is called Scotty, they called him, a Rhinelander living in Silesia, well, Rhenisch. It's not really a name at all. It's a nickname, a joke, a sign of disrespect.

When my father went to kindergarten, he received a *Zuckertüte*, a paper cone full of toys and candy, just as every other German boy and girl since Bismarck has done when they take the plunge. He was pretty proud. In kindergarten he was taught how to sit straight, how to recite his ABC's, how to make sure his parents were good National Socialists and who to tell if they weren't, and was taught to sing the children's chant "*Das Kleine Negerlein*," the little nigger boy. Actually, it was a game. Ten children stepped into the middle of a circle made by the rest of their class, sang, "Ten little nigger boys crossed the Rhine, one fell in the water, then there were nine." At that, one of the children stepped back into the surrounding circle. On it went, until the last verse, when the last "little nigger boy" was run over by a coach. Some game. Thing is, the song first got its kickoff in Philadelphia in 1868, when the songwriter Septimus Winner wrote the original version: "Ten Little Indians." Here's a typical verse: "Six little Injuns kicking all alive. One kicked the bucket and then there were five." It was immediately adopted for a bit of London music hall by Frank Green: "Ten Little Niggers." The song became a hit. Children loved it most of all, and it crossed the channel immediately. Winner wasn't averse to sticking it to Germans, either. One of his greatest hits was "Der Deitcher's Dog," with its mocking opening "Oh where, oh where ish mine little dog gone," and its rather literal conclusion, in which the dog ends up as a sausage. The song had its roots in an old German folk tune, through which it is linked to the postwar homesickness hit '*Ich hab mein Herz in Heidelberg verloren*" ("I Lost My Heart in Heidelberg"). During the Second World War, when my father was still running around in his lederhosen, a satirical version of "Das Kleine Negerlein" popped up. People were hauled off to jail for singing this one: "*Zehn Kleine Meckerlein*" ("Ten Little Grumblers"). It disassembles pretty well all of the propaganda of the Third Reich, starting with, "Ten little grumblers had a glass of wine. One of them aped Goebbels. Then there were only nine," and finishing with a bitter flourish: "One little grumbler told this poem out loud. For that he went to Oranienburg, and then they were ten again." That's to say that the whole lot of them were reunited in a death camp.

Things hadn't improved much by the time I got into school in the Interior. There was no singing about the *Negerlein,* thank God, but we did troop across the school field, around the Manitoba maple growing wild behind the town hall, and into Ike's General Store. With a big maple butcher block in the back and wilted lettuce on the side, it got its name from Ike Sing, the Chinese grocer who ran the joint. At Ike's, we bought penny candy with our 5-cent-a-week allowance. The best ones were "nigger babies," baby-shaped black licorice candies. We made a big show of being tough by chomping their heads off and making loud satisfied noises, before chewing up the rest of their bodies. The girls thought we were disgusting.

On it went: one of the stories my mother read to me was *The Story of Little Black Sambo.* Naïve and generous to a fault, Sambo was tricked by a bunch of vain tigers into giving up all his clothes so that he had to parade around, humiliated, in his underwear. Luckily, the tigers were too vain for their own good and chased each other so quickly around a palm tree in the hot Indian sun that they melted into butter. Sambo's dad found the butter and brought it proudly home; on their pancakes that night they all had good golden melted butter.

Little Black Sambo was written by Helen Bannerman. Born in Scotland in 1863, Helen married a surgeon in the British Indian Medical Service in Madras. The climate in the lowlands was bad for her children's health. Everyone knew that: it would make them go as daft as natives, praying to crocodiles and smearing their bodies with blood—ugly words from an ugly time. My mother knew that, knew about Stanley and Livingstone and their black bearers in Darkest Africa. It was all part of her education in how to be British, which was how she was educated to be Canadian in the 1940s. Bannerman knew it, too. Every summer she took the train with her little daughters up to the hill town of Kodaikanal. Indian trains can be awfully slow. To ease the girls' boredom on one of those trips—sometime before 1899, when the book was published in England—she wrote *The Story of Little Black Sambo*. The girls adored it.

Black Sambo went into publication around the world. You could buy records of it and books with lavish illustrations in which Sambo was as black as coal and the trees were as green as lettuce. Kellogg's gave away a Poor Little Black Sambo Board Game in their cereal boxes, complete with little push-out game men, a spinner, and a dad who looked like Harry Belafonte. In California in 1969, we dropped by a Sambo restaurant beside the freeway, where I ordered pancakes slathered in butter, drank a tall pink strawberry milkshake and looked out through smoky glass at the parking lot and all of the cars whizzing by, while a waitress in an impossibly tall hairdo and a starched pink uniform with a white collar laughed that I hadn't been able to finish all my food and my parents explained that my eyes were always bigger than my stomach, you know how it is with children, and I wanted to crawl under the table and die.

Thomas Hardy, the novelist, had a lot to say about the dream of the land. During the Great War, he was an embittered old man, looking for some sign of permanence in a world gone mad. He found it in arguably the worst of all possible places to look, in landscape, that locus of madness and ignorance where life is ruled by love, work, the changing seasons and towering clouds; he found it in a painting by Constable, with cattle fording a muddy stream. It might have been romantic nonsense, but it was nonsense with deep roots. Hardy found sanctuary there. After watching a man and a horse ploughing half asleep on their feet in France, he took solace in the memory of seeing the same thing fifty years earlier during the Franco-Prussian war. Eternal war, eternal earth, and the man of the soil who took no part in the killing that civilization enacted in its rituals as it trampled over the fields around him: it was all Hardy could cling to.

Everybody clung to it. In Hardy's time, the citizens of Northampton extended the round nave of their Norman church and added oak choir stalls. Back when a quarter of the money of the world flowed through the English Midlands, there was enough money to remake the dream of history any way you liked. Angels were carved in oak above the seats of the choir, each holding a different instrument. After proudly showing me the battle colours of the regiments that captured Quebec hanging against the stone walls ("You Canadians should be pleased to see that") the rector clambered up on one of the choir stalls to pull a flute from an angel's hands. "There was an amazing attention to detail, wasn't there," he said in a stage whisper. "It can actually be played." He put it to his lips.

—

In that mannered world, a poet could leave poverty behind by sending around his calling card and having tea with the daughters of lawyers and iron merchants—a kind of court jester. The American poet Ezra Pound lived that life in London in 1908 after hitting London society to talk about fairies with the Irish romantic poet W. B. Yeats. Ezra wore a pirate's earring in his ear and trousers cut from a green velvet curtain. He thought he was a troubadour. Fathers hurried their daughters out of his way. Throughout it all, he clung to a dream of the land. He married Dorothy Shakespear, a rich girl who dressed in velvet and wore flowers in her black hair. Her father, a prominent London lawyer, was furious. Ezra embraced the mechanical poetics of Italian futurism, grew hard and angry, and suggested that his friends slaughtered in the trenches had been worth more than every book ever written and every statue ever chipped out of marble. He observed the Rothschilds and Krupps profiting from the war and grew bitter and reckless. Still his dream of the land as the wellspring of aristocratic privilege, through the ability of the aristocracy, steeped in classical mythology, to carry on earth-based religions despite all the vagaries of culture, was so strong that he clung to it as an antidote to power. When Mussolini first walked off the farm, drained the swamps, got the trains running on time, and even when he paraded around in Africa like Mark Anthony, Ezra wrote about how without leaders there was no art—and without art no leaders. Neo-Nazi websites are still going on about that, how as an artist Hitler was more qualified by his calling to run Germany than anyone else, how he, gosh, sketched out the design for the first Volkswagen on a dinner napkin, grasping intimately what the educated could not even see. Even the Second World War couldn't beat the idea out of Ezra's head: how the peasant rises up from the land and re-fertilizes a decayed civilization with new blood. Ezra worshipped Nazi monetary policy, damned Churchill as a puppet of the Jews, and spent the war broadcasting anti-American propaganda from Radio Rome—as a patriot, yet. For that last act, the American Army threw him into a reinforced, double-welded cage in the open sun in the middle of the plain in front of Pisa. His cage was twice as strong as that given to any of the US Army's other guests in Italy, the rapists and murderers and criminally violent, because the army feared that the remains of the fascisti would storm the compound in the night to set Ezra free to serve as a lightning rod for a new fascist republic. But Found was harmless. The Italians knew that. He had spent the Great War sitting around in London society, sipping tea and explaining to young society women that all creativity was male, that women had never created anything, that they could do crafts, could decorate, but no more, because the male brain was a giant repository for sperm, which flowed up through the spinal column. When the pressure of the sperm had built up enough, a man could create. There were exercises you could do to increase the flow. After the war, the United States Government tried Pound for treason. He wouldn't budge. He spent thirteen years in an asylum for the criminally insane. He served his guests tea out of tuna tins behind the piano. He shared quarters with Napoleon and God. He didn't relent. When he was finally released, he went straight back to Italy. He stepped off of the boat, with the swallows of St. Francis high in the air above him and his wife and his mistress waiting for him, and he gave the fascist salute. His was the last of the grand tours. Cocky bastard.

Hitler was gaga for that dream. He wanted to depopulate the Ukraine and refill it with German families tossing up stooks of hay onto their wagons in the evenings, tucking their children into their eiderdowns as the birds settled into the trees and cows murmured contentedly from their stalls. For Hitler, the modernist movement was a movement to claim for every petit bourgeois the right of a landowner in the European East, with two thousand Polish serfs. Every bloody Polish serf wanted that power, too. Bruno did—and *he* was a communist. His sister, Martha, sure did. Everybody did. Everyone is guilty. The British Columbia government, which shipped the children of the Gitksan, the Halkomelem, the Cowichan, and the Secwepemc off to residential schools where priests beat their language out of them, is guilty. The Doukhobors burning their houses and walking naked down the roads of the Kootenays when the British Columbia government tried the same trick on them are guilty of the same confusion between the sanctity of the land and its use as a barbed wire fence. When George W. Bush said, "You are either for us or against us," in reference to his aggressive war in Iraq, he knew that perfectly. Land, and the confusion between its myriad faces and the earth, is the greatest lever for bending people to your will. In that sense, land is the fence between cultural belonging and wilderness. People can identify with a dream like that. They nod their heads and say "You can't make an omelette without breaking eggs." Margaret Atwood knew that. The monks who planted the first fruits and flowers around their monastery on the Reichenau knew about the strength of that logical conflation. My father knew that antidote to growing bushed. Every immigrant who came to Canada knew that, and if they didn't know it before they came, they learned it fast: if you walked out of the firelight, you were on your own.

That is my country.

~The True North~

My father got his first glimpse of the borders of that country in 1954.

"After a year in Ottawa, Karl and Hans and I, Little Hans—there was Big Hans and Little Hans, a big joke—were heading west in a '38 Plymouth. We called it Jonas. It looked like a whale, too. It was a big adventure: we were crossing the North American plains in winter. It was something you read about in a book. We were going to drive through the Rocky Mountains and down into South America."

My father is telling this story in 1969. Already, I'd heard it so often I'd memorized it: how it was snowing so hard they couldn't see the road, how for hundreds of miles they saw nothing except snow and black trees, and no towns. As my father put it, "There was nobody there. People had tried to warn us about the road, but we just laughed at them. The road was closed, but we drove past the barriers. It was stupid."

Several times the trunk fell off Jonas. It was really just a trunk, strapped onto the car with leather belts. Jonas was the kind of car which had a crankcase filled with sawdust, and which the Okies had driven while fleeing the dustbowl for the dream of the fruit orchards of California. Just as it would have been on an old black-and-white episode of *The Three Stooges*, whenever Jonas crashed the boys broke out laughing and ran out into the blizzard to retrieve the trunk where it lay in the snow like Windigo curled up and gnawing off his leg.

"We were so worn out from driving ten hours straight at twenty miles an hour through the blizzard, it felt as if we had driven off the end of the earth."

It was the worst blizzard in years. Curly and Larry and Moe could hardly tell the road from the snow. The endlessness of snowflakes driving at the windscreen and curling off over the roof, coupled with the boys' realization that if the car stopped they would die within hours, sent them deep into their selves. The worse the road became, the less they talked. By the end of the day they were not talking at all. They had become hypnotized by the driving flakes.

"That night, we slept above a garage. We climbed up the shaky wooden steps in the wind and crashed on the beds. There was frost on the window and the smell of oil coming up from the workshop. In the morning the temperature had dropped even farther. We staggered down into the blizzard to start Jonas, but Jonas wouldn't go. Up to this time I'd drained her every night, but I'd been so worn out I'd forgotten. We pushed her into the garage and kept the room for another night while she thawed out."

When my father spoke those words, it was early afternoon—a Saturday. The sun was beating at the roof as if we were Helen Bannerman's brain, but my father was already laughing in anticipation, for he knew well enough that the next morning the Three Stooges would be awoken with the sound of the engine firing, and would break out with a roar of laughter. Those of us listening laughed along as the boys slammed out the door, down the icy steps, and into the shop. There in the gloom and the oil, with the fanbelts and the bolts scattered over the floor and the tires stacked up willy-nilly, was Jonas, in a cloud of exhaust. She was running fine!

"Boy, I was lucky. All night I'd cursed myself as the dumbest jerk in the world. I had nightmares of being stranded there all winter at the end of the earth. I was really scared. But there was Jonas, running, and the mechanic slamming down the hood and wiping his hands on the back of his overalls. He grinned at us. I was so happy then. I could have kissed the guy.

"'All I can figure,' the mechanic said, 'is she is so loose that there was room for the ice. There wasn't a drop of antifreeze.' He shook his head in disbelief."

My father shakes his head in disbelief, too.

Without a further thought the boys piled into Jonas and drove out into the hard, cold snow as the mechanic swung the doors shut behind them, and we went along with them. They were on their way. They could have been on the North Pole.

"We felt we were on the North Pole," Little Hans said, offering his heart to Margaret Atwood's Windigo on a platter.

As they drove west, Jonas slowly disintegrated around them. They were tired and bloodshot, the Boys from St. Catharines, driving west in a blizzard to escape the chill of an Ontario winter. For hours at a time they just stared out of the windows in a stupor, drugged by the distances they had driven. The fields, the lakes, the muskeg, the Shield, the first grain fields, were all under snow. Snowdrifts cut across the roads. Every time they went in the ditch, two of them jumped out, lifted Jonas up in the back and gave a big push. That was the only break in the monotony as they hurtled across the continent.

"Winnipeg was bad. It was the coldest place yet. We had driven all that way, yet just as we crossed Portage and Main Jonas's muffler fell off. It was a Sunday night. There was no way we could fix it then, but the cops gave us a ticket anyway, two big guys who sneered at us. That made me so angry. In the middle of the night some other cops found us sleeping in the car and booted us out of town. We didn't care. After the reception we got, we were happy to go."

At Moose Jaw the boys saw a big plume of fire. They drove off the highway and towards it down a side road. Suddenly, all around them, in the wheat stubble, the mud and melted snow, were bits of bodies scattered around and the broken-up parts of an aircraft, for a half mile around the road, and men with ambulances trying to sort them out. There were people moving, dark, staggering around amongst the fires. And the boys drove on!

"Can you believe it! It never struck us that we were needed there! We were all a bit shaken up. It was like seeing something on the moon."

They drove deep into the West.

"The prairies were big. They went on forever." The blue-eyed boys played skat in the back seat. Unlike the unending game off Iceland, the game was low key: there was laughter, but it was swallowed by the space they were driving through. Then off they would go in the ditch and the cards would scatter and they'd tumble out into the drifts, push Jonas out, and drive off again on the black ice. Often it would be snowing so hard the windshield wipers couldn't push the snow aside.

When they got to Claresholm, the Rockies rose on the horizon. It was like magic, as if they were deep in Africa—except cold. They stopped, and worked for the rest of the winter, pitching hay and feeding cattle. They were in their big adventure at last. When the mallards came back to the sloughs, and as the hawks hunted across the borders of the fields, they drove the big diesel tractors into the horizon. Behind them the soil was dark and rich. The hours were long in the yellow sun.

Then disaster struck: it was Big Hans. He said he was not going to leave, as they had planned: he was going to get married instead! This was betrayal! You cannot imagine: together they had planned to drive the world, and here one of their own had abandoned them for a girl. For a girl! It left their hearts heavy. Out of guilt, Big Hans leant Karl and Little Hans his car.

They left Jonas with Big Hans and drove north. Sometimes the road west of Edmonton vanished into a sea of mud. There'd be a bulldozer idling at the side of the road, waiting to push them through. The biggest sinkhole was a hundred yards across. They felt their isolation then and felt a great urgency pressing them on, the first hint of the great storm of responsibility that comes over us with adulthood. They drove on, but it felt like they were putting off the inevitable, as if they had very little time left. Once they'd crossed the Rockies they couldn't face driving south: that would be to admit that the dream was over, that they'd have to take their places somewhere in this huge land of rough, uninviting towns, and settle down, and stay put. They knew that. They knew they'd have to accept Canada. They were afraid of that. The towns were ugly and horrible. It was a different civilization. They knew there was no longer any dream of South America, and that there was little time: there must be some girl out there for each of them, ready to snatch them away. They were trapped. With that fear in them, and the intensity brought on by the pressures of time, and the confidence and recklessness brought on by their companionship, they decided they'd drive up the Alaska Highway into the Yukon, and see the North.

"It was our last fling! It was still a new highway then. We stopped long enough in Fort St. John to send a note to Hans in Claresholm. Then we drove off without waiting for a reply. Fort St. John was just a log cabin, full of furs and spare tires and guns and flour. An old Indian woman ran the place. There was a sign that said 'STORE.' We couldn't see a store anywhere, though. We sat there in the car laughing about that. In a couple minutes, the old woman came out from the back and unlocked the door. That was the store, hanging on the backs of the double doors! Our tires were shot, so we bought new ones, for the bad road ahead. They cost a lot, but we figured that was better than being stranded in the middle of nowhere. What a hole."

They drove into blue and white mountains and green glacial rivers and long, long hours without darkness. Every day that they drove, slowly, over the roads of razor-sharp rocks, there was less darkness than there had been the day before. The skies were lit with golden light. Red shadows played over the snowfields. The sun balanced on the horizon—a flaming golden ball. While they watched all that, their tires were being cut to shreds.

"The gas and food we bought along the road cost a fortune: day by day we watched our money dwindle. It disappeared so quickly we soon came to laugh about it: it was so preposterous! We told ourselves that when we had spent half our money we'd have to turn around. We had loaded the car down with provisions in Fort St. John, and had bought heavy winter coats. We figured we were set."

They were set. The car had been laden like a U-Boot leaving Lorien for six weeks in the Atlantic. Despite their precautions, however, the provisions ran out as quickly as their money. They ate their way through it all. They spent most of their time driving, alone, while the other slept, as the North of the continent unfolded around them like a map that was being uncrumpled piece by piece.

"We were far, far north of the Arctic Circle, and had exactly one half of our money left. We knew it was desperate then, for half of the money did not include the food we had already eaten. Worse: we had a flat tire. When we went to get it repaired, the mechanic said, 'Your tires are junk. They are absolutely cut to ribbons. You have to buy a complete new set. They cannot be fixed.' So we said 'okay.' What else could we do?

"'That will be $200,' the guy said. We couldn't believe it. We'd bought our entire set for $50 down south in Fort St. John, and that was a lot! So there we were, almost in Siberia, with Hans's car. We asked what it cost to fly south. That was every penny we had! We bought the tires. We agreed to look for work, to get some money together so we could get out on the road again. The only work was at a mine, so we decided on that."

That's where they learned what it means to live in Canada.

In 1954, mine work in the Yukon was like railroad work in the 1970s: a lot of ex-cons were working there at the end of the world and the end of the road.

"In those days there were few safety regulations. When Karl asked me, 'What can we possibly do for work?' I said 'Don't worry, I'll take care of it. You just say what I say and we'll be alright.' We set ourselves up! The miners took full advantage of us. We were hated Germans. For two weeks they had their fun with us. They didn't care if we survived their joke or not.

"We walked into a mine office and I said, 'We want to work.'

"The man there said, 'There's no work.'

"'We're miners. I've worked in the mines in Germany.' That is all I knew: the word *miner*.

"When the man said to Karl, 'What do you do?' Karl did not understand. He knew even half as much English as I did, so I said, 'Oh him, he's a miner too!'

"'You're hired then!' the man said, with a smile. 'Go down to the supply hut. Get your equipment and show up for work!'

"After that no one paid us any attention at all. What we did not know was that in the Yukon, *miner* meant an explosives expert."

In 1969, my father is gnawing his way through Ukrainian sausage and mustard, chewing the words with his food as he speaks.

"So there we were—we had never been in a mine of any kind at all in our lives, had never been underground, and were about to get a ridiculously high wage each day to do the most dangerous job in the mine."

My father tears off a chunk of bread as he says it and slathers it with Helen Bannerman butter, then starts in on it as he tells us how they stepped out of that wooden shack onto the permafrost. The sky was cold and hard. Under it, they trudged across to the supply hut. The yard was littered with rusted and broken-down machines. Big dump trucks were driving slowly back and forth from the mine. The smoke from the bunkhouses plumed up in the air, white, against the blue sky. My father says the sky seemed so very close there, at the top of the world.

On any normal day, my father would be at work in the orchard, mowing grass, spraying, bossing a thinning crew, but today he has company: Americans. After wiping the last of the mustard off of his plate, he leans over the kitchen table and paints them a picture of the supply hut, bright yellow and set a considerable distance away from all the other buildings. They see it all: Karl and Hans standing there for a moment with the blue light pouring in through the door, looking at all the walls stacked with strange equipment. The Americans are mesmerized.

Hans sweeps them up in his tale: "Step by step we explored the contents of the shack, and outfitted ourselves: first a pair of boots each, steel-toed, spiked, then a hard hat, then oilskin pants and an oilskin jacket. We were beginning to feel more like miners already! Then there was the dynamite. There was a case of that for each of us. And the blasting fuses. They were marked: 5 seconds, 30 seconds, 5 minutes. We slung long rolls of each over our shoulders. Now we were feeling really confident! We each pulled down a shiny, greasy new shovel and a new pick."

Hans belts the words out like a stand-up comic. The Americans fill the silence of his pauses with laughter. They are right on cue.

"Then the explosives man came into the shack. He shouted, 'Who in the fuck are you? What are you doing here?'

"'I'm Hans! This is Karl.' I tried to shake the man's hand. He got a good look at us there in that gloom.

"'Are you the new miners?'

"I tried to sound tough under the hard hat and all the equipment. 'Yes. We are the new miners. Where do we work?'

"The man stood there for a moment sucking on his chewing tobacco, and then he said through orange, tobacco-stained lips, 'You go blast out a ditch across the road over there.'"

The man took the boys out in the doorway and pointed it out. "And then over to the bunkhouses, for water. I want it six feet deep and straight. Can you do that?"

"Sure," Hans said.

"I want it done by tomorrow."

Hans smiled and shook his hand again, and so did Karl. Then they trudged off with their new boots and their shovels, their cases of dynamite and their coils of fuses. Setting his dynamite down beside a rock outcropping, Hans picked up a shovel and tried to dig a hole, but the blade just hit the permafrost underneath the moss and sprang away. Karl picked up one of their long picks and had a go at it. The jar of the pick shattered through him, and he threw it down, his fingers stinging with the vibrations. They stood there feeling a little stupid for a moment. Then the man who had hired them got in a 4 x 4 pickup and drove up on the road towards the mine. When he got to them he stopped, shut off the engine, and climbed out. Without saying a thing, he walked over to them. For a moment, he stood beside them, as they all stared down together at the chips in the soil.

Finally the man spoke, "How's it going?"

"Damn hard ground," Hans said.

"You'll have to blast it," the man said.

"Can't get into it," Hans said. Karl nodded energetically, as Hans gave his best bright smile.

"Blast on top," said the man. Then he took pity on them. "You're sure you're miners?"

"They don't have such hard ground in Germany!"

"Well, you'll figure it out!" He turned and walked away, back to his truck. "By the way," he said, turning back for a moment. "Don't use the five-second fuses."

"Okay," Hans said.

"What did he say?" asked Karl, as the truck bounced away over the rough road.

"Shit, I don't know," Hans answered. "I have got to blast on top. I have to use the five-second fuses."

When the lunch table calms down, Hans continues. His blue eyes sparkle. We are a great audience. He loves us.

"We set sticks of dynamite where we were going to blast, unrolled the fuses, then looked at it all, puzzled. It was August, the beginning of winter, so there was snow in the air. As the flakes fell around us, we wondered how to connect the dynamite to the fuses. That was no problem: we each had a jackknife! While I cut the fuses with my knife, Karl started boring holes into the end of the dynamite with his. I followed after him, sticking the fuses into the holes. We were so proud that we had figured it out! When we had it all lined up, I walked back to the car and got some matches out of my smoking pouch. I sent Karl to flag down the traffic on the road. He stopped a whole line of big trucks and pickups. With the miners all watching us, I lit the fuse and ran behind the rockpile, waiting for the dynamite to blow. We waited five minutes, ten minutes, but nothing happened. I ran back up and looked at the fuses. They had all burnt away! The dynamite still sat there. I swore and ran back down and waved the traffic through. I grabbed Karl.

"'Shit, would you look at this!' I said.

"Karl just stared.

"Finally, I said, 'Well, the dynamite must be no good!'"

The Americans are roaring. Hans offers them another beer. Dorothy gets up to fetch it from the fridge.

Back the boys went to the blasting shack and got another case of dynamite—each. They laid out more fuses, and whittled more holes into the ends of the sticks. By this time everyone who drove by cheered at them, and they waved back, laughing. They did not have a clue what the men in the trucks were saying. The men had made bets, though, on whether the stupid Krauts would blow themselves up. I've heard this story so many times its blasting fuses are laid out in my head: as the stupid Krauts were setting the fuses into the end of the dynamite again, the explosives man came back up from the supplies shack; he slowly made his way up over the rockpile; when he saw what they were doing he instantly went all tense; his voice went shrill for a moment.

"Don't do that!" Then he calmed down a bit. "You need some blasting caps! Shit, don't do that ever again, okay?"

"Okay," Hans said. Then he knew he had a friend, someone who would help them through this initiation. He also realized that no one else expected them to make it out of there alive, and that there was no way out of that: they were stuck in that trap, and had to see their way through to the end.

In the kitchen, my father has pushed his chair back. The hot air pulses against our heads like a hammer. I am starting to drift away.

"I started to get really scared," my father says.

The Americans clamour appreciatively: "Damn rights. I'd be scared, too."

Hans grins. I grin, too, although distantly. I know how this one's going. The sun beats down on the top of the house, through the attic, and fills my head. I feel unwell.

"I went back with the man," my father continues, "and got some blasting caps. He showed me how to stick them into the ends of the dynamite sticks. He sent me up there with a box of them. I got back to Karl and shouted out, laughing, 'I have what they need!' I opened the box, and showed Karl.

"Karl said, 'Ya, but how do you use these?' Karl was always more practical than I was, but I knew English, so I was the brains of the operation.

"'Shit, I don't know! Pretty stupid looking little things! You stick them in the end of the dynamite, that's what he said.'

Journeys Through a Dark Century - 177

"'Ya, but how do you stick them to the fuse?'

"'Shit, I don't know that! You figure that out. I'll stick them in the dynamite. You stick them to the fuse. Okay?'

"'Okay.'"

Giggles. Knowing glances.

"So we did. I went ahead and stuck the caps into the dynamite sticks, and Karl came after me and bit the caps with his teeth to stick them on.

"When I got to the end and saw what he was doing, I said, 'You're crazy!'

"'It works.'"

Hans had to agree. It worked alright.

The Americans are shaking with almost soundless laughter and smashing their glasses down on the table. Beer splashes. Dorothy brings a rag and wipes it up.

Hans and Karl got the whole line rigged up that way. Then Karl went down again and stopped traffic. The traffic was a bunch of investors who had flown in for a personal inspection. They were all stalled on one side of Karl. All the mine trucks were stalled on the other side, heading out with ore. Once they were stopped, Hans ran up behind his rockpile and lit the fuse. It came very quickly. They had used that five-second fuse! There was a terrible bang, and chunks of ice flying around. One of the chunks smashed through the windshield of a bigwig mine car. Before the smoke settled, Karl waved all the cars through. Together, the boys walked up to their dynamite. Nothing had happened! As they were standing there, another man came up, all grim. He had just got off shift at the mine—an old fellow.

"You guys made a big bang," he said.

"Ya!" Hans laughed, and then Karl laughed too. They were proud of the noise they had made, but a little uncertain, because it had done nothing.

"Didn't make a hole, though."

"That's for sure!"

"What you need is mud. Put that dynamite down. Put mud on top of it. That will do it."

Hans looked around—the place was frozen; there was no mud. The wind swept a little low fine snow over the ground. The sky was pale and thin.

"Anything else work?" he asked.

"Some people use shit," the guy added. "That'll do it." And he walked away and waved.

The Americans are groaning, as if reading from a teleprompter.

—

The story has taken hold of my father now. He can't stop. It is out of control, like a runaway train.

"It is hard to believe, but for four days, as the whole camp watched us from a distance, we laid out the dynamite and took a dump on top of each stick. We just thought it was a Canadian thing. Then the day came. Once again we closed down the road. Karl's English was getting really good. He went down and shouted out: 'Stop! NO! Bang!'

"The investors were still around and they were caught in the lineup again, but from the opposite direction: this time they were on their way back from the mine. As Karl stood there on the road, smiling at the drivers, letting them know by his smile that it was going to be alright, I lit another fuse. This time it worked! This time everything worked! The force of the blast went down into the ground instead of up in the air and we blew chunks of rock and permafrost a half mile. With them we threw up a big pile of shit, too. It splattered all over both of us, and all over the cars. The mine officials had to sit in those stinking cars for three hours, while Karl and I cleared the debris away so they could drive on. The whole time no one lifted a hand to help us. All the miners, all those ex-soldiers and ex-cons, sat on the backs of their trucks, or leant their heads out of the cabs, and laughed, 'What a shitty job, eh! Is that how you do it in Germany? So that's why you lost the war! Boy, you've got a lot of shit!' Our faces were burning with shame and humiliation. We cleared the rock away. After three hours it was clean and everyone drove off. After that, we decided to build a fire, melt down the mud, and use it instead. I don't know why we didn't think of it in the first place."

The Americans are wiping their eyes with the backs of their hands. Their wives are tittering quietly. My mother laughs out loud.

So it went on for the afternoon, and so it went, on and on, for the two weeks of their apprenticeship, there at the mine in the Yukon. As the days went by they became very quick and proficient at the blasting.

"We had to blast the waterline right up to the bunkhouses, and had to do it without wrecking the buildings. We went together to the guy who had hired us, and told him the problem.

"'That's no problem,' he laughed. 'A good miner could muffle the sound! A good miner would put something over the blast.'

"We nodded knowingly and went out. As we walked away, Karl leaned over and asked, 'What did he say?'

"I shrugged. We stood among the junked machines, in the starlight. It was early one Sunday morning. Everyone else was off shift. Not us. We were racing to get our job finished.

"'Well,' I said. 'Look at it. All the force of the blast goes down, so all they need is something to muffle the sound. That can't be that hard!'

"We looked around. After half an hour all we found was a whole bunch of cardboard boxes outside the cookhouse."

As the temperature in the house rises and energy seems to flow out of us like water draining out of a well, Hans tells how they carried a whole bunch of boxes back, laid them out, one box upside down over every stick of dynamite. They were feeling very clever by this point and congratulated themselves on their genius.

"We stuck a second stick of dynamite under each one, just to be sure. If one was good, two was better! We figured on getting it right the first time, and saving ourselves a bit of work."

"At 6:00 AM we let the blast go. It did not all go down, though. The first stick of dynamite blew those cardboard boxes all to bits. Then I knew we had had it." Hans pauses and surveys his audience. They guffaw. Hans has them in the palm of his hand, when he delivers the punchline: ". . . because there was a second stick under every box!" From here on in, the laughter of the Americans and Hans's words are coming out all mixed up at once: "Sure enough, the second stick smashed out every window in the bunkhouse. We ran away fast! We figured we were dead! A few hours later, we came back. By that time, the whole rest of the water line had been dug and all the glass had been replaced in the bunkhouse. We couldn't believe it."

When the Americans collect themselves and ask him what happened next, Hans takes a long drink of beer and goes on, but calmer now. Now he is just giving the facts.

"We went into the bunkhouse and it was alright: we had finally become members of the gang. It was strange! The man from the office came down and said, 'Ya, you guys are okay!' He hired us on full time! That was our training period at the mine. That was how you got new miners in those days. We were lucky we were not killed. That is how you had your fun."

My father shrugs.

After their trial period, Hans went underground. Down there, no one treated him as if he knew what he was doing. It was no place for mistakes or kidding around. The man from the gate took him to the supply shed, and outfitted him properly. He explained every piece of equipment he needed, what it was for and how to use it, and every piece of clothing, and all the rules, how many whistles to clear out for an explosion, how many for the explosion, how many for all clear.

Hans worked for six months inside that mountain. He never saw the sun. His last month, December, 1955, was a living hell. Karl had been working above ground as a driller's helper at a new rock face, taking out core samples in a vertical line down the face of the cliff.

"They chose Karl because he knew no English. They thought he wouldn't figure out their scam. Each sample was noted in a ledger. It was slow, methodical work, with the roar of the drill and the shouting to make yourself heard. As they worked down the cliff, Karl noticed the driller made a note whenever they hit a vein of ore. When they got to the middle of the vein, Karl thought he lifted out the cores and set them aside and did not enter them in the ledger. Karl told me that when you looked at his chart there was a perfect rise and fall graph, except that the peak of the graph, the core of the seam, was missing, but you wouldn't know that."

Karl and Hans talked about that, behind the bunkhouse. As they talked they both realized that they were completely and utterly alone and had no one except each other. They were stone cold sober.

In the farmhouse, you could have heard a pin drop. Hans is speaking softly now.

"'Don't say a word about this to anyone,' I said to Karl. 'You know what they are doing—they are milking the stock market! They are keeping the profits for themselves and not sharing them with the stockholders! Go back to work in the morning and don't say a word!'

Pause. Heads shake. Hans is not smiling anymore.

"Karl had to work alone with the driller all day long. He had to pretend he didn't notice a thing, but he concluded that there were really two ledger books, one that the big mine bosses took away, and another that was sent to their head office. Worse yet, Karl stumbled on the boss, with his ledger book. After the boss left, the driller came back up to him and said, "This didn't happen. There was no meeting here. Do you understand?" Karl didn't understand the words very well because he knew hardly any English, but then the guy said, "Cause if you don't understand, I am going to fucking kill you. If you mention a word of this to anyone, I am going to fucking kill you!' and he drew a finger across his throat. From that finger and from his tone of voice, Karl understood perfectly well, although he was really only guessing, just like he was with those ledger books. It was then Karl was sent to work underground with me."

The sprinklers are swishing outside in the heat. My father's voice is low and sober now.

"The first time they tried to kill us an air hose came apart when we were walking down a passage. It whipped and smashed around. We only escaped it by sheer chance: someone grabbed us from behind and dragged us into a dark tunnel, and said, "Christ! Watch yourselves! Someone's trying to kill you!" My chest was badly bruised for a week, where the hose had glanced against me as I fell back."

The heat is rising. Hans wipes the sweat from his forehead and takes another slug of beer. My mother is noisily clearing away the dishes from lunch.

"When we came out, the hose was still writhing like a yellow snake. There was no one else there so we went down, deeper into the mountain, to a main chamber and hit the emergency shut-off. We walked back up the trainline, picking our way over the coils of the hose in the darkness. I spent a week in bed. Karl went down into the mine every day. He was scared to death. He always watched his back."

"A few days later, they tried to kill Karl. He was walking down the trainline, which was also the main entrance to the mine, when the train rounded the corner. It was a shift change, so there was not supposed to be a train running at all. Karl turned and ran, but the train was overtaking him. It filled the entire passage. There were no side passages and nowhere to turn off."

Hans times his phrasing, pausing for effect like a ringmaster in a circus. He snaps his whip.

"Just as the train came onto him, Karl squeezed to the side. There was a bit of a depression there. The train pushed by, scraping against his chest. His lamp was smashed, and the driver looked at him and yelled, 'You son of a bitch!' Karl followed the train out in the darkness, running his hand against the walls of the tunnel to find his way. He went to me then and said, 'You have to come back to work. It'll be better if there are two of us.' I was too sick to work, but I went. We worked side by side, under the mountain."

"It was terrible," the American wives say, in hushed voices. The cuckoo clock ticks behind them.

"That was the North," my mother says knowingly, rummaging around in the cupboard behind them and beginning to take down the ingredients to make icing for the carrot cake she's made for afternoon coffee: icing sugar, food colouring, a brick of cream cheese out of the fridge, her beaters, bowls, spatulas, measuring cups, spoons. She bangs and tinkles away as Hans goes on with the third attempt on their lives:

"A week later, the bells were sounded for all clear. We were working deep underground. The foreman had told us to work in Chute 7. As we were walking down the chute a voice called to us from far behind, up the stope, 'Where are you going?'

"'Chute 7.'

"'You can't go there! They're going to blast in Chute 7! Everybody's cleared out! Didn't you hear the whistle?'

"'We heard the whistle for All Clear!'

"'Well, they're going to blast down there in five minutes.'

"'Five minutes!' We couldn't get out in five minutes!

The timing of Hans's delivery is perfect. My brother and I, lanky, teen-aged, pimply, are mesmerized. The Americans are enthralled. The American wives are holding their breath. Like a stage manager in a theatre, my mother is smearing icing on the cake. Hans's hands are gesticulating across the table. His eyes are blazing.

"'Follow me!' called the man. We did. We all ran together into a side passage, high up. It let out onto the side of the cliff, a stope for dumping out the waste rock, and for air. We scrambled out, breathing hard. When the explosion went off, the whole of Chute 7 came down. When we returned to camp, everyone was surprised to see us. That was the real clue!"

The Americans are furious. "How could they get away with that! That's scandalous!"

"That's murder," their wives say.

I am in awe.

"They figured they could get away with anything," says my mother, plunking the cake down on the table and laying out the forks around people's elbows, then added, "they usually did."

"Dorothy," says Hans. She turns red in the face and he sweeps his audience up again in his story. Plates clatter onto the table as she sets them down.

"'It's the middle of the winter!' I whispered to Karl later. We spoke in German so no one would understand us. 'There's no way out of here. We can't drive out.' There was a guy who had a taxi. He said he would take us out in a few days, when the weather warmed up.

"'We'll pay you double,' said Karl. That clinched it.

"It was 50 Below that night. We got about three miles before the car stopped, in the middle of the frozen river. There was no way to get it going again. The snow was blowing everywhere. You couldn't see a damn thing. I stayed with the driver, while Karl walked back to camp. One of the Indians working in the kitchen said, 'Yeah, I can get you out.'

"'We'll give you our car,' Karl said. 'If you take us to Dawson City!'"

The rest of the story unfolds like the opening of Jack London's *White Fang*:

> A vast silence reigned over the land. The land itself was a desolation, lifeless, without movement, so lone and cold that the spirit of it was not even that of sadness. There was a hint in it of laughter, but of a laughter more terrible than any sadness—a laughter that was mirthless as the smile of the Sphinx, a laughter cold as the frost and partaking of the grimness of infallibility. It was the masterful and incommunicable wisdom of eternity laughing at the futility of life and the effort of life. It was the Wild, the savage, frozen-hearted Northland Wild.

Quite the bit of hyperbole just to describe how, when the temperature drops below minus 40, the air becomes as still as a liquid. The boys didn't walk out of the mine into that liquid stillness, though, moving through it with surety and power; they stepped out into Jack London—better yet, into Karl May. Every good German boy curled up on the heated bench of a green-tiled stove while the rest of the house turned to ice knew May's stories by heart: *Old Surehand, The Slave Caravan, Winnetou, Among Vultures, From Baghdad to Stambul,* among a hundred others, or *The Oil Prince*, which opened with:

> Anyone who wanted to take the open road over the Rio Colorado from El Paso del Norte to California, came

first, before he reached Tucson, the capital of Arizona, to the old Mission San Xavier del Bac, which lay approximately nine miles from Tucson. This mission was founded in 1668 and is such an imposing construction that it fills the traveler with astonishment to think that he has come across such a monument of civilization in the middle of the wilderness.

"It was those names I remembered most of all," says my father. "I had them memorized. With names like that you knew he was telling the truth."

What a guy. Born in poverty in Saxony in 1842, May was in and out of jail from the age of six, when he stole six candles from the school chapel and was kicked out on his ear. By the time he had finally made something of himself with his romantic stories of adventure in Arabia and the American West he had invented his own history. In his 1912 autobiography, he wrote how he learned his first stories from his grandmother, who had inherited a secret esoteric tradition from certain rare old books. Almost a century of research has uncovered not a single copy of those rare books, mind you. No matter: in 1896 May had visiting cards printed with the name of the hero of his Wild West novels: "Dr. Karl May, AKA Old Shatterhand, Radebeul Dresden, Villa Shatterhand." May even answered fan mail with fictional references to his past and passed on the experiences of Old Shatterhand as his own. His publisher's catalogue proudly displayed a picture of May posing with his Indian hero Manitou's silver rifle, with the inscription: Old Shatterhand with Manitou's Silver Flintlock. What a card.

May's Wild West was populated with Germans who had escaped from a cramped homeland to a world of freedom. The sun shone off of their bronzed skins. They could see a hundred miles across the mesas. They were the characters of Dresden's great romantic painter, Caspar David Friedrich, standing motionlessly on a foggy shore looking out to sea, except under May's hand they were animated. They had actually left the frozen, two-dimensional space of the paintings and the motionless space of German society, and could move, and act, and *realize* their dreams in a land full of Arabs and Indians and clever, clever Germans. My father could identify with that, big time. So did his mother, it seems, because when I was a year old, my mother got worried letters from her mother-in-law in Germany, suggesting they leave the orchard in Cawston and move somewhere safe, such as Kuppenheim, where no one was shooting flint-tipped arrows at you all the time. "It's no place to raise children," Charlotte wrote. My mother had never read Karl May. That was her problem, obviously. She had no sense of proportion.

For writing those letters, my mother called Charlotte "A silly German," and accused her of seeing a naked Indian behind every rock, and of being unable to apply any logic and proportion to the situation. Oh, dear. Karl May's Germans weren't silly, though: they were never at a loss for wisdom or knowledge, were able to solve any practical or diplomatic problem, and lived among Indians free of the poisonous taint of civilization.

In the 1930s, May's books received official state sanction. They didn't outsell *Mein Kampf,* but they came close. In the *Heimat,* you can still go to a rock quarry outside of Dresden, paint your face with coloured makeup, put on a headdress of goose feathers, receive an Indian name, and whoop it up along with Karl May's ghost. You can go to Charley's Saloon, drink a schnapps at the bar, take lessons in tossing whiskey back in one slug, be photographed in Western costume, see the General Store, the hotel, and the Western church, and even pan for gold. You can spend evenings around a campfire, walk a trapline, throw horseshoes, and learn to shoot a bow. You'll puff at a peace pipe, eat Indian food, and if it rains, fifty of you can sit around a campfire in the comfort of a big tipi, and all that for $30 a day or $160 a week.

May's final heroes were Hans and Karl. It was 50 below. The sun hadn't risen for months. Their breath had frozen to their faces. They were in the North. They were on the run. How exciting.

With fingers numb with pain, the skat players unloaded the taxi in the middle of the frozen river. Hans May and Karl Shatterhand were wearing the heavy Yukon jackets they had bought from the old woman the spring before in Fort St. John. Like that, they set off by dogsled under the Northern Lights. They nearly froze to death.

"The trip took us five days. Every morning the Indian said, "I'll leave you here if you don't pay more!" What could we do! The dogs were vicious. We were really afraid of them. We figured they would eat us while we slept. The Northern Lights flickered over us the whole time. Some nights the snow covered us all as we slept under the overturned sleds. We really thought we would die there in the cold. We started taking turns sleeping, because we thought the Indian would murder us in our sleep, for our money!"

They eventually did make it to Dawson City. By this time they wanted to get out of the North as quickly as they could.

"We found a pilot sitting at a table in the corner of a restaurant and said we heard that he flew people out. He just grunted, so I asked him if he'd fly us out, today.

"'We have the money,' I said.

"He said, 'I'm not going in this weather!' Karl and I were still afraid. We figured that since we had left in a big hurry, the miners would know for sure that we knew something, and would follow us. We thought we knew damn well what they would do with us.

"'What will it cost?' I asked."

Now my father was playing the fool for the Americans, laughing at himself as the words sputtered from his mouth, and the Americans laughed along. Digging at our mother's cake, my brother and I were quiet, so we'd be allowed to hear the end of the story instead of being sent out to work the afternoon away in the green shade of the trees.

"The pilot named a ridiculous figure, but we paid it. We would have paid anything, and he knew it, too, just by looking at us. We took off in the darkness. The storm rose up behind us in a black wall. It was a wonder we didn't crash. At Fort St. John, the storm hit as soon as we landed. Snow filled the runway two feet deep. The airline gave us a choice: stay there for a week, or start shovelling the runway and get out when it was clear. We sure weren't going to be stuck in that hole for that long! We didn't want anything more to do with the North. We started shovelling. We shovelled for thirty-six hours. When the runway was clear we took the next flight, a regular commercial flight.

"It was just like a movie! We got on the plane, and flew in the face of another storm, south, to Vancouver. We looked terribly out of place. Even for those days in the North we were all dirty and unshaven and our clothes were frozen with snow. I had grown a red beard on the sled. We stank of sweat and smoke and dogs. No one wanted to sit with us! We arrived in Vancouver in the fog and the rain. When the plane landed on the runway, the lights of the city burned around us, and the plane taxied up to the terminal. It was raining, but I didn't care. We ran down the steps and kissed the ground, we were so happy to be back and to be alive. We had a few dollars left.

"Karl said, 'Let's go hire some girls and get drunk,' to celebrate. I'd had it with that, had it with the North.

"'Go ahead,' I said. 'I'm going into the city.' I spent three days in a steam bath in Chinatown, soaking the dirt out of my pores. When I had finally sweated the last of it out, and paid the Chinese the little money I had left, I looked up Karl, to see how he was getting on. He had some loose change left, so he telegraphed Big Hans in Alberta: *Send Money Stop*. Hans did!"

That's what he told the Americans.

There's a photograph, though: Little Hans standing in the doorway of Robert Service's cabin in Dawson, a rifle cocked over his arm, dressed in his middle-class German clothes: pressed white shirt with pointed collar open at the neck, black slacks, polished black shoes, black jacket, narrow belt. He was clean-shaven. He grinned. His teeth sparkled.

Oh well. Hans and Karl took the bus back to Claresholm. When they got there, it was the Chinook. There was water everywhere. Big Hans quit his job, and they drove off together. Karl May sat in the back seat, his flintlock on his knee.

"We took two cars through the Rockies and through the Kootenays. It was like old times in the snow, driving, except this time there were mountains. Jonas was Big Hans's car now. She belched out blue smoke the whole way. Coming down into Golden, we knew she had to go, so the next day in Nelson, we went to a wrecking yard. The man said, 'Sure, I'll take it, but you'll have to pay me $20.' We didn't have any money, and we sure weren't going to pay anything for a man to junk a car we had only paid $30 for in the first place! We told him that. He thought about it for a bit.

"'Okay,' he said. 'I'll take it, but I need the registration.' Registration! We had never ever heard of registration. 'You get it from the guy you bought it from,' the wrecker said. Not the guy we bought it from! Jonas was a hot car, and we hadn't even known!

"At last, I came up with a solution. That afternoon we took Jonas up on the cliffs south of Kaslo where the road winds in and out high above the lake. I set myself up with my camera on a corner, and when no cars were coming either way—we had to wait a long time—Karl drove Jonas up to the cliff and jumped out. As Jonas rolled over the edge and down into the deep lake, I took pictures—a whole roll. Afterwards, I took my film into the newspaper in Nelson and said, 'We were driving by Kaslo. We saw this accident. It was a car with a woman in it and a couple of kids. I took these pictures just as the car crashed!'"

The paper paid $35 for the film. Jonas ran on the front page. The RCMP sent divers down to find it, but it had sunk down into the cold, deep lake, among the sturgeon.

—

Two days later, Hans was winding down Anarchist Mountain in Osoyoos. When he swung around the face of the cliff and the Southern Okanagan spread out below him, with green orchards ringing the blue lake and sagebrush and antelope brush hills spreading up towards mountains grey as clouds, he recognized it at once. It looked like the Bodensee. It looked like Paradise. There was no sign of Windigo anywhere. Little Hans had come home.

~Secret Stories~

The story of how Little Hans met Dorothy is founded on a lie—a lie so big that there was no way anyone wouldn't believe it. It begins in a peach orchard in Osoyoos.

"I had never seen a peach tree in my life," my father told me. "For us in Germany, peaches were exotic, like oranges or something. You never thought you would ever see one of them. So I walked up the driveway and asked Louis Hart if he could give me a job. I told him I was a horticulturist from Germany; I had a degree. Louis stood in the doorway of his farmhouse, with the tractors and equipment in the shed behind, and eyed me up. His foreman and a few workers were walking across the yard. He was in a hurry and didn't have time for me.

"'Do you know how to prune peach trees?' he asked. 'I had a couple guys pruning my peaches, but they were ruining the trees.' He spat snuff. 'They don't know a thing about peaches.'

"'Sure, I know how to prune peaches.' I smiled. 'We pruned them all the time in Switzerland.' That was a lie, but he didn't know that. 'I'm really in trouble now,' I thought to myself.

"'What about this guy with you?' Louis asked, pointing at Karl. I looked at Karl. He didn't look like he knew shit about peach trees.

"'No,' I said. 'He doesn't know shit about peach trees. But I do.'

"Louis spat again. 'Come with me,' he said, and slipped on his boots and pulled on a mechanic's cap. We walked out into the orchard together. A light wind blew through the trees, coming up from the lake. It was the early spring and the blossoms weren't out yet. I thought to myself, I'd better keep my eyes open, so as we walked I ignored what Louis was saying and looked at what he had done to the trees. It looked terrible, you know. It looked like he had half killed those trees. But I saw the saw cuts and the kind of cuts he had made, what he had cut off and what he had left, and what did I care, I needed a job. So he showed me a ladder and gave me a pair of pruning clippers, and said, 'Here, prune a couple trees. I'll be back in an hour. If you do a good job, you're hired.'

"So I happily started cutting away at those trees. I didn't have a clue what I was doing, but I did exactly what he had done to the other trees in the block. After an hour, I had finished two trees. I figured I had damn near killed the fucking things, so I was really worried when Louis came back. He drove his truck up this time, parked it, and came out, with a cigarette dangling between his lips. He stopped, cupped his hands around a match, and lit the cigarette, shook out the match, then stood there for a minute taking a couple puffs on the cigarette as he looked at what I had done. Finally he spoke. I was a basket of nerves by that time. I thought he was going to kill me.

"'Son of a bitch!' he shouted. Now I was really worried! And then he laughed. 'You're the first man I've ever seen who knew how to prune peaches! You're hired.' I didn't know shit about peaches, of course, but he wasn't smart enough to know that. He was just able to recognize that I did exactly what he had done! 'But not your friend. I don't have any work for him. He can stay in the cabin with you. I'll give you work for six weeks. After that, I can't promise anything.'

"So I pruned the peaches, and Karl and I lived together in Louis's cabin. There was no work for Karl, so it was really tough. Every day he went out looking for something. He got hired a little bit, here and there for a few days, but that was it. There wasn't much work in the orchards in the winter in those days. So, then I finished pruning the peaches, and Louis came to talk to me again.

"'You're a good worker,' he said. 'I'd like to keep you on, but I don't have any more work for you right now. You can be my foreman in the summer, and run my thinning and picking crews, but right now I don't have any work. Here's what I'll do: the two of you can keep living in my cabin as long as you like, and when I have work again for you, you can have it. Why don't you drive over the mountain to Chopaka,' he added, clapping me on the back. 'Go see Kohler. He needs pruners over there.' So that's what Karl and I did. Every morning we got in the car and drove over the mountain, right over the Richter Pass, to Kohler's ranch—and that was the old stagecoach road, too. I thought it would shake the car apart. I pruned the big old Starking Delicious trees and Karl chopped up the prunings on the ground. It was a really rough road in those days. We got a lot of flat tires, and we went in the ditch a lot, but we thought nothing of it. So that's how we got through that winter."

By the 1980s, when I was in my twenties and it was my turn to live that dream—and before I discovered how to stand perfectly still and let history flow through me—I drove all over British Columbia to find some place where I could grow apples and be alone with the land: through the Fraser Valley, up Vancouver Island, into Lillooet, the Cariboo and the Kootenays, and up to the Skeena, where I had heard of a perfect climate zone at a town called Cedarvale. My bride, Diane, and I bounced down the gravel roads, splashing through puddles in our tiny blue car, but all we found was one old farm with sour, worm-choked apples in a cardboard box on a windowsill, and the light as if it was squeezed from grass. In pickers' cabins in Cawston, Penticton and Osoyoos I found a few rusted iron beds, antique fridges, a few scraps of newspaper, and empty tins. When I got to Peachland, Greata Ranch had been abandoned for decades. The Chinese bunkhouses stood empty, their paint peeling away into the bunchgrass. In 1980, a developer had even bought the place up, sculpted twenty acres with a D-9, buried the topsoil under yards of sterile clay, and had framed in a set of lakefront condos. When interest rates rose to twenty-one percent, he walked away. The condos sat unfinished for a decade, the plywood warping in the rain, before they were torn down. For ten years, the place was up for sale. We often drove over the mountains to trespass in the old orchard rows and the shallow benches, where a few shoots, sagging with a few sour seedling apples, struggled up among the wormwood and Russian thistles. The sagebrush had rooted in the old orchard rows, yellow-flowered and soft. We sat there and ate summer apples and cold chicken as blackbirds sang like rain. I felt as if we had gone back eighty years in time, that with the blink of an eye we'd see the old crews with their horses pacing down the rows of stumps towards us, loaded down with apples, and pickers would climb up into heavily laden trees. I could hear them within the air.

When we walked back to the car, I felt as if I was walking with the dead, waiting like them for the developers from Hong Kong and Toronto and Vancouver. Time slowed almost to a stop. The seedheads of the grasses caught the blue and purple light as it flowed over the long, hilly benches. Along the highway, irrigation flumes, which once brought water down from creeks in the high country, ran with early moonlight and skitters of ochre, heat-withered leaves. I scooped aside the puffy white flowers of wild clematis and fingered the tin: the technology of World War I, that called the men home, to die, was still not rusted under its zinc shell.

Twenty-five years earlier, though, Karl and Hans settled in quite comfortably in Osoyoos. They worked six days a week, ten or twelve hours a day. On Sundays they went to church. At that time, there were a lot of Doukhobors in town: after their communal communities in Grand Forks and Castlegar had collapsed under the strain of residential schooling and religion, they had come over the mountains to work in the orchards.

"Those Doukhobor girls were really good looking," Dad laughed, when I was twelve years old. "Until they turned eighteen. After that, they started to put on weight. By the time they were thirty, you thought they weren't even female anymore. They were just big and ugly and fat. Before that, though, they were thin and very pretty. Karl and I learned really quickly that the best place to pick up girls was at church, so we went to their church. We had our pick of them! It was really hard to leave Osoyoos!"

But they did. Karl went to work for a carpenter in Penticton. Hans was hired to manage Frank Laird's orchard, and Braeside Orchards, on the granite outcroppings and clay cliffs above Skaha Lake. In those days, the eastern shore of Skaha Lake was the richest apricot land in the British Empire, and proud of it. Braeside Orchards was the kind of place that would have warmed W. Somerset Maugham's malaria.

"It was my first night. After work, a bunch of us were sitting around a fire on the beach, bullshitting and drinking beer, and the guys started to give me a hard time. I was the new guy, so that's natural. I was bullshitting them, too! They asked me who I was going to take to the dance on Friday night—the next night—and I said, "What dance?" I didn't know anything about any dance. So they told me, and gave me a hard time, so I said, 'Well, I'm going to take Dorothy Leipe.' I didn't know Dorothy from a hole in the ground, but I'd seen her walking, clip clip, down the road towards Penticton that morning, dressed up, on her way to work in the law office, and I'd asked Mrs. Laird who she was.

"'Oh, that's Dorothy Leipe,' she said. 'She lives just down the road.'

"I didn't tell the guys around the fire that, of course. They all laughed, because I had just come to town. How could I know Dorothy Leipe? It was a joke. 'Have you asked her?' they asked me.

"'No,' I answered, 'but I will right now.'

"So I went into the house and phoned the Leipes. I got your Grandma on the phone. It was 10:30 at night, and she was in bed. Everyone was in bed. They were all asleep! I asked if I could talk to Dorothy.

"Your Grandma asked me who I was, so I explained that I was Johannes

Rhenisch, and that it was really important that I talk to Dorothy. She said that Dorothy was asleep, so I told her it was really, really important! So she woke her up! Can you believe that! Your Grandma!

"So then I got Dorothy on the phone, and explained who I was, and asked her to the dance, and she said yes! So, I went to the guys, and said it was all arranged.

"I took Dorothy to the dance the next night. We had a good time. I invited her to the Penticton Vees hockey game on Saturday, and she said she'd come. Now, back in those days, of course, the Penticton Vees were the world champions. They had just beaten the Russians. Going to a Penticton Vees hockey game was a real big deal. The whole town went. They had just built a new arena for them, too."

My mother continued the story—when I was forty. "So, Hans and I showed up at the arena. That's when his problems started. Out in the parking lot, two young women came up to him, 'Oh, Hi, Hans!' they called, and he said 'Hi' back. When I asked him who they were, he said they were two friends from Osoyoos. He got us seated, and then excused himself to go to the concession. He said he'd get me some warm coffee. He was gone awhile and came back with some coffee, but it wasn't long before he said he had to go to the washroom, and he'd be right back. It continued like that for the whole game. He hardly saw any of it, because he was always running off to the concession to get me something, or slipping off for a minute, and then he came back and sat with me for a while before running off again. Out in the parking lot, after the game, he must have felt badly, because he told me the whole story: he had invited both of the girls from Osoyoos to come to the game with him, but he had forgotten, so when he saw them in the parking lot, he knew he had problems. He spent the whole game running from one to the other of us, buying us coffee, getting us snacks. By the end of it he was broke and exhausted."

When I asked my mother what she did then, she giggled. "I just laughed," she said. "He asked me if he could take me out again, and I said, 'Yes, you could.' Six weeks later we were married."

At that point, my father reached over and turned off the tape recorder. "We've heard enough," he said.

The wedding was the toast of Penticton German society. All the Germans in town—including the Germans that Bruno and Martha had come over with to start the commune in 1929, and even a few my father had played skat with on the boat over from Hamburg—gathered at the Pruesses' stone-flagged terrace, in their villa high above the lake. It looked like a hilltop in Majorca. Everyone wore dark suits. Everyone was relaxed.

"It was a shock," said my father. "One minute I was a young guy with a hot car and a good job; the next minute I was married. Not only that, she was sick. I didn't have any money for a honeymoon, so I got permission to camp on a private beach on Okanagan Lake, just north of Peachland, all by ourselves. I drove the Volkswagen down there, and set up the tent, and spent the next two days in misery, because Dorothy just lay in bed moaning. 'What have I done?' I thought."

A year and a half later, Hans became manager of Jim Dawson's orchard at Similkameen Station. For four years we lived there, on the edge of the hill above the willow swamps of Frank Richter's third ranch, halfway between Keremeos and Kohler's ranch at Chopaka. Elm trees, planted along the top of the slope to cut the relentless valley wind, shaded the house and cast ever-moving shadows through the windows. Funded by Dawson Construction, which had done much of the paving that had opened the Interior to modernity, the place was prosperous. It was postcard perfect.

Journeys Through a Dark Century - 199

Hans was part of the program: with a diploma in horticulture, he had a knowledge of fruit-growing techniques, and a European's love of modernity and technical innovation, which became the byword for the industry for four decades. The old farms, which had coasted along for so many decades as the economic ties that bound them to empire gradually deteriorated around them, had become almost worthless. Children raised on those orchards had left for the cities. There was no one left to work the land, and few who knew it: the colonial dream had failed; even the replacement of the colonial dream by Bruno and Martha's generation had failed. In the 1950s, the farms were being overtaken by a new technical generation. Capital and the efficiencies of specialization and chemical production had returned to the land to recolonize it. Hans stood at the forefront of that movement. It blew over my mother like a wind.

For his part, my father tried to harness the modernist steamroller by buying farm after farm. He planted cold-hardy Antonovka apple trees with seed he imported from Poland so he would be the only survivor of the next freeze. He joined the Packing House Board, the Irrigation Council, the Executive of the British Columbia Fruit Growers' Association; he started the Horticultural Forum, an annual fruit-growing conference to educate farmers in modernist technique; and year by year he put on weight, became a drunk, grew ever more angry and short-tempered, and was paid less and less for his fruit by an antiquated socialist fruit-marketing system set up in the '30s, before the world turned away from Soviet Russia, when the "Russian experiment" was on the lips of the working classes. The Canadian experiment united producers, marketers, and packers in one regulated organization, which sold all fruit from one selling desk and shared the profits.

If there were profits. By 1966, Hans and Jim Dawson and Hans Kohler and other large modernist farmers in the valley were going broke. They fought long and hard for the right to pack, market, ship and sell their own fruit, but against the smaller farmers, who needed the system's protection, they got nowhere. By 1971, my father and his friends were desperate. Even economies of scale could not protect them from the devastation of American production, subsidized by hydroelectric treaties between British Columbia and Washington. Things just got worse and worse. By 1973, all the orchardists in the valley were on the line. The spinoffs from the British Columbia Hydro profits, which had been used to build highways to open up the land for industrial development, had not materialized, just as they had failed to materialize in Egypt, in South America, and in Africa, where the game was also played. It was at that time, immobilized on his living room couch from a skiing accident, that my father agreed to join the United Fruit Growers movement, as its founding chairman.

"It made me so angry," my mother told me two decades later, after she had lost the farm, the land, and her dreams—the ones she had married Hans to protect. "They took advantage of a man who was on crutches and drugged on painkillers. They appealed to his vanity and he agreed to join their organization. It was an agenda completely against his nature, and he was the one who was ruined by it, not them. He took the fall for it, and they knew it. He was the front man for their politics. They used him to protect themselves." Then my mother tried out a word she had never used before—"The bastards!"—and found it right. It fell off of her tongue like a rock.

The UFG was a powerful political force in the Okanagan. Its goal was to persuade the government to change fruit-marketing legislation. As it stood, a farmer could sell retail fruit from his own farm, but could sell to no one else, at least in lots of more than ten bushels—about half the production of a single tree. To make sure that rules were followed, the

Fruit Board had its own police force. The Ministry of Highways had even built pullouts for the Fruit Board on the highways leading out of the valley. As the light sifted through the pine trees above them, men in light green shirts and black loafers, with clipboards and barricades, stopped all holiday traffic. Fruit in excess of ten bushels was seized and loaded onto waiting trucks.

The revolution began with secret meetings in farmhouses throughout the valley, followed by a Saturday folding application forms, stuffing and addressing envelopes, and licking 3,500 stamps. That was my job. They tasted pretty bad.

Within a week, the membership drive had split the industry in half, with farmers on each side claiming those on the other side was using mafia tactics to bring them to ruin. My father went on TV daily, led convoys of farmers to Vancouver in protest, sold my mother's canning cherries illegally on the streets of Vancouver, took up serious drinking, and actually did change legislation, changed the Okanagan forever. In the process, though, he lost his farm to Fruit Board seizures and crawled off to the States, licking his wounds. Even a quick look at the membership list of the United Fruit Growers, however, ought to clarify the battle lines: Rhenisch, Tilstra, Tomé, Treitl, Wagner and Wallin, Wuensche, Czuczor, Wingelmann, Dutra and Sebastio, Sousa, Stoll and Strafehl, Szanto and Souto—over a thousand immigrants, all with their backs against the wall, all of them paid three cents a pound for apples that sold for twenty cents a pound at the packinghouse gate and forty cents a pound in the supermarkets of Vancouver, all with the banks closing their doors to Canadian farmers in order to cover their South American debt; all of them shopping for clothing for their kids in the Sally Ann, all of them living in fear and shame.

Among the fruitgrowers who joined the United Fruit Growers was pretty much the entire Portuguese community of Oliver and Osoyoos, who had come to Canada after the political turmoil over the succession of the Portuguese dictator Salazar and the collapse of his fascist economic model, and who had got their start picking asparagus for my father at Inglewood. The fight was about who got to sell the immigrants' fruit. Not the Ferreiras, de Silvos and Webers, the Witzkes and Benzlers, the Soutos and Klettkes, and not the Garcias, Rosins or Rothes, either, that much was clear. The movement was a right-wing revolution against the rump of Empire, using the passive resistance techniques of Gandhi to convince a social-democratic government to disband a socialist agenda: kind of a hard sell!

——

While members of the British Columbia Fruit Growers' Association were lobbying government for full police powers, above and beyond the ability they already had to seize fruit and to search the books and premises of any grower at any time, a renegade trucker, his rig shorting out and running rough, with shot brakes and threadbare tires, pulled into our orchard at 2:00 AM. I was fifteen years old and loaded his semi up in the starlight. At dawn, I guided him behind our shed and covered his trailer with branches from the apple trees, making the truck unrecognizable from the air. TV crews came up from Vancouver and filmed me moving my sprinkler lines through the mud. Big lines of pickups, three-ton trucks, and Volkswagen campers packed with cherries, a hundred and fifty of them in a row like the diesels lined up on the road to Moscow in October, 1941, wound around the switchbacks at Whipsaw Creek, over the Hope Slide, and down through the silage fields and hop gardens of Agassiz to Vancouver. When it became clear that the police were going to impound all hundred and fifty trucks before the farmers could sell their fruit in the morning, a Vancouver retailer—another right-wing immigrant—offered them his warehouse as a parking lot for the night.

In the morning, fifteen thousand people came. Seventy tons of cherries were gone in one hour. The farmers drove home with the first cash they had had in five years. This was personal. My father and Charlie Bernhardt, the head of the British Columbia Fruit Growers' Association, fought it out every night on Kelowna television: Charlie would get on, my father would start to yell and scream over the dinner table, would turn purple in the face, and would pick up the phone to phone the television crew, to tell them how it really was, and my mother would rush up and pull the phone out of his hands, and only let him have it back after he calmed down.

The Minister of Agriculture, Dave Stupich, seemed to be beside himself with frustration, too. In March, 1974, he wrote to UFG secretary Olav Wallin, "This legislation was introduced on the insistence of the primary producers themselves, and the majority of those concerned today is still strongly in favour of it. Since it is obvious that you have little if any knowledge of the reasons for such legislation, may I suggest that you talk to some of the older growers who remember what it was like trying to make a living under the kind of 'freedom' you advocate." Twenty years later Stupich was charged with embezzling money from charities, during that period, to finance the New Democratic Party. Oh well.

"I came to Canada for freedom and democracy," my father told me in 1980, after he had moved to the States. "I came to Canada to escape the fascists. When those bastards put me out of business, I discovered that they are here, too. There is no democracy." I watched him retaliate by insinuating himself into Washington fruit culture, introducing himself to the owner of a three-thousand-acre plum orchard. The pressed hand was taken, but without enthusiasm; the attempt at networking failed in a stony face—a tall man with a military bearing, an old soldier. Behind him plum trees stretched in dark, shady blocks—big, old trees, so overgrown they were almost wild. Most of them had broken branches hanging to the grass. Sometimes whole halves of a tree were missing.

It wasn't an orchard; it was a forest. The place smelled of pesticide and rotting grass, of the resin of pitch that had oozed out of old limbs.

When my father came back from Washington, betrayed by his best friend, without a farm, without a penny, without any vestiges of pride or self-respect, he said, "A man can change countries once when he is young. You can't do it a second time. That is too much to ask any person to do."

— —

There is another story. In this story, my parents hide. They are immigrants. They don't know the rules. They don't play baseball. Everyone else plays baseball. Hans even fires a worker once when he borrows a tractor in the evening to go to a ball game. The games are in the knapweed field between the school and the cottonwoods by the slough. The air hangs green between the mountains. Frogs sing in chorus. Cool air is starting to rise off the water. Taught about machinery by soldiers in the wartime German army, Hans repeatedly fires new tractor drivers by the droves as soon as they adjust the throttle on the tractors. The first time they lift a hand to the throttle, he drags them off the machine, shouting that a diesel engine must remain at 1500 rpm forever. They shout back. It gets ugly.

This is not a fairytale. In this story, Hans makes moonshine in his basement. When the police come over in the evening, he serves them coffee bucked up by a good shot of hooch. They come back a lot. The neighbour starts asking questions. Hans just shrugs. In this story, he grows up in the black market, buys an orchard on a never-never plan from a major in the Canadian Army, and outwits him. In the end, he gets the orchard for nothing. He sends his children out into poisoned trees. He dismantles the social safety net of the packinghouse system, blows up marmots with dynamite at 4:00 AM, takes apart the old Upper Keremeos townsite for scrap lumber, uses the blasting ticket he earned the hard way in the Yukon to buy two cases of dynamite and blasts out the Lombardy poplars lining the old Keremeos cut-off road. In this story, a tree that produces a box of apples is said to produce six. Hans discards thousands of dollars of machinery on the dump, because he refuses to have a sale, refuses to have people see him down and out. In this story, Hans says that the CIA has a file on him, that they have a file on Dorothy, that they have a file on me. The RCMP has Hans's number for speeding recklessly. He takes to hiding in orchards with his lights off while the cops, in hot pursuit, scream past. The corporal vows to put him behind bars, if it's the last thing he does, so help him God. Hans does not see the mockery that is society: he has no part in society at all.

There is, mercifully, a third story—an epic tale about a successful farmer, a horticultural genius, a man with the golden touch, the brightest young farmer in the valley, who runs experiments for the Ministry of Agriculture in his orchard, who sells fruit trees grafted onto rootstock from Poland, introduces modern fruit-growing methods, reforms the packinghouse system, initiates horticultural forums to improve orchard quality, advocates for individual farmers with the United Fruit Growers. In this story, he is a hero. He should be canonized as a saint. For writing anything otherwise, one old member of the United Fruit Growers suggested that Harold should be "taken behind the barn and shot."

Beyond all the politics, the story of this northern shoulder of the world is the taste of a Winesap apple in the late fall when the snow lies on the branches. The fruit hangs down heavily to the ground and the apples are almost ice in the hand. Cougar hounds, kept in backyards, bay on fall nights as stars swing over the valley. There is the taste of bear meat on Bruno's table, the way a river moves through grass in flood, the way you can thread a hook through a grasshopper and pull trout out of that grass as wood ticks hang off the end of the grass stems at your back. This is not the history of Mackenzie King and Lester Pearson and the Suez Crisis. It is the grey gravel slopes above the Similkameen River north of Hedley, the Nicola River west of Merritt, the Thompson River north of Lytton, each tree spaced at a perfect distance from every other tree, in a musical pattern dictated by root growth and rainfall. There are ten thousand stories, a hundred thousand stories, of people living on this land and making a life here. It is what women made here when their men grew bushed. This is what Martha and Dorothy made when Bruno and Frank were feuding out in the barn, what Dorothy made when Hans was crumbling into rage, what I made when at twelve years of age I was completely alone with the trees. This history lies between men telling the old ghost story of Ogopogo and Dorothy saying, as she looked out of her window in Oliver, over the trees tossing in the light, after bankruptcy, after the decade in Vancouver saving up money to buy another farm, "I am finally back home."

Home is not British Columbia. Let's get that straight. It is not "The Heartland" or any other advertising slogan. In "Home," a girl wakes up in the morning with six inches of frost on her eiderdown; the air in her cabin is 60 below zero, Fahrenheit. She has newspaper pinned to her walls to keep out the wind. A hundred metres away in the farmhouse, her mother is making oatmeal for breakfast—the same oatmeal her father feeds to the workhorse in the barn. The air cuts the girl's breath like a knife. Out in the barn, mice rustle in the hay. The wind off the glacier blows down through the farm on July days, rustling through the dandelions, settling in the stalks of the rhubarb. In "Home," a girl picks the red stalks of the rhubarb, brings them in and cuts them up. Her mother bakes them in a pie, and the pie is served later, after dinner, as the smoke from the woodstove sifts through the room like maple sugar, joining with the shadows and pulling them over everyone like wool. The rhubarb's acid dries out the girl's mouth and her eyes open with surprise. Fifteen years later, her son's mouth opens to rhubarb pie in the desert air, with the same sense of surprise. Home is a place where you don't farm for money, but to live. It is a place where you plan to live for a long, long time, and where you plan for your children to live, a place between the desire for home and the desire for profit, between immigrant culture and the British culture that receives it, between the garden of Eden on the Reichenau and the native earth its image was projected across, between the city and the country it feeds upon: it is the earth itself, as all of history speaks through it. No one speaks to it except those born to its history, and no one else has the right to speak of it. No one else can.

⸺

There is the official British Columbia, the one with an official flower (dogwood) and an official bird (Steller's jay), with its encylopedia and its museum (royal) and its official history (archived). It has Chambers of Commerce and the Coquihalla Highway (toll), historical mills and ranches and gold rush towns, tour guides and golf courses and casinos—the British British Columbia, the one with all the words in its pocket.

There is also an unofficial British Columbia, where the immigrants live, where the sun is green and orange in the lower sky, where long shadows stretch out from the horses as my mother leads them to the barn, with Hudson's Bay Mountain like a giant wing above her in the high northern sky. The alpine peaks of the Coast Range tower above the desert mountains rimming the river in Lillooet, as if they were the voice of ancient gods. Native and immigrant earths mingle in this country. Winds of apricot petals drift across farms in gritty spring wind. There is the taste of tomatoes picked out of a field, with a dash of salt out of the shaker in your back pocket. It is the British Columbia without a word to its name, or where the names are lost.

From that loss to film crews descending on the Okanagan to film the sacred dreamtime—to try to catch the Ogopogo on digital video—is just a short step. From there to an American film crew invading Keremeos and Chopaka to film *The Shipment* on Frank Richter's first and fourth ranches, a B-movie about a small farming town in Arizona, stolen drugs, the Mafia from New York, complete with a buffoon buggering cows, is an even shorter step. From there to living with no history at all is just a heartbeat.

When I look up above the aspens outside my house and the chill blue winter stars spill over the roof like the seeds of spearmint scattered across sandy ground, I am looking at the same stars that my grandparents, Hans and Charlotte, saw above Freiburg in 1933, that night after the SA marched triumphantly through the streets, and the same stars that Hansel and Gretel saw through the high branches of the beech trees of the forests of the Mittelgeberge. This is the starry night that Vincent painted, when he went mad. These are the shingle-nail stars that shone down on Braunau am Inn, when young Adolf Hitler was skipping school, as the cool water flowed down out of the Alps; and the early morning stars that hang low over the buildings on the outskirts of Kuppenheim, slowly swinging over the old pastures and orchards as if they were spoken by God, where it is still the Middle Ages; and the stars out in the Chilcotin, in territory never ceded to Western civilization, which has never been owned.

In the Sticks

Spring is burning season on the Plateau. Men stride across the fields, directing the fire with pitchforks, flamethrowers, shovels, matches, and strategically thrown buckets of water. From the bunchgrass basin lakes of Clinton and the salt pans of 70 Mile to the basalt columns of Dog Creek and the clay cliffs above the green water of the Fraser at McCallister, red tongues of flame lick at fenceposts, flare up into swaying walls of fire when they hit the thistles in the ditches, and send pools of smoke drifting through the trees and across the roads. Cars drive into them as if into a white-out. Even the smoke of one small ditch of weeds between a horse pasture and the road turns into a huge blue-white cloud that quickly dissipates to spread for kilometres. Even with the doors and windows locked, it seeps into my house, wraps around me, smelling like Joan of Arc on her way out of this world.

Just clear of ice today, Williams Lake reflects the yellow sodium lights at the rail yards on the edge of the city. Houses slouch against the April hills, flickering palely through dark trees. The clouds are low, but dry. They could travel another three hundred kilometres before they even started to drizzle a few slow, white drops of rain. At Sugarcane, on the low, marshy ground along the San Jose River, the Williams Lake Indian Band is burning grass. Long, orange lines of flame lick over the shore, streaming up ten feet into the air. Flames burst into the thick smoke, igniting it; red plumes twist above the fire and over the water. It is as if a whole year of grass, swaying as ducks call softly in their night fear and summer rain, lashing in from the south, bends the grass flat to the soil, is projected in the air, playing out in a half hour, at great speed.

Sugarcane is an unlikely reserve: the low ground is too swampy to grow much usable grass; the rest of the reserve is dry, good for grazing for about one week a year. It isn't curled there into the low hills because the Secwepemc had always lived there, though, mind you, but because all the arable land in that cultural centre of Secwepemc life was pre-empted by white ranchers. With the stroke of a pen, the Secwepemc were denied the grassland east and south of Williams Lake, the best grassland of the Interior, off of which they had lived for thousands of years. The Secwepemc only got Sugarcane because, against governmental orders, the Indian Commissioner, Malcolm Sproat, bought a ranch for them. As the geographer Cole Harris details in his book about the formation of Indian reserves in British Columbia, *Making Native Space,* even though it was the worst agricultural land around and the farmer who sold it concluded what was obviously a great business deal, Sproat had to fight political and personal pressure from other Williams Lake ranchers for a decade to get even that much.

It's likely the Secwepemc knew the Cariboo before there were any trees on it, that they watched the trees come—the giant cedars of the Quesnel River, the cottonwoods pouring out fluff from their amber bud cases along Williams Creek, the aspens dotting the moraines above Lac La Hache, the moss-draped black spruce of Bridge Lake, the lodgepole pines and Douglas firs of the Big Bar Lake eskers, dropping their needles on saskatoon berries and bear scat. Now they watch them go, on the back of Kenworth trucks sitting heavily in the ruts of Highway 97, growling past Sugarcane towards markets in the United States to pay for the stumpage fees that feed British Columbia's habit. The debate: *Who do the trees belong to?* is being fought with Caterpillar skidders from the United States, Husqvarna chainsaws from Sweden, capital kissed by Hong Kong banks, stalled treaty talks in Victoria, legal judgments in Ottawa and corporate lobbyists in Washington, and, against all of them, by the Secwepemc and Wet'suwet'en and Tsilhqot'in, who are pretty clear that the trees belong to them.

They do. At Soda Creek, a half hour north of Williams Lake, the rocks leading down from the Secwepemc village of Xatsu'll to the fishing holes on the Fraser are worn down into deep tracks from 8,000 years of bare feet stepping down to the water. The ancient city of Ur, proclaimed as the first city of civilization, excavated with trowels and toothbrushes by Agatha Christie and Leonard Woolley in 1928 and blown up by the American army and plundered by the Iraqi people to be sold on eBay in 2003, was only half as old as that. For all but the last hundred of Xatsu'll's eight thousand years, caribou ran free on the plateau. When the Secwepemc came here, there were no trees at all; the caribou grazed the tundra. When the Europeans first arrived, the caribou were sifting through spruce trees, munching on the long skeins of black lichen that hung from their branches like cobwebs. The branches of the trees grew so thickly together that the snow scarcely struck the ground between them.

If you walk through the barbed wire fences behind my house, you'll soon come to one of the largest Secwepemc trees. Spared for seed stock, she is six feet thick at her base and towers above a tiny creek which eventually finds its way to the Fraser, the log booms below the designer houses of Vancouver's Marine Drive, and the sea. The weedy sticks around her are her daughters, fighting for light, in what was once an open forest, with grassy hills and glades of light. Here and there through the bush, there are other families like this. A very few of the seed trees are her size or even larger; many of them are over five hundred years old. The Secwepemc never signed any treaty passing them over to any other people, and knew them for three hundred and fifty years—that's sixteen generations—before anyone else even came along. In other words, the Secwepemc have known those trees since Henry VIII started dealing his wives out in a game of blackjack. The Secwepemc probably knew the biggest of those trees for far longer—for twenty-five generations. Britain was a new French colony. The world was flat.

In short, contact with native land did not occur a hundred and fifty years ago; we are making contact right now, with every Kenworth that gears down past my house, streaming with resins, heading into the mills in town or, if the tree is big enough, two hundred kilometres south to the plywood mill in Savona. The colonial farm that Elspeth Huxley grew up on in Kenya before the First World War, with its dogs sunning on the porch, its long evenings of mosquitoes, and the hopeless planting schemes to bring a monetary return from native land, is the same one I knew in the Okanagan in the 1970s, when many of the first Macintosh trees, planted in 1909, were still alive. Their apples may have been small and green—and worthless—but they had a taste of fresh hay, sweet and sparkling, with a tang of frost on distant blue hills: the kind of apples you could build a civilization around. They've gone the way of all the others that would not survive the heat and the two weeks it took to ship them to distant markets: Raspberry Sweet, Victuals and Drink, American Mother, Golden Russet, Winter Banana, Grimes Golden, Cox's Orange. Apples that thrived in the humid climates of Ontario, Belgium, and England grew soft and full of bitterpit on the Okanagan benches. No one who had half an idea what an apple could taste like—wild, hard, woody, and stolen from a hedge that tangled along a road—would touch those things. Over six generations ago, the American environmentalist Henry David Thoreau wrote an essay, *Wild Apples,* about the relationship between wild apples and a true community of free men. Today, beautifully red, starchy Red Delicious apples are grown on a diet of hormones and petrochemical fertilizers. The trees are held up with wires. They are heavily capitalized. The other half of the remaining land of the Shuswap, the Kootenays, and the Okanagan consists of ruined fencelines, overgrown pastures, apple trees gone wild amidst ingrowing poplars, and seventy-year-old farmhouses with cracked roofs. This is the colonial reality: you settle wild land, attempt to produce items of value to some distant culture, to which you export them, while struggling to import and maintain the cultural values and traditions of that foreign culture. It's like communism: it should work, but it doesn't.

The annual Clinton ball started as a way for ranchers to get together for a social event now and then—part of the ballroom circuit. Down the valley, the local gentry thought nothing of riding the thirty miles through the sagebrush and prickly pear from Walhachin to dance the night away in Ashcroft. It was like the circuit of social calls that society people made in London a century ago—send your man around with your calling card in the morning, and maybe you would get an answer written later in the day, sprinkled with some rosewater and delivered by a boy who stood there, like a minor character in one of Shakespeare's plays, bowing and scraping and picking his teeth, waiting for a tip. The favour was returned at a later date, when the Ashcrofters picked their way east to Walhachin. In the mornings, they all saddled up to hunt coyotes, or maybe have a round of polo, just the way they used to do on their estates back in England, with crisp lips and shining leather boots. Now the property of the City of Vancouver, the Ashcroft Ranch has been designated to hide Vancouver's garbage from Vancouver for the next century— a half million tons a year—while the Clinton ball is still the makeshift affair it used to be, except now it is tradition, and a darn good boost to the local chamber of commerce, too, don't get me wrong—and there's no doubt the Clinton Chamber of Commerce couldn't use a boost. This is a town on the way down. In Clinton, it is still 1898. In Clinton, the Boer War hasn't even been fought yet. In some place not ground down under the colonial heel, you would have got a tradition of dress-making out of that ball by now, or a ballet company, a couple dance schools, a few orchestras, a chair of music at the local university, a couple novels, even a book or two of poems. In Clinton, you celebrate the fact that nothing changes. Nothing does.

For their shot of culture, other Cariboo towns are content with musical theatre. That's a tradition with deep roots: travelling theatre acts that shipped themselves across the continent to San Francisco picked their way north through the mud to Barkerville, the venereal disease capital of the West, and why not—it housed the same miners, the same technology, the same whores and whiskey, the same young men digging deep into the gravel to sluice out a poke, the same soft vaginas to tease it back, and the same fantastic wealth for a few and poverty for the many. The idea stuck, and it stuck good. In 100 Mile House and Williams Lake, the big arts event of the year is the annual school musical theatre production. People come out in droves, with a fancy family dinner beforehand at the A&W, a few double teenburger value meals with upsized fries, to watch their children and grandchildren learn the ropes.

In 100 Mile House a dozen years back now, the production of choice was *The Sound of Music*, complete with dirndls and lederhosen, a massive set of plywood and paint that filled half of the high school gymnasium floor, topped off with the whipped cream of some good, old-fashioned Austrian kitsch, and who can do it better than the Austrians, eh? The whole stick-in-your-craw-'til-you-choke thing about dirndls and lederhosen, the happy-fucking-peasants-screwing-in-the-mountains shtick, the oom-pah-pah, and the small-town Nazi beginnings of destruction that swept over Europe, all those black-laced ironies that were built into the original show, were lost on 100 Mile, where to dress up means to put on a clean T-shirt. It might still say "Ron's Mufflers," but damn it, the thing is clean. Bleached, yes. Faded, oh sure. But clean. You slick your hair back. You clap after each song and each scene. You watch the music break up into its parts and float up to the ceiling and hang in the air like rain clouds torn by storm, while the sound falls over you in cold driving gusts.

You'd think the Austrian kitsch shtick would touch the Cariboo's heart. After all, the big old colonial house at Alkali Lake Ranch—brick and gingerbread under a steeply-pitched roof—was built by a wealthy Austrian to keep his daughter from going crazy out there among the Indians, no doubt flint-tipped arrows sticking into the sod hut or something, you just don't know, do you, painted feathers poking up from behind every rock. This Karl May angst was all lost in a little song about the *Edelweiß* and the kids showing us what they have learned in all those voice classes on all those winter evenings after school, Mom running here, Mom running there, in between skating lessons and music lessons and getting home to water the horses. In 100 Mile House, the whole arts community is based on education. Instead of the streetside cafés back in Old Vienna, 100 Mile has the DQ and the A&Dub. Everyone claps 'til their hands are sore. The production lasts close to four hours. It is a marathon. You don't take your art lightly in the Cariboo. You endure it.

People scrape the mud off their boots before they come in the gym door to watch the show. The programs are photocopied. Want one? Two bucks. This is Austria, not some mud-streeted peasant town in the East, for God's sake. Kids go in pairs to every business in town, extracting donations with the skill of a dentist over a root canal. Major sponsors get a full page and a thank-you basket, with cheese in tins, wine, and a half pound of coffee, *Seattle's Best*. In return, the kids learn the inner secrets of how to fit into colonial society. Productions of late include *Grease, Bye Bye Birdie, The Sound of Music, The Music Man,* and *Oklahoma!* Melodrama, shock theatre, romantic heroines, sly but lovable villains, rugged heroes straight out of Karl May who live against the grain and see the light when everyone else does not: our kids are ready for the world.

The world is a collection of genteel subdivisions laid out above the

Williams Lake Golf Club, with a view over the log yards and working-class slums lining the railway, across the black, dirty, smoking thing we have made of the Williams Lake River, and over the swamp set aside as a fishing reserve for the Secwepemc people sometime after their village sites were illegally pre-empted in 1861, back when they were called the Shuswap, because who in the fuck can say Secwepemc anyway. In Williams Lake, you can't hear yourself think: in the trailer courts above the sewer plant and the river, in the middle-class 'burbs butting against the highway to Prince George, the day-and-night grinding of logs fills your life. "The noise of the city," one realtor calls it. The working-class subdivisions are a loose jumble of tumble-down houses with peeling latex paint, weed-grown yards packed tightly with sprung tires, twenty-year-old pickups, their fenders eaten with rust, square-box American cars, singlewide trailers jacked up on cinderblocks, and three-room cabins set along winding streets jack-knifing up a dry and dusty hillside. These are not a slum. They are view properties. The people who live in them are proud. They look out over the hills to the north and west, where palatial homes with designer paint and matching wallpaper are set on five-acre parcels, their plate glass windows burning with the evening sun as if they were made of liquid gold. Down the hill in the blue television glow of their shag-carpeted living rooms, the millworkers look out over the wood-waste electrical plant anchoring the northern edge of the city like a nuclear reactor containment structure at Chernobyl, with its three-hundred-foot-tall chimney tethered by cables and topped with a flashing blue arc light to ward off planes, surrounded by a hundred acres of logs stacked fifty feet deep—remnants of forests the size of a small European country, like the Czech Republic.

Those are Tsilhqot'in trees. Treaties not yet signed with the Tsilhqot'in are lighting the streets of Williams Lake with yellow sodium vapour lights.

Here is a curriculum that might free our children:

- Literature: Germans, Hungarians, Canadians, Brits, Yanks, Vietnamese, Japanese, Chinese, Russians, Mexicans, Hawaiians, everything that was written in the last hundred years—the memory of most of our families in this place; the Wawa love poetry of the 1930s
- Social Studies: The Secwepemc, the Haida, the Nlaka'pamux, the Okanagan, the St'át'imc, the Carrier, the Lil'wat, the Tsilhqot'in, the Cree, the Nisga'a, the Kwakwaka'wakw, the Halkomelem, the Sto:lo, the Gitksan, the Indian agents, the land reserve system, the real estate agents, the Chinese towns mirroring every white town across the Interior
- History: the cattle ranches, the wheat and tobacco farms, the orchards, the little blue opium bottles, the Utopian communities of the Emissaries and the Doukhobors, the years of radical labour unrest, residential schools, the Chinese head tax, the missionaries and smallpox, the golden years of the lumber industry, the years of the Hardware Store czars, the waves of immigration, the power of the Columbia River dams bankrupting rural economies, anything, everything, to show us how we have come to the present world of farmgate wineries in Okanagan Falls and Buffalo burgers in the Happy Eater restaurant in Alexis Creek, where Anja, a tall blonde-haired pilot from Schleswig-Holstein, makes pizzas for the reserve on Friday nights

The spreading grasslands stretching the twenty kilometres from Riske

Creek to the Chilcotin River and then east to the deep cut of the Fraser where mountain sheep clatter down the cliffs to green water is as rich a grazing and cattle country as anyone has ever found on earth, and the whole of it was staked out by a couple ranchers. Four hundred fifty acres, nestled in a bowl inside the farms, was set aside for the Toosey people. When the Tooseys spoke to sympathetic priests, who took the government their plea that such an allotment was inadequate, the duly elected members of the British Columbia Legislative Assembly suggested that the reserve be made even smaller, as it was as good a reserve as could be found in the country, although five days before the reserve was laid out, a settler had recorded two hundred inches of water, effectively rendering the reserve's farmland completely worthless.

And we're still at it. Michael Crichton's flick *The 13th Warrior* was filmed in the Cariboo. Shooting started excitingly enough, with the prow of a Viking ship sailing up the highway on a flatbed truck. I saw it highlighted through the trees—like Erik the Red striking out for Hudson's Bay. Rumours flew through town on black wings—a movie was being filmed upriver at Alexandria, a Viking movie. We were all darn proud, because this would be a great place for Vikings travelling deep into Russia, no question . . . well, you could see it there, where the spring bunchgrass comes down soft as dew to the river, the sky is always thin and distant, and the water flows past flush and green, milky with glacial flour, strong and deep like a serpent. It must have been the serpent thing that did it.

The movie was mayhem. They filmed it west of Alkali Lake. They could have filmed it on a sound stage in Philadelphia. It would have made no difference. Cro-Magnon man (Vikings, blond, strong, rah rah team) and Crichton's Neanderthals (eaters of the dead, cannibals, dark, short, living in caves, riding Appaloosas, boo), fought it out in Scandinavia and—Bingo!—we got another ghost story. That kind of gothic nonsense is the last thing we need around here, where even Coyote is having a hard time being taken seriously these days. It's as if the Methodist missionaries had got hold of all of history and remade it in the way that Stalin used to disappear people from photographs; it destroys our ability to read the story of our confrontation with the landscape and the story of the social landscape and social mores that come from that confrontation. That is our history. Anything else is prostitution.

A Garden of Roses

Those evenings in the log cabin in Evelyn, when the wind howled past the house at 60 below and Frank and Bruno screamed at each other across the dinner table, with potatoes and overcooked canned peas, and maybe some tripe or some pig's lung, while Martha yelled at both of them to shut up, and the grease hung in the air, my mother was reduced to tears and silence. The house rocked with poverty and hurt and pain. The stove roared and the wind surged through the chinks in the logs. Martha, who had dressed so gaily in gypsy costumes when she was secretary for the theatre in Breslau, with her bobbed hair and her fine, clear skin, was reduced to a caricature of a Russian peasant woman, in a dress made out of old flour sacks, with her hair tied down with a kerchief knotted under her chin. She looked sixty-five, not her actual forty-five years. Frank vowed never to raise his voice to his children, ever. He became the picture of restraint. Dorothy vowed never to speak of it, and never, ever to allow an argument over dinner in her own house. For both of them, life became a constant effort to make the past disappear.

Talk about pain! In 1945, when he was thirteen years old, my mother's cousin Hans left the Hitler Youth for a Russian POW camp. His father, Joe—head of civic works for the mountain spa town of Reinerz—was with him there, in the typhoid. Hans and Joe eventually left the camp together—for years of forced labour in a uranium mine in Joachimstal, in Czechoslovakia. They were a long way from home. The mine killed Joe. In the years he was there, the Russians let him go home twice. Each time he sat in the apartment, coughing, doubled over. On his second visit, in 1952, Martha had had enough: either she had to wait for Joe to die, or she had to do something. She was a practical person. She did not like to wait. She dragged her two men over the border in the night. All they had was one knapsack of hand-cut Czechoslovakian lead crystal and money from her brother in Canada: my grandfather, Bruno. The money was waiting at the Red Cross refugee camp in Hamburg, should Martha and her men make it out. They did. Their guide was a farmer. He led them out through the forests, away from the machine guns and the barbed wire, and sent them across the river in the starlight.

Joe had contracted TB at the mine. The Canadian government was leery. Martha spent the next year dragging Joe from doctor to doctor and Red Cross station to Red Cross station and back and forth to the Canadian consulate, trying to get clearance for him to move to British Columbia. In the end, Bruno had to promise the Canadian government to fully support Martha and Joe and Hans, and had to sign notarized documents promising that they would never be a burden on the state.

Joe would never work again. He had always been a sick man, a kind of wiry jack-in-the-box figure—a caricature of an emcee on a decadent Weimar Republic cabaret stage. He was very funny, in that old Silesian self-deprecating way, and prone to depression, to a kind of shrinking away—the Silesian national disease. His physique had proven unequal to the Russians. He smoked cigars like Groucho Marx.

Joe died of lung cancer in 1963, in a collapsing weatherbeaten house smelling of cattails on the floodplain of the Similkameen River. I saw him once: sitting in a rocking chair, shrivelled up, not saying anything at all, while Bruno smoked his pipe in the shadows on the far side of the room and I came running in, five years old. I was suddenly afraid, in the presence of such inexplicable age. The room smelled of something broken. Brokenness flickered in the air. It was thin and blue. I wanted to run out. I did not see the hope that was there, expressed only through me. I felt only the cloying and stern regard, and the foreignness of those men, who were a long way from home. I hated that feeling. I wanted to be rid of it. They wanted me to sit down.

Hans spent thirty years working on the Canadian National Railway out of Kamloops. For thirty years his home was a bunk car, shunted onto a siding at Hope, or Spuzzum, or Golden. A lot of the time he roomed with ex-cons. Over the years at that work in deep river valleys without the sun, he grew to be famed as the laziest man on the trains. "He has two speeds," men said. "Slow, and Dead Stop." That is not what I remember. I remember he used to be cosmopolitan. He had style. He was very funny. He would roll down the long, frozen driveway of the farm every Christmas with a new car—a Rover, a Jaguar, a Volvo, a Saab—before anyone else here had heard of those makes. The sky rose up around the orchards those days, high and relentless. On the grey mountains the mountain goats clambered across the scree. After you watched them for a while, you grew dizzy. You felt a great space flooding around you.

Hans retired to a small blue Ford pickup and his mother's three-room tar-roofed house below the hill in Keremeos. There would be no more impossibly beautiful cars. The big semis geared down behind Hans's bedroom window in the yellow sodium vapours of the highway night. There, thirteen winters ago, he neglected for two days to take his high blood pressure pills, and had a stroke that "burned out half of his brain," as the nurse put it. The stroke left him unable to drive, unable to cook his food or pay his bills, but left him with a haunting, pure memory of his boyhood in Silesia during the war, and the hard years of punishment afterwards, and those first years in Smithers among the tall spruce trees—when there was nothing there for young men, or old ones either, when his father sat in the small clapboard house above the swamp on the edge of town, and did nothing more than hold the arms of his rocking chair still and breathe very slowly, while Martha washed floors in town.

When the young nurses came to Hans's small vinyl-sided house after his stroke, the first thing they saw was his mother's dead cacti sitting on the windowsill. The plastic curtain was rotted by the sun and lay crumbled in pieces on their spines. The raising of cacti was a very German practice, a means of sharing in an exotic world. I saw one of those cacti bloom once: a fragile flower, as if it was made out of bright Japanese silk. It seemed artificial, such a small, unlikely hope. When I saw it I was sitting in the red-carpeted living room, staring at an oil painting of a golden river running over blue stones and flanked by fall beech trees. It was New Year's Eve. Everyone was around the kitchen table speaking a peasant German from the East. I didn't understand a word. I pushed myself down into the couch and stared at the cactus flower, and then the painting, and then the cactus flower. Time passed very slowly.

In his last year, Hans greeted the nurses at the door, wearing an old dress shirt unbuttoned at the front, with no cufflinks, and wearing no pants, and, as they put it, his penis hanging out. The nurses had to ask him, gently, to get dressed. He did. He did everything they said. He even took his pills, if they watched.

My mother says he had always been like that. "He never had a chance. First the war and the Hitler Youth, then the mine, and then Smithers. Only if there had been more for him there, and he didn't have to take the job on the railroad—he was bloody lucky to get that too, no one wanted to give a job to a German at that time—he might have drifted into a more normal life."

But he didn't. He spent thirty years dealing cards and telling dirty jokes, while everyone else, to the last man, moved on. Year after year, he dealt out the poker hands and smoked cigars, as men used to do in Silesia, all the time with the big silver rings on his pale fingers and his hair slicked straight back. For others, that life of bitter brutal work in the beautiful middle of nowhere was a life lived with drunken angry passion punctuated by the occasional moose and the low thunderous chatter of the passing trains that signified nothing in the end, while for him it was the beginning and end of time.

—

I still clearly remember Martha's funeral in Penticton. The funeral director was a tall man. His only words with Hans were to ask him to pay the bill. Then he stepped into the next room and read the eulogy off a standard card. He stopped at the blanks awkwardly, holding up a sheet of yellow notepaper to read her name, Martha Schreiber, with a question mark the first time, while she sat there before us in a brass urn surrounded by one hundred dollars' worth of flowers for which Hans had paid five hundred bucks.

Afterwards, Hans invited us all out to dinner, meaning something fancy, with steak and baked potatoes, and the whole family there, for the last time probably. We ate at the El Rancho: a low-slung kind of asphalt-fringed Washington State motel that used to be the definition of Penticton elegance, with a diner in the front and a low-ceilinged dining room in the back. A lariat hung on the wall. All through the dinner Hans scowled and picked at his chow mein, but there wasn't much that could be said.

We left. My cousin Mike is now an electronics engineer in Ottawa and says he will never go back to Smithers, ever. I have found my way to a life among birds and trees. My mother eventually got out of bankruptcy and her years under the sulphurous rain of the oil refinery in Port Moody, to return to the strength of a farm in the Okanagan. Frank has late in life fought his way clear of the temper of his father, that old communist from the '20s, when communists were rough men and fought on the streets in the violet night, where the trains roared through the cities of Silesia and there was no way back to the land except to come to Canada and the blue lakes that reflected the clouds. We all could leave. Hans could not. He had to stay there.

—

I find myself thinking more and more of all the men who spent their few bright years of freedom beating their bodies into the rails outside of Savona and Blue River and Kanaka Bar, telling stories of "this crazy German guy they worked with on the fucking railroad" when they were back in their concrete cells or in a bar on East Hastings, where men talked over the green felt either totally slurred or with an absolute perfect grasp of language, an eloquence and force denied to them at all other times, while the heavy pool balls clacked and the blue smoke settled lower and lower from the ceiling fans so that their heads were in the smoke and below that their chests and hands glimmered, ghostly—stories of this stupid Kraut they worked with turning switches outside of Boston Bar and Lytton and Matsqui and Monte Creek, saying the names with disdain, but with awe too, the awe that comes to men who have worked in such places of true brutality and have survived, men who have gone where few have, who know the place intimately and find a life within the pain.

—

I like to go to Savona above Kamloops Lake, which is burnt country, where the whooping cranes come to the mudflats in March and October as they pass through. I like to wander through the junkyard, among the old railroad and mining machinery, and finger the hard and rusty metal with the slag-burnt, cut-off bolts in the gravel, as the raw sun overhead smashes at the tops of the mountains again and again. Hans used to pass there once a week on the train. When the bunk cars were shunted onto the siding, he used to come to the wrecking yard and talk. It is a harsh and bitter museum: all that heavy cast iron, so cleverly fitted, all for the purpose of blasting mountains away and carrying them off and crushing them. Hans would wander there on Sundays when there was nowhere else to go and nothing else to do—except to play cards. But he had grown tired of that.

My family has been on the run ever since the Industrial Revolution drove them off the farms. Obviously, to serve the train and the whole industrial complex necessary to sustain it, as Hans and Joe, and even Joe's father, had done, was no release, and brought to them only the train and the smell of coal, while the denial of that, the attempt to create a paradise on the land, as Bruno did on the bush farm and then on the orchard, led only to rage. One winter Bruno even built a makeshift lathe, so he could turn the parts for a good lathe, so he could build an entire tractor out of used airplane parts and rivets. As a machinist out of the poverty of the '20s in Germany, he did not know how to weld. Mind you, as a machinist in the '20s he was mostly out of work, so he hardly had a chance.

"He was hopeless," said Frank. "That damn tractor broke down once while he was out mowing dandelions, so he left it there, for a week, right where it quit, before he fixed it."

I remember him walking out under the trees that spring, with the pink and white blossoms above him and the humming of bees in the air, picking dandelions into a canvas apple-picking bag slung over his shoulders. I ran to my mother. "What is Grandpa doing?" I asked.

"He is picking flowers to make into wine," she said. I went outside and watched him again. From my father, I had picked up that he was a fool, but I thought he was a magician. I thought I would never know that much.

In the late '60s, Bruno finally got his sailboat—that old North-German sea cadet's dream—and sailed up and down Okanagan Lake, cutting junipers off the cliffs to turn into bowls on his lathe. All Hans got in the end was his childhood. He didn't even get those bright years on the trains outside of Alexandra and Spences Bridge where the steelhead swim up the Thompson River just outside the engineer's window and the grasshoppers flash off the cutbanks and into the cab of the diesels as they pull up the grade past the old villages with their one abandoned church, a couple log cabins, and a huge graveyard full of smallpox and crickets and the odd snake.

Tonight the train echoes faintly through the trees on the far side of the lake, where the valley widens out to Sugarcane and Williams Lake and eventually down between clay cliffs silhouetted by old tires and junked cars to the Fraser at Xatsu'll. A pair of Canada geese call to each other softly just on the edge of the ice. They've just come back to the lake after a long winter. The sound pools like water lapping at a shore. As I hear their calls I know what it meant when Uncle Joe's dead eyes stared at me as I ran into the room, with the scent of the sun and the sky in my hair. Now I am staring back. Sadly, now that I want and need to talk to Joe and Bruno, to sit down there in the smoky dark, with Bruno's steel etching of the Breslau city hall staring at me over his shoulder, they are gone, and I have to find them in myself and in the world, where they sit, for a long time silent, like elders in a synagogue, speaking in dialect, watching every move I make with intense interest and concern.

———

My mother, my grandparents, and my great aunt never called my cousin Hans by his proper name. To them, he was always Hansemennschen—literally, "Hans the little man," or, better, "Big Hans." At first glance, it is intimate and endearing.

"In Kuppenheim, we didn't speak German," says Michael, pouring wine, sloshing it into our glasses. "We spoke Kuppene. It was a dialect, of course, but such a terrible dialect. It is older than either French or

German. There are people in France and Belgium who still speak like that, too. It really is an ugly thing. It sounds like a throat disease." He laughs at his own joke.

Eberhard laughs, too, more quietly. "Five kilometres from Kuppenheim, no one knows what you are talking about." We are sitting in Michael's apartment on Johann Sebastian Bach Street in Freiburg, drinking a bottle of Grey Riesling from Alsace: a heavy wine, like perfumed amber in our glasses. "We all had nicknames. Your father, Johannes, became Hansel, Michael became Michel, I became Eberle, Charlotte became Lottl, Margot became Margottl, Siglinde became Siggi, Brigitte became Brigittl."

"I wish I had been born with any other name than Michel," confesses Michael. "That's the name you give to a stupid farmer when you want to make a joke. You know what I mean? What name would you give to a man like that in English?"

"Harold," I answer, with a shock. We stare at each other for a moment, then solemnly clink glasses. I take a sip. The wine tastes like fog in oak trees. "What would I be called in Kuppene?" I ask.

"That's a tough one," Eberhard pipes in. He thinks for a couple minutes, mulling the words over in his mind, staring at me and at his wine glass, while Michael shakes his head. "No, it's not possible."

"Harry," says Michael. "He'd be called Harry. A lot of people in Kuppene had English or French names: Michael and Richard and Margot."

Harry. Christ.

Hansemennschen, though, has a bit of Russian in it, and a thread of Yiddish seeping through, with the *mensch* shtick, and Hans's mother's voice in a cloying parlour room in Reinerz during the war, when Hans no longer had to wear the short leather pants of a little boy, yet was not a full-grown man. The name stuck. There's also a connection with the German folk character Hansewürst—Johnny the Wiener. Straight out of the Middle Ages, Hansewürst is a bit like Punch and Judy, a bit of a buffoon: the uncouth, fat, insufferable, slow-witted hero of a mocking slapstick comedy, the dark side of commedia del 'arte. He was Lazy Hans, the village idiot, the braggart, the boaster, the glutton, the fool, who remained popular in Germany right through the nineteenth century, a fast-talking, word-mangling liar who never ran out of lies. Like Hansewürst and like his father, Joe, before him, my cousin Hans made people laugh. No one expected much more from him than that.

"Even when he was fifty years old, he used to bring his washing home every six weeks. His mother was old and could hardly walk, yet in that tiny house below the hill, in that little room in the back, she had to do his wash from the railroad—two big dufflebags of it covered with grease." My mother is angry, dismissive, as she tells this story. "Sometimes he'd have to leave again the next morning. He'd expect every piece of wash to be cleaned, ironed, and folded. And Tante would do it. She'd stay up all night. She was always worried about Hansemennschen." My mother raises her voice, until it is thin and vibrating and high-pitched, just like Tante's, *"What will he ever do without me? Poor Hansemennschen."*

It seems that his mother was right to ask.

——

"I met a man a few years back," says Frank. "He had a CN jacket, so I said to him, 'I have a cousin who used to work on the CN. He worked there for twenty-five years.'

"'What's his name?' asked this guy. 'I've been a crew boss all around BC and into Alberta: I bet I know him.'

"So I said, 'Hans Schreiber.'

"'Yes,' says the guy, in a slow, thoughtful voice. 'I know him.'

"That's all he said, so I said more, to tease him out—to let him know that he could talk to me, if he had more he wanted to say. 'That is if he did work,' I said. That did it.

"'We had to let him go,' says the guy. 'In all my years on the railroad I have seen a lot of lazy people, but he was the worst. We couldn't work with him any longer. We'd send him out on a two-hour job, and it took him all day. I have no idea what he did out there. We finally had to buy him out. We made a special deal with the union. He was hurting all of us.'"

In 1967, Hans quit the railroad for a year and opened a jewellery shop with a friend in Kamloops. Hans made cufflinks and big clunky men's rings set with heavy stones. It wasn't long before the store flopped, but not because no one wanted jewellery like that—that kind of heavy, European dreck was the height of taste in a Canada made out of European refugees. The business failed because Hans's friend left him to run it on his own—and Hans was no good with the books. That's the reason Hans gave me one evening in his mother's laundry room. He had taken me back there to show me his cufflinks, his wax forms, and his gold wire—stored in a fishing tackle box with a fold-out tray. Everyone else was up front, reminiscing about the good old days back in the Old Country—how poor they were, how fat the geese were, the songs they sang. It was New Year's Eve, 1974. Hans was bored. He had rigged up a shelf above the washer and the dryer, with all his tools, his boxes of gemstones, his silver, his soldering irons, everything he needed for his craft. He touched them lovingly as he laid them all out on the lid of the washing machine, among the soap flakes. Money wasn't really the issue, though: Hans was gay in a time when homosexuality was close to a death sentence, that's all. Alone in Kamloops, Hans went back to the trains—in those days, railroad society was one of the only places outside of prison in which men could love men, but, like a prison, it was often a place where men loved men as an expression of force, not of tenderness.

Hans died alone in the Extended Care wing of the Penticton Hospital, in a room looking over the Penticton Industrial Area, just down the hill from the depot where Penticton's handicapped spent their days smashing recycled glass in big bins with a sound like the percussion section of a symphony tuning up. At the end, Hans didn't even know his name. He was violently angry, and often had to be restrained. He had five days' growth of beard. Food had dribbled down and caked to his face. He threw his food down and fought against the nurses and pissed himself and didn't recognize my mother when she came, once a week. He never said goodbye.

——

"After the war," says my mother, "my uncle Max was kept on by the Russians. He was an engineer, in the days when an engineer knew how to take a locomotive apart piece by piece and put it back together again. They needed him to rebuild the country." She says it with pride.

Everything was made out of iron in those days—locomotives, picture frames, chairs, beds, cooking pots, roasting pans, shovels, picks, axes, needles, planes, knives, all of it frozen, black, in shape. For a century, tracks had stitched themselves across all of Europe. Dostoevsky saw it as the death of Russia. Tolstoy did, too—in protest, he sacrificed his heroine, Anna Karenina, under the wheels of an engine as it rolled squealing into St. Petersburg's Vitebsky Station, its black smoke and steam rising up and collecting under the arching glass. An age of the world, and much of its beauty, died with Anna, and everyone knew it. The cities were hell. Everything was heated and powered by coal. You carried it up in buckets to your fireplace. It got into everything. You coughed it out. The ceilings turned yellow with smoke. You couldn't breathe. If you were rich, you could live out in the country, between Gleiwitz and Kattowitz, like Rudolf Rhenisch, or in Linden, like Georg Koernig, with a villa under the fruit trees and polished, inlaid wooden floors set in Baroque designs of conch shells or water lilies. If you were half so rich, you could afford to travel once a year to a country villa. You would stay in a small hotel overlooking the river, take a boat cruise, breathe the good air, pick some wild flowers, try the local wine, see the sights.

—

On the Volga, south of Moscow, the Vistula, south of Warsaw, on the Elbe, north and south of Dresden, on the Danube, the Salzach running through the river grasses in Salzburg, on Lake Constance, in Montreux on Lake Geneva, where the old houses are so ornate they look like giant wedding cakes and the boardwalk is actually a botanical garden—British Columbian rhododendrons flowering next to Chinese Ginkgos next to Indian grass—everyone was dreaming of the Loire. At Giverny, Monet even planted water lilies in his garden, to bring the dream home.

"All of Moscow used to come here," my cousin David said as we strolled along the Montreux boardwalk. "There used to be direct trains from Moscow." He stopped to point out the rococo decorations of an overhanging roof, dropping one half of his mouth into a smile. "There are no direct trains from Moscow anymore. Actually, there are no direct trains at all, although they're talking about bringing one in again from Paris. The aristocracy came here for holidays from all of Europe, and of course they all had to show each other up. Each one wanted to look richer and more sophisticated than the rest. They spent impossible sums on the houses. All that is the past. Now the people who come here are middle-class."

In Poland, it was the same. As the Germans rolled into Warsaw with their tanks and their horse-drawn artillery in the fall of 1939, Jews fled into the countryside with fake passports or no passports at all. They came starving out of bombed-out ruins, with anti-tank ditches dug into every street and anti-aircraft guns and sandbags in the city parks. They broke into country houses on the Vistula, with pink roses shedding the last of their petals on flagged doorways and the river moving slowly north. They thought it was a fairytale. They had forgotten that a world like that could still exist. They hid there for a few days, as if they were on holiday, then they got on with their war.

In Russia, too. The British spy, Conrad O'Brien-ffrench, the playboy recruited for his ability to infiltrate the Nazis from the high-society end by skiing with them in the Austrian alps, and who eventually joined the communal cult of the Emissaries of the Divine Light in 100 Mile House, came upon his friend Kathleen of Monivea in China in the 1930s. She was living there in exile, after her estates on the Volga—roses again, long sweeping lawns, parquet floors—were seized by the Bolsheviks. She had barely escaped with her life. White Russian friends who lived with and off of her in China while their brothers and cousins were driving taxis in Paris had convinced her that because she was English even the Bolsheviks wouldn't keep her property forever. They wouldn't dare. They dared.

And so it goes. The Elbe on both sides of Dresden, north to the porcelain factory at Meissen and east to pretty Pillnitz, with sour wine growing on the damp slopes and country houses among the oaks—is packed with villas, summer houses, and pensions. A century ago, a steamship trip along the river had the emotional power of a cruise up the Yangtze or the Nile—a little bit of August's pleasure palace for everyone. It was like a bargain tour package is today to the shores of the Black Sea: one week, four people, a room with a view, three meals a day, swimming pool, a chocolate on the pillow before you turn in for the night, $500, cheap like borscht.

Even Doctor Zhivago started out living in a country house like that. When the Revolution came, he was shanghaied by the Red Army. After his release, he escaped the poverty and political indoctrination of the new Moscow by fleeing to the garden house of his family villa, surrounded with rose bushes deep in the Ural Mountains. Buried in the fields of God, in Mother Russia, he slept the sleep of Sleeping Beauty, to wake when the world was again in balance. Then his princess came—Lara, a woman he had met back in Moscow and had met again when he was detained by the Reds in the retreat from the West. She was his soul mate—his salvation and his ruin.

"Don't talk to me about this damned soul," said my uncle Gerd in 1994, sorrowfully, as we walked down the old Roman road outside of Stuttgart. Sweat poured down our faces as we passed through light and shadow, puffing slightly, walking off a heavy lunch. "Just think of all the horrors that have been committed because of that soul. Every war that has ever taken place has been on account of this soul. Don't talk to me about it!"

My father takes up the contrary position. "We're getting better," he says. "My grandfather was a son-of-a-bitch, and my father was a bastard, and we all, every generation, try to straighten it out a little bit. By the time it gets to your grandchildren, we ought to be pretty decent people!"

When the Kaiser abdicated in 1918, the teenaged doctor-in-waiting Hans Rhenisch gave up his noble title: a minor count. Like many young German nobles of his generation, he was looking past war towards a dream of a modern, unified Germany, in which the will and mass of the people, the *Volk,* was more genuine—more robust—than the will of a landed elite. He was also a pure romantic. In 1924, six years after abdicating, Hans turned his back on the East completely, fleeing Kattowitz for the safety of medical school in Freiburg. Rhine maidens sat out on the rocks, their long golden hair hanging over their naked breasts, luring sailors to their deaths. A hoard of gold lay in the bottom of the river. Castles were broken on every hilltop. A people, crushed but proud, lived there along the river, where they could brood. Nine years later Hans was ensconced in a country villa, far from urban life—a hunting lodge set amidst formal rose gardens, on the edge of a small town with mud-streets. Storks nested on the roof.

⸺

After the war, with winter coming on and Alfred Leipe cursing the German Post Office from a refugee camp outside of Dresden, and new refugees streaming in from the East, just weeks after Auguste had hobbled through town with the ghost weight of her Bible pressing into her back, the communists brought in bulldozers and levelled what the Americans had left. Overnight, Dresden became a ring of villas surrounding a plain of crushed brick, like the fields of salt the Romans sowed around Carthage so it would never rise again—except this time the desert was right downtown.

Over time, the communists left it like that: a memory of who they had once been. They replaced the city with an allée of chestnut trees, to remind themselves of the allée upriver that led out of lowland fields to King August's pleasure palace at Pillnitz, where August had set up his mistress. His guests travelled upriver on a little Chinese junk with a buxom Venus on the prow, landed at a set of broad steps leading down into the water, like you might see on the Ganges, where celebrants step down to bathe in their god. At Pillnitz, two sphinxes guarded the flanks of the ramp, looking more like women with tails and baboon's heads than sphinxes. The guy who carved them had definitely never seen a sphinx.

August's guests came up for weekends of tea parties—the cocaine of its day—and titillation. Fountains spouted in the centre of the court, scenting the air with the tinkling waters of the ancient rivers of the world: the Nile, the Tigris, the Euphrates, the Ganges. If that didn't turn all the women into nymphs and the men into satyrs, well, forget about popping oysters. If you came overland to Pillnitz, you rode past marshes sculpted into broad pools of water to bring the sky down to the earth, along the broad allée between its two long lines of chestnuts, and out onto swirling gardens with sprinkling fountains turning the power of the river into a dance. The palace was a minuet, with orange trees and palms

That was the allée the Dresdners extended into their downtown. In fact, they replaced their city with it, bringing into its heart the energy of the villas that still lie up against the hills and up and down the river, remembering a king who brought pleasure, not war. On the edge of the devastation, the communists erected the Dresden Technical University. Its grey stone buildings stretch for miles, set behind screens of trees. Between the streets in front of it, however, you can still see the foundation walls of houses, overgrown with weeds, in soil too poor to even grow a decent thistle. Along the river, the key public buildings have been rebuilt: the Zwinger Pleasure Palace, with a bone china organ that sounds like someone's best man hitting his glass with a spoon to get the bride and groom to stand up and kiss; the Semper Opera House; the Baroque Cathedral with its saints, lined up, silently, on the roof; the Residential Palace, where the king hung out when not playing cards upriver late at night. The round Frauenkirche, the woman's church, which the communists left in ruins as a reminder of the brutality of capitalism, was rebuilt, finally, in October 2005, with money raised by charity concerts given by a Dresden violinist. The pink sandstone walls are chequered with the black blocks that lay in a heap in the weeds through fifty years of coal smoke. The Church of the Holy Cross, on the old market square four blocks north of the river, was still a shell when I saw it with Eberhard, full of wooden braces, catwalks, and struts. It smelled of a damp basement.

—

No Baroque palace worth its salt was built without a grotto: a fountain, a pool, a cave of some kind. It was the source of power for the Baroque tea house, and for the chastity belt, the open-air opera house, the poor man's palace, God's rose garden, which is British Columbia. From the grotto, the power of the four rivers of the ancient world could flow to invigorate the inhabitants of the palace with the force of life. There'd usually be a boat, and Venus down there, riding a rather sexy conch shell, like a pearl. The whole civilization was thinking like the randy poems of Catullus, which generations of German boys had to learn by heart in Latin class in public schools, learning terms like *metaphor* and *simile* to package up what was just the honest, unabashed truth.

On the roof of the Semper Opera House, in Dresden's grotto, Dionysus—or Pan, if you like, the randy god of wine and orgies—and his companion Ariadne ride two pairs of sphinxes with bits in their teeth. The beasts rear back and raise their paws, as if Dionysus and pretty Ariadne can hardly hold them from over-running the city. True, actually: in the fall, the Elbe is a trickle between long flats of stinking mud draped with reeds, but in the spring it drains a huge area of Central Europe, rising up to the top of its banks, almost ten metres above low water. Once a decade, it floods. In 2002, an irrepressible wave five feet high flashed through the lower city. In Pillnitz, brown water filled the tea house waist deep.

Riding the backs of his sphinxes on top of the opera house, Dionysus raises a solemn arm. In the square in front of him rides the King of Saxony himself, August the Strong. Stone-faced on a stone horse, with a proud stone smile, he is taking his time—in fact, he's frozen in it—savouring the ceremony, leading Dionysus out of the Elbe as if he is unwrapping a Christmas gift for his mistress. Wrapped in coloured paper and ribbons, the gift is an opera house shaped like a music box. Inside, musicians play their hearts out, the people sit in ranked rows, turning to joy with the music—all caught inside Dionysus' dream.

To achieve this effect, August turned his entire city into a poem. Instead of building his grotto in his palace garden, with a cave and Venus and a golden boat, like Mad King Ludwig of Bavaria erected at Linderhof, or in his basement, with a room plastered with mussel shells, as Frederick the Great did in the New Palace in Potsdam, or even in a courtyard alcove at the bottom of the main stairs, with Triton fighting with a dragon, as did the Prince-archbishops of Salzburg, August left his grotto as the river itself: a serpent among the poplars. When August was dreaming of sex, August was dreaming about the land.

After August lured the debutantes of Dresden upriver and they sat around sipping the buzz of Lapsang Souchong from yellow china cups peasant artists had painted to look Chinese, once they had tittered and played cards in the yellow tea-room opening onto the sphinxes, after the starlit walks in the maze of the garden and the Nile palm trees, their energy and innocence were lured back down to the city. Dionysus was at August's command, and together Dionysus, his sphinxes, his chariot, the music box, the little musicians playing inside, strum strum strum, and the whole dream of music, poured out of the river and flooded into the city, fertilizing it. Art had found its ultimate patron.

"The Saxons complain about how hard they've had it in the last fifty years and how we in the West owe them a piece of our prosperity," complained Eberhard late at night in Kesselsdorf. Behind the bar, the waitress, Barbara, refilled the salt and pepper shakers and polished the glasses, again. "It's all bullshit," Eberhard continued, as I picked at the bar nuts. "The Saxons were some of the worst Nazis. They got what they deserved." I looked up at Barbara: milky skin, framed by hair as black as coal, a kind of unstated laughter that filled her fingers as she picked up another glass, trying to make a new life: a picture of grace.

"Would you like anything?" she asked.

"No thank you," said Eberhard.

The Italian painter Canaletto spent decades in Dresden. He saw the

Elbe flood and recede, flood and recede, flood and recede. In his heavily varnished paintings, he documented how the city was transformed into a party favour: records of mud bars in the channel, long stone quays, sailing ships with grey and tattered sails framed against a black midafternoon sky of approaching storm. In Pirna, an hour downriver, he painted a girl leading a cow through a grassy field beside the fortress. Eberhard, Anassa, and I took one look at that painting in Dresden's Zwinger Palace and piled into the car: we doubted if the Yanks had ever bombed that. We were right. Pirna had died a slow death instead. Fifty years of communist administration had reduced every building in a once proud tourist town to ruins. People were slowly fixing the buildings back up, giving them new doors, windows, roofs, and their first coat of paint in sixty years—bright yellows, oranges, blues, and greens. That was every fourth house. The rest were grey heaps of peeling plaster, bleeding wattle, and sprung doors. On what had been the mayor's door five hundred years ago, framed by a stone inscription from the Psalms and stone fruit cascading down the lintel, someone had scrawled almost illegibly in pencil the names of the people living inside, and what room they could be found in. The door didn't shut. On the window to the left were the remaining two-inch-tall gold and black letters of a self-adhesive sign: "Hairdresser." Half had fallen off. This was the People's Paradise.

Eberhard was annoyed. He picked up his pace to get back to the car. "Give it fifteen years," he said, standing very close to where the peasant woman had stood in Canaletto's painting, with her bright cheeks and her cows grazing beside a derelict castle. "Then I'll come back. Right now there's nothing here. This is too much like the Rhineland after the war. I've built it up once. I can't bear to build it up again."

With Eberhard leading the way with long polyester strides, Anassa and I retraced our steps, under the curious gaze of other sweaty tourists and waitresses puffing as they carried trays of beer and glass dishes full of ice cream. The tables were decked with green umbrellas advertising

Italian mineral water. The heat flowed over us like fire. I just wanted to sit at one of those tables and let the whole day end there in indolence. My eyes stung from dehydration, but Eberhard, lost in a private maze, was in a rush. He was just one step short of being in a panic. If he hadn't been seventy and trying to be the good host who knew his own country well, I had the feeling he would have broken out into a run.

All along the streets were shops, selling tourist artifacts, but, strangely, no kitsch: no cuckoo clocks or little dolls dressed up in folk costumes, no purple lace doilies or keychains with a map of Saxony and the word Pirna stamped on them in gold or red. What these shops, which had moved back here to the ruins after fifty years of neglect, were selling was definitely upper-class: blown glass from Frankfurt, gold jewellery from Cologne, crystal from Prague, the latest fashions from Berlin: a simple silk blouse with one button at the neck, $300. The next three windows were cracked and empty, or boarded up.

As we left, another string of sun-dried tourists struggled up from the boat.

By evening, we still had not had a drink. We were almost delirious. The ozone had dried out our eyes. They felt scratched, as if the entire day had been spent walking against a wind of sand blowing across the Mediterranean, smelling of dates and salt. Pirna was far behind us. We were winding back from the kirsch orchards that stretched for miles along the road west of Pillnitz and the vineyards that rose up the hills to the beech trees on the ridges. Behind us, the sphinxes settled slowly into the umber dark above the river. I imagined them coming alive, when everyone had left and the moon played through the empty windows on all of August's collected kitsch: the fluffy yellow wig, the big red velvet thrones with the golden arms and lions' feet, the gilded ceremonial armour set with jewels, the ivory-inlaid rifles and crossbows he received as gifts back in the days when conflict of interest did not bring down governments but was just good politics, the writing tables inlaid with ivory, the writhing gold leaf—as if under the king's touch the world was coming to life and light—a sexually charged world in which every movement was compelling and dangerous. After a weekend you could get back on the funny little junk that didn't really look like a junk, ride the Venus with the big breasts back down to the city with its churches, and step off, changed, a little tired, a little gritty around the edges, and could forget what had happened out at Pillnitz as if it had all been a dream.

And then the storm came. For an hour we wound back inch by inch in the blue smoke of exhaust, past miles of villas and holiday cottages above the grey mudflats and the charcoal river. The road was completely clogged. I sat there, drifting between worlds, looking out of the window at the garages built into the blackened retaining walls below the upper row of villas and the "No Parking. Keep Entrance Clear." signs and across the road to the rows of holiday houses and pensions, yellow and pink and peach and apricot, with their "Room for Let" signs in the front windows, and wondered how in God it would all eventually look when every one of the houses had been built back up, and why on earth anyone would want to come and spend their holiday there, with their bedroom window opening on a parking lot. What had worked well in 1914 wasn't going to work well any longer. Dresden, I thought, was in for a big disappointment.

——

It was 6:00 PM, late July. The sky above the city in the distance was black. Lightning flashed and reflected across the belly of the clouds like bombs blowing up in wave after wave after wave of attack. As we slowly crept down a hill and past giant beech trees lining the front of a big villa on the river—set off behind lawns, overgrown flowerbeds, and broken, ivy-covered walls—the sky grew steadily blacker above us, as if a river of night was flowing to engulf us, and then the clouds split with a tremendous crack, five hundred feet above the car. The car shook, Eberhard jumped at the steering wheel, giving a little moan, I screamed out, Anassa snatched at the door, and the rain poured over us, so strongly that the wipers couldn't push it off. Only the red blur of the taillights of the car ahead of us was visible. The drumming of the rain on the roof was like a herd of wild horses as the lightning cracked again and again. Dionysus was upon us. All the way into the city we drove through rain. When we finally got there, the city was rising, cloudless, into late evening light. Long yellow beams and broad bands of shadow thirty kilometres long shot out across the plain and broke up into fields and trees and towns. Anything white sparkled, like wave crests.

One of the few Dresden landmarks to survive the bombing was right downtown, a half kilometre from the train station at Ground Zero: the back wall of the royal stables. Back in 1898 it had been done up with tiles of fine Meissen china painted yellow, black, and white, portraying the march of the princes, from the first knights through the great Saxon kings (even August the Strong with his huge blonde wig), up to the turn of the new century, with the mayor and architects and other worthies of the city in their business suits. It was a time of pride: in industry, in unlimited progress, the march of man from savagery to ignorance to knowledge, from poverty to wealth, from war to luxury. The pride wasn't just felt in Dresden, either, but all across Germany: in Cologne, the cathedral, unfinished for three hundred years, was completed with donations from Krupp and Siemens and other big industrial concerns from the Ruhr. Even today, the big stained glass windows are named the Krupp Window and the Siemens Window, around the whole, huge space they enclose and scarcely light.

"Next to Rome, Cologne is the richest diocese in the Catholic Church," said Eberhard. "They have a saying here in Cologne: 'When the Bishop in Cologne coughs, the Pope jumps in Rome.'"

"I hate this place," said Anassa.

When we returned home, my father agreed wholeheartedly. "Did you see those old men dressed in red? They made me so angry I wanted to kill them. They walked around like they were holy and better than everyone, asking for money for the poor. For God's sake, at the centre of the altar, there was that big box made out of solid gold. It looked like a coffin. What a bunch of hypocrites. What do they keep in there?"

"I don't know," I said.

"Me neither."

In Dresden in 1945, workers scraped the rubble from the mural of the March of Progress. The entire mural was black from the fires, yet underneath the soot it was clean and clear, as if it had just been fired the day before. Once again, Meissen china had pulled through. The wall was lovingly restored by the communists. The march of progress was something they could understand. It was prophetic, a sign from Heaven, if you could accept that piece of romanticism—and you could, with a wry Saxon smile.

"Now do you see why I left Germany?" my father asks.

But he didn't. Not really. He still smelled like flowers! Back on the farm, he always had a big bottle of Eau de Cologne on his dresser—a last vestige of upper-class life.

"Why does Dad use that?" I asked my mother, when I was eight. I couldn't stand the smell.

"Because," she said, and rolled her eyes, opening the door on her secrets just a crack. Then she added a completely different thought: "Your father likes it."

He sure did. There, where dirt and tumbleweeds blew into the sheds, he sprinkled 4711 Eau de Cologne onto his hands from its gold-capped, blue-labelled bottle, and slapped it on his cheeks and neck. When I said it smelled terrible, he just laughed. I tried some once myself, sneaking into the room while my mother was out, but I was soon caught. Like a skunk, I left a trail.

In retrospect, a dirty farm was probably the best place for that stuff. The Baroque European aristocracy never washed. Never ever. They were very scientific—to wash in water was to open up the pores of the body and to allow disease to enter. For proof, just look at the peasants: *they* bathed. Instead of washing, princes and countesses scraped the dirt and dead skin off of their bodies. They had a whole array of scraping instruments for doing their toilet, running them over their curves like a sculptor running a knife over a model of a musician's bust. Each body was a statue, and a work of art. It took hours each day, while the peasants were out splashing in the millponds. The aristocrats also built little chapels in the backs of their grounds, where they retired from the hard work of an artificial life, dressed in rough cloth that chafed the skin, ate bread and water, prayed, whipped themselves and begged forgiveness for what they had to do in the service of the state. To cover up their smell, because there was a lot of smell, the aristocrats doused themselves with Eau de Cologne. My father said they used to gargle with it.

——

At the last, perfumed end of the Baroque, in the 1920s, my grandmother, Charlotte Koernig, sat around with her friends in the afternoons, in loose, flowery dresses, drinking tea and eating kuchen off of Meissen china. While they talked, they drew ornate—and flowery—greeting cards in albums to celebrate the gathering. In their Art Nouveau parlours, they talked of spirits and of the other world trying to get through to them.

They read each others' tea leaves. There was nothing else to do to fill their time—by then, the Baroque tradition had become only the civilization created to maintain it, with its schools, its armies, its factories, and its art. My grandmother threw it all in to become a doctor. I have a picture of her in front of a row of test tubes in Freiburg in 1926. Her hair was bobbed. She held a test tube in one hand. She looked like Madame Curie. She looked damned determined. In the afternoons, though, she was still obliged to serve tea.

It was the very decadent end of the decadent end of the Baroque, its one last splash before the Nazis used its elements to design their tanks and motorcycles and desk lamps. By the time the tradition filtered down to Charlotte, the whole goal was to be refined. The leading poet of the age, Rilke, begged from the Princess Marie von Thurn und Taxis-Hohenlohe the time and space to be a tortured poet. He wrote the half-romantic, syrupy, precious poetry of the upper class of the early twentieth century. It was not a poetry in touch with common life, but rather with a world of spirit. Its practitioners talked a lot about the *Soul*. In the twentieth century, this was called art—a world of compressed emotion, bursting out in a flower, snow, rain, or a tiger pacing in a cage, as if they were the first flowers, snow, rain, and tiger seen in the world. Out of magnanimity, the princess gave Rilke the time and space he had asked for in her castle Duino above the sea outside of Trieste, because without poets to lead the way into a sublime world of angels she was just playing croquet. Rilke forsook love to stay in the cold and fog of that sombre castle. There was no view. He could not see out. It was all very Depressing and Deep. A century earlier, the aristocrats of Vienna had given Mozart the same blessing, and had taken it back from him at night over games of cards. Mozart died a pauper on a king's salary. The aristocrats who fleeced him must have shaken their heads at the tragedy of it all, and dealt another hand. A half century earlier, when the Baroque was new and bursting out all over, it fed directly off the peasantry. Flowers were all the rage. Peasants stuck them in clay pots. They wilted; they were thrown out. The aristocracy had the peasants paint them on the pots. It was far simpler. They lasted forever. On the basis of this discovery, August the Strong sucked Europe's aristocracy dry, because only he could help them fully realize the material vision of the romantic longing for the romantic longing for the romantic longing for the land. Flowers were everywhere: ornate golden flowers crawling up the walls and across the ceilings of aristocratic houses, kitschy little flowers on Meissen china, worth its weight in gold—it was even called White Gold.

But it was madness. In Schloss Favourite, where my father played in the ornate golden halls of fake marble during the war that destroyed at last his entire class and culture, ladies once sat sipping tea from Meissen cups in the trompe l'oeil room. As a housewarming present, the Duchess's sister had sent the Duchess a coffee table (a new invention) inlaid with sliced gems in an oriental pattern of dragons, jade lakes, bonsai trees, and Chinese women with bound feet. It decorated the place in the same way a swank house today might have a low Japanese table from IKEA and a few throw pillows to sit on, and Takamitsu on the Blaupunkt and ginseng in the teapot. Not to be outdone, the Duchess ratcheted the whole imitation of Meissen pottery up and had her peasant workmen finish a whole room in precious gems. As a finishing touch, they decorated the floor with a score of sleight-of-hand effects—a hand of cards, a bee, a dragonfly, beetles, snakes—to make her guests laugh with recognition at the cultivated joke, or shriek, so the rest of them could laugh and make a fuss.

They call it industrial art now. For $15 each, Eberhard, Anassa and I went on a tour of the State china factory in Meissen: the apprentice (male) turning the cups and plates in moulds; the apprentice (female) gluing on flower petals, the handles of cups, the heads of angels, the legs of cupids; the apprentice (female) laying on the stencils and painting the petals bright pink and the leaves bright green; the apprentice (female) applying the final glaze before firing. After we staggered out, we hit the museum: a coffee service for four costs $10,000 to $18,000. For that you get a coffee pot, four cups with saucers, a creamer, a sugar can, and four small cake plates. Six women in black suits waited behind counters ready to take our money. We held onto it.

Young artists apprentice for four years, painting flowers, studying colours, before they learn to fill in the patterns on plates and cups so that each one is exactly the same. We learned that.

Eberhard was enthralled. "Now I know how it is done!" he chirped. "I always wondered how they could make each one the same. Can you believe they are all still done by hand? Of course, they have a stencil. Of course!" I am filled with horror. Anassa's eyes are glazed over.

The factory was bombed by the Russians, captured, and left in the control of the Russian Army, which manufactured china for a few years, sending the lot back to Moscow and seizing the entire historic collection of pottery as booty. When the German Democratic Republic was founded, the Russians gave Meissen to the communists as a wedding present. The historic collection didn't follow until the '60s. After that, the communists ran Meissen as a state industry until the Wall came down in 1988. Along the way, they tried to modernize the factory, with machine-pressed china cut to designs that suited an assembly-line process, but finally had to give it up and return the whole process to its original form: each piece hand-turned, hand-painted, hand-glazed, and hand-fired. After the wall came down, the factory was transferred to the state government of Saxony, which operates it now as a state corporation—part of their heritage.

Even Eberhard's enthusiasm couldn't last. "If I see one more kitschy flower, I'm going to scream!" he groaned. "Let's get out. Are you ready?"

"Ready!" We burst out laughing onto the street, in a thin drizzle that turned to steam in the hot air.

On the way out of town, looking for lunch, Eberhard drove us down the main street of Meissen. Like Pirna, it is in the process of reconstruction: the row houses, wall-to-wall, three stories high, curving around the street, set back on sidewalks two feet wide, leaving open only a narrow gap of sky above, are mostly grey. Here and there a few houses have been repaired, and painted with bright Art Nouveau colours.

Suddenly I knew I had seen that street before. I knew it like the back of my hand. I raked my mind, and then I recognized where, and when. The houses streamed past as if unfolding on a newsreel, and I was riding in the back of one of Hermann Goering's big black Daimlers; only the crowds were missing; above me and around me were the Nazi flags and swastika banners and ribbons and floral banners stretching beneath the balconies and across the street, and all the people leaning out of windows, cheering, that I had seen a hundred times in photographs from the election of 1933. This was that street. Shit.

We stopped for lunch at an old hotel, *Der Adler*, "The Eagle," in a small town in the country. The stairway up to the rooms, lined with black-and-white photographs from the 1930s, was blocked off by a big vase of sunflowers—impassable. The factory in Meissen was still spinning in my head.

"I feel at home here." Eberhard said, looking around with sharp, darting, bird-like motions of his head and his small brown eyes. "I don't know why."

I laughed. "It looks like your old house in Kuppenheim." I pointed to the banister and the high ceilings.

He smiled. The waitress came. We ordered drinks. The menus were thick with down-home German cooking—spiced roast beef, hunter's cutlets, red cabbage, potato dumplings.

"You'd never get this in the Rhineland anymore," Eberhard beamed. "You could go to twenty pubs and not find this. They're all owned by foreigners now, Italians and Greeks and Turks. You can get pizza anywhere, but you can't get this."

The waitress came back. We ordered the lot. We were going to get stuffed.

Eberhard dropped his voice. "Fifteen years ago, you wouldn't get a drink in a place like this. It would have been boarded up. Pubs were considered frivolous. The communists only allowed meetings of three people, not four. If there were more than three people, it was considered subversive."

I tried to imagine the Germans not sitting in their pubs. The damn things were everywhere.

Eberhard kept on. "If you wanted to go for a drink, you had to knock on the door, with two friends. You waited for fifteen minutes—don't ask me why it was fifteen minutes. They said they were afraid to open up for you, afraid it was the police, but they opened eventually, so I don't get it, and if there was anyone else in there they wouldn't open. They'd give you a bottle of beer, and then stand there and watch you while you drank it."

—

"Life was simple then," says the German novelist Stefan Schütz. "You knew that every third person worked for the police. If I met with one friend for coffee, a close friend, I knew I was safe, because there were only two of us, but if there was a second friend there, the conversation was completely changed: all of us knew that one of us was going to write a report to the police about everything we said.

"When I got to the West, I told myself I was in a different place now and would have to write something different. The problem was, I didn't know what people in the West wrote about. I didn't know anything about

Western culture. I had heard that *Ulysses* was a great Western book, so I set out to write a German *Ulysses*." It's a big book called *Medea*—one seven-hundred-page paragraph. Schütz won Germany's Döblin prize for it. He became a star. It was all politics. "It's the first and last money I've ever made as a writer."

Schütz is the direct theatrical heir of Bruno's contemporary, Bertolt Brecht. In 1992, Schütz followed his wife, Ute Birnbaum, to Alberta, where she taught Brecht for two years, first at the University of Alberta and then at the arts colony on the hills above the green copper roofs of the Banff Springs Hotel. Schütz went for long walks down by the river. The result was a radio play, called *Peyote,* which I translated.

I met Schütz in Banff in 2003. He was jumpy. The conference centre staff would not let him smoke. "I can't write when I can't smoke," he confessed. "It's crazy. The only place on campus they let you smoke is in the Native Education Centre. I used to spend a lot of time there, smoking and trying to write."

On the surface, *Peyote* tells the story of a German tourist who shelters from a storm in a derelict cabin by the Bow River, except the cabin is not empty: it is the home of a drunken, stinking Indian—or the ghost of one. The entire story is told by the Indian—or the ghost—who is very keen on stealing the tourist's fat leather wallet and Rolex watch. The Indian (ghost) takes the tourist on a rambling series of shamanic initiations, taunting, mocking, and abusing him the whole time. On another level, the book is a peyote trip, delineating step by step the entrance into the spiritual world revealed by this drug—the old Indian is peyote itself. On another level, there is no Indian at all, only a German writer at his desk, making everything up out of Karl May. On a more abstract level, *Peyote* is a damning critique of colonialism and native/white politics. No one comes out of this story looking good. That is Schütz's one trick: he takes the world apart until there is nothing left except the brutal honesty of a man who does not want to live any longer with any illusions at all.

"I didn't have a childhood," he said. "Not a normal one. I grew up without any sense of how people lived. I had to learn it all on my own. For years after I was exiled in the West I lived above White Cross Square in Hanover. I could look down from my apartment window and see addicts lying in the streets, people shooting each other with pistols, and drug deals being made in the doorways of bars. It was a great place to be a writer!"

When I met Schütz, he and Ute were back at Banff to put on a Brechtian workshop for young native actors from across Canada. Things were not going well.

"The producer walked out three days ago," said Ute when I walked in on the opening night of their big show, the culmination of six weeks of intense work. "She said we were abusing her actors."

"It isn't heritage," said Stefan, drawing the word out, her-i-tage. "I don't understand this her-i-tage."

"We're here to teach Brecht," said Ute. "We want to give them something."

"I don't know what this damn her-i-tage is," said Stefan. "What is heritage?"

For an hour I tried to explain it. It was amazingly hard to do. I gave up.

"I'll tell you about my next book," said Stefan. "It's called *The Employee*. I used to think that anyone who worked in the capitalist system was not a human being. I really believed that. I believed for a long time that it was impossible to live a human life within the closed constraints of a system like that."

I sipped my bitter tea. It was growing cold and a thin skim of tannin was floating on the top. It stuck to my teeth. "What made you change your mind?" I asked.

"9/11," he said. "I watched those towers fall, and watched people's reaction to it, and I thought, 'My God, those people working there actually did have a life. Of sorts.'" He smiled through his bushy orange moustache. "Not much of a life, but, still, it is a life. It might only be a part of a life, but it is a life. So, that's my next book: *The Employee.*"

"Do you have a publisher for it?" I asked, as a way of asking if I should be thinking of translating it.

"No. I write for the drawer now. I went to my publisher and showed him my manuscripts—I have three finished novels lying in my drawer—and he said, 'Stefan, you are our best writer, but no one wants that kind of thing anymore. People want entertainment. It won't sell.'"

"That's terrible," I said.

"Not really." He smiled "Behind the Iron Curtain I used to write for the drawer, to hide my manuscripts from the police. Now I write for the drawer in the West. It's the same thing." He shrugged.

He put on a jacket, and we went out to watch the marmots whistle in front of the ballroom. Wealthy people from Calgary in black suits and chiffon dresses danced behind glass. Stefan pulled vigorously at a cigarette.

— —

In Berlin, Brecht had set it as his task to dismantle the edifice of theatre and polite society. Instead of polite, middle-class entertainment, in his productions he left the theatre lights on and had his actors heckle the stage from the audience and the audience from the stage. This was theatre that had clawed its way up from the beer hall. For him, theatre was an attack on the presumptions of the elite—the distance they maintained between themselves and the working class was, he figured, exactly the distance between audience and actors. For Brecht, everyone was onstage. No one was an observer. He wanted them to hurt. He wanted them to understand very clearly that it *was* about them, and that it *was* personal.

In exile in the Baltic fog of the Faeroe Islands, with the Nazi army frolicking back home on the Ku'damm and stealing pastries from Jewish shops and licking the cream and honey off of their fingers before wiping them on the lace curtains on the way out, Brecht wrote about a cherry tree, blooming in his garden—beautiful, Japanese, eternal, the blossoms killed by a late snowfall. It was Easter morning, 1935. Brecht wrapped a sack around the tree's trunk. In 1965, in exile in Canada, Bruno wrote of a cherry tree in his orchard, throwing out a few blossoms after the killing frost of the previous December. Both of these poems are rooted in a poem, *Cherry Blossoms in Moonlight*, by Barthold Heinrich Brockes, written in 1727, about a cherry tree with branches so filled with blooms it is as if they are covered in snow. Brockes uses it as a symbol of the beauty of Heaven, so much greater than any beauty on Earth. Even Goethe had a go at the theme, using the occasion of cherry blossoms in moonlight as an excuse to ask a girl for a kiss. Eschewing any sense of eternity for a present as bittersweet as a cherry picked from a limb, he wrote, "This is the moment. I want a kiss. I say, kiss me now." Before exile drove him away from the sentimental romance of German poetic tradition, Brecht wrote a different poem about a cherry tree, *The Cherry Thief.* In that poem, he is woken before dawn by the whistling of a man stealing cherries from his tree. Brecht looks out his window, the thief raises his hands in greeting, both filled with cherries. Cherries bulge from the thief's pockets as he continues whistling down the road. The image haunts Brecht. It haunts me.

Ute had selected ten scenes from Brecht, and had cast them with her native actors.

"They are all scenes to do with justice. I wanted there to be something that would inspire them."

They were a mass of communist set pieces about the injustice suffered by workers in inner cities in Germany—Breslau and Berlin, Dresden, Hamburg and Cologne—in 1928 and 1931. It was bizarre to see them cast with natives dressed in reserve rags.

At the party held afterward in the Indian Friendship Society Lodge, I told Ute: "I can see where the anger is coming from. Perhaps it would have been better to have used the techniques of Brecht, and applied them to native tradition, and made something new out of that. The natives are going to have a hard time seeing this as anything other than another piece of colonialism."

"But it's Brecht," she said. "If you're going to understand Brecht, you have to go through the fire. There is no other way. No, it has to be like this."

Stefan pulled me aside in the hallway with the coats. "I'm going to write another book," he said.

I laughed. "I know. *The Employee.*"

"No, not *The Employee*. Another one. I'm going to call it *Apparatchik*. I lived for too many years with the apparatchiks, those petty party bureaucrats. They're nothing compared to the apparatchiks in this building. They gave me a cubicle to write in downstairs, because they pitied me and I needed a place to write where I could smoke, but I didn't get any writing done, because I had to listen all the time to their goddamn petty bullshit and all their crap about their heritage. *Apparatchik*. They say that *Peyote* is just cultural appropriation. They won't even read it. *Apparatchik* is going to blow them all to Hell!" He wasn't angry. He was conspiratorial.

After that, we went out for a drink with the cast. There was one place at the arts centre where you can get a drink: a tiny bar that opened from 6:00 to 10:00 on weekends. Ute slipped upstairs for lipstick and a white fur coat. Stefan and I watched the stars. He smoked another cigarette and pointed out the silhouette of Buffalo Mountain behind me, and indicated in the valley below where he used to go for walks while he was writing *Peyote:* there and there and there. When Ute came back, she was transformed into a kind of thickset Greta Garbo, with white hair.

We piled into the bar, and in the bar I understood what had happened to all of us. The cast of Ute's Brecht had all shed their reserve clothes for the latest fashions from Bloor Street. These were beautiful, young, urban people. They looked good, and they knew they looked good. In fact, they were there to look good, positioning themselves so that the light caught their hair just right. They smoothed down a blouse, a pair of slacks, and spent most of their time orchestrating whom they were going to sit with, how they were going to be seen. I was enthralled. Thomson Highway, the native playwright, who now lives in Britain, was there that night, with a table in the corner. The table sat six. After ten people crowded around, eight were left out. Ute, who also needed to be seen, commandeered a table between the pool table and the window, set us up on that, and watched over us for the next hour as all her actors kept an eye and an ear trained on Thomson. Stefan introduced me as his translator. I asked the actors what they thought of the book.

When I couldn't hear above the terrible din that echoed off of the walls as if amplified in a train station, one of them, big, generous, good-natured, leaned over and shouted into my ear, "I'm reading it right now. It's pretty good."

"Is that what people think?" I asked.

"The term cultural appropriation has been tossed around," he shouted.

"But why?" I shouted back. "There isn't a single Indian in the book!"

"I know, but no one's going to spend the time to read it closely enough to see that. They're going to look at the first page and say, 'Another drunken Indian!' and close the book."

It's a crying shame, but we had other things to worry about. Stefan was at the bar, ordering Scotch. He is diabetic. He shouldn't order Scotch. We hauled him out under the stars.

I ordered dumplings, *Klöse*, at the Adler, for my mother's sake. Every Christmas, my mother, my grandmother, Martha, and my great aunt, Tante Martha, argued about which one of them would host Christmas dinner. In the end, they always settled on the same truce: Christmas Eve was at our house, with roast ham, a tree hung with sugar cookies, and all the lights off except for three candles, before we opened our gifts as the first snow fell against the glass; Christmas was at my grandmother's, with roast pork; New Year's—my grandmother's birthday—was at Tante's, with whipped cream and long games of Hearts played with the huge deck of trick cards Hans had bought to make us all laugh, and the crystal serving dishes Tante had lugged across the border in the night. All three dinners included potato dumplings.

We didn't call them potato dumplings, though. We called them *Klaisel*.

"You are betraying your Silesian roots!" laughed Eberhard as I pronounced the word the only way I knew it. "No one says *Klaisel*. It is not a German word. The word is *Klöse*."

"But my grandmother always called them *Klaisel*! I'm sure of that."

"So am I. But that's Silesian dialect. Silesia doesn't exist anymore. The only people who still use that word are you bunch over there in Canada!" He was almost wiping the tears out of his eyes.

Every Christmas Eve, we had dinner at 5:00. At 4:30, at first dark, my grandmother showed up, in her black overshoes and thick Berber wool coat, stomping in the door, stiff with arthritis from all the years of hard work in the damp with bad shoes. She hadn't even squeezed in through the door, her voice ringing out in laughter as she called out "Hello!" to everyone while my grandfather came in behind her, puffing on a pipe and carrying a box of gifts, before my mother called out, "Mom!" That's all she said, but she said it in a tone that expressed all the anguish of those Christmases to her. She had been crying since 4:00. The *Klaisel* had fallen apart again in the pot. Every year we insisted on *Klaisel* with

Christmas dinner, and every year my mother tried. Every year she failed. She rolled the mashed potato dough out the day before, sealed it in long tinfoil tubes, and laid it in the fridge. She added salt to the water, she left salt out of the water, she put one in the water at a time, three in at a time, she tried everything, and every year she made potato soup. Every year my grandmother hung her black coat on a hook behind the door, rolled up her sleeves, bustled over across the big farm kitchen to the stove, and rescued her.

I was there, too, laying the silver out so carefully on the table. I watched those two bending over the stove, lifting the *Klaisel* out gently with a slotted spoon, as if each one was a hand-painted Easter egg from the Ukraine, and laying them in a bowl. At dinner, we lit the candles, turned off the lights, and nothing ever tasted so good. My mother would have a sip of wine and go red in the cheeks, because, after all, it was Christmas, and because it was Christmas I would watch it all.

At dinner, Bruno sat at the head of the table, amidst all the plenty, the family, the crystal glasses, and drank a glass of beer with my father. All around the table, we had finished our second course, while Bruno was still clearing off his plate meticulously with his fork and knife. When he was done, the plate was so clean it could have been slipped back into the cupboard. All the bitter years of struggle to achieve this kind of plenty had taught him only not to appreciate it. To him, those were the Christmases of defeat.

"Don't ever, ever watch that show again!" Bruno barked at my brother and I once as we were watching *Hogan's Heroes* on TV, that old sitcom about a German POW camp. The Germans at the camp are fools, outwitted time after time by Hogan and his men. The parade of fools includes Colonel Klink, the commandant, a Prussian dandy with a monocle, and Schultz, the fat Bavarian guard, eager at any time to accept bribes of Red Cross chocolate. Tamed guard dogs, the pompous SS in their ugly black leather coats: Hogan got the better of them all, funnelled the Resistance through the network of tunnels under the camp, and won World War II.

We were shocked. *Hogan's Heroes* was our favourite show. We laughed at it with our father all the time. Our grandfather was cutting: "The Americans didn't defeat the *Wehrmacht*," he said that evening. "It was the Russians. The Americans could not have defeated anything."

Wehrmacht. I had never heard that name for the German Army before, and had never heard my grandfather so upset, had never considered that any part of him had remained German, or proud, despite all the Nazis had done, or that there was any distinction between Germans and Nazis, but it had, and there was.

—

When Hans Schreiber came for Christmas, he smoked cigars. They gave off an oily, blue smoke that made our eyes water and our heads go dizzy and made me sick to the stomach. He had his hair combed straight back like a Silesian dandy and cracked jokes the whole time. Slipping out of the corner of his mouth, they were his only form of conversation. I worshipped him. Bruno smoked his pipe, the thin blue smoke spilling out of the bowl like liquid ammonia—but only after he had spent fifteen minutes cleaning the bowl with his penknife, scraping the tar out of it, then another five minutes lighting it, taking deep puffs on the stem to get it going, like a bellows. The two of them sat there on the couch in the reflected glitter of the tree. My brother and I sat between them, awkward in dress shirts and cufflinks, coughing, while outside, right behind our backs, through the huge plate-glass windows, the stars swam like fish through the branches of the elms. Our father bent over the stereo and put on Christmas music from the Rhine, recorded during the Occupation and sold to refugees around the world, "O Tannenbaum" and "A Rose is Blooming," a little bit of the *Heimat*, with the bells of the Cologne Cathedral tolling at the beginning and end of each side. He sat quietly, and sang along, although at all other times he was loud and brash. Martha sat back in a deep chair, and stared into her hands, like a silent statue. The music sounded foreign and so distant.

Looking for an insight into that time, last summer my cousin Thomas and Anassa and I were on a mountaintop high in the Vosges, walking away from the Natzweiler-Struthof concentration camp. The only concentration camp in France, it was used as the main processing centre for members of the Resistance. They were forced to quarry granite and bring it down the steep slope in improvised wooden wheelbarrows. As the prisoners passed, a turncoat prisoner guard—a *Kapo*—randomly stuck out a foot: a prisoner would trip, spilling his granite blocks, the kapo would shout *Alarm!* and one of the SS guards would shoot the prisoner dead—for trying to escape. For his sharp eyes, the lucky guard got extra rations and a week's paid leave, off of the mountaintop. The hospital block, God help you, housed a dissection chamber; the victims were dissected still warm—immediately after execution. Extra corpses were preserved in formaldehyde and shipped whole to the University of Strasbourg. Natzweiler-Struthof imprisoned about a thousand prisoners in ten barracks ranked in twos down the steep mountainside. A further 258 prisoners were housed in twelve satellite work camps—lumber mills and quarries. Three of those were within easy walking distance of my father's boyhood house in Kuppenheim.

Thomas hadn't known that. It wasn't until the night before we drove up out of the burning Rhine to the cool of the Vosges that I told him how my father used to tease the dogs there as he walked past on his way to school and back, how he'd watch the inmates through the barbed wire, how our grandmother, Charlotte, as the official camp doctor, had taken pity on a sixteen-year-old Russian girl whom the guards had picked out to be raped; to save her she had asked that she be assigned to her as a maid. Thomas knew none of it. "Dad says that Maryushka hid an escaped Russian in the attic for three months," I told him. We were sitting on Thomas's veranda, under the clematis flowers, as a big moon rose above the Rhine. "For three months our grandmother pretended that he wasn't there. Three times a day, Maryushka took food up to him."

"I thought it was a Frenchman in the basement," said Thomas, out of the shadows of the one candle set on the table between us.

"That was Pierre." Thomas said he'd heard the story, but he hadn't heard the name. I repeated it. "Pierre. But that was earlier. This was a second prisoner."

Pierre had been badly wounded while escaping. Our grandmother answered a knock on the door in the middle of the night, dragged him in, and nursed him back to health in the basement, for six weeks. When he was healed, he pruned my grandmother's rose garden, weeded the flower beds, taught my father the names of all the flowers and left for France.

In Natzweiler-Struthof, our voices were swallowed by the heavy air, but the gravel crunched loudly beneath our feet. "I really doubt that this story is true," said Thomas above the grating rustle of his footsteps. "A woman like our grandmother, with her job and her connections, could have had a German maid at any time. It doesn't make sense. You only got a foreign maid if you couldn't get a German one."

We walked on in silence. My emotions were crushed by that dissection table, and by the toilet—a small concrete room dug into the hill beside the crematorium. The concrete was black, hastily poured, by the inmates who had built the camp. The plumbing was sixty years old. The toilet stank and it hardly flushed. The door latch was operated by a cord—sixty years old and rusty. After I had flushed and tried to leave, after my urine flowed down and mingled with the dead, I tried to open the latch. It was stuck. For a moment, I felt myself trapped there, back in 1943, felt that the door would soon burst open and Thomas and Anassa would be gone and the noise and grinding filth of the camp would crush in upon me. Then I took a deep breath and tried the door again. It barely opened, but it opened. I stepped out ashamed.

By the time we walked back out the gate and into the parking lot, I was angry, angry at the tiny solitary confinement cells, too short to stand in, too narrow to sit in, with their iron grates, which lined the halls of the camp prison—angry that someone had sat down at a drafting table and planned the whole thing out while his art-deco lamp burned brightly.

"Who knows," I said to Thomas, at last.

"*We* never will," he answered.

More silence. "I think our grandparents knew more than most," I said. A softer silence. "At the very least."

An even softer silence yet. "I think you're right."

But that's not exactly the same as history—or truth.

The history is brief. Hans and Charlotte met in medical school in Freiburg in the mid-Twenties. They raised a family, after a fashion, in Kuppenheim, and were broken apart by the war. Hans was badly wounded. After the war, Charlotte stayed on in Kuppenheim; Hans married his physiotherapist and started a new practice in Constance, not far from the Reichenau.

Truth, though, is anyone's guess. Under the destroyed fortress of Freiburg, where the beech trees sprout from the walls on the hilltop above the lacy trees caught and splayed in the light above the cathedral spire, Eberhard once gave me a book of quotations from Dostoevsky—*Words like Mirrors*. It was Easter. The Wall had still not fallen in Berlin. My father still did not have his little chunk of concrete in a little white paper box. Stalks of pussy willows and hazel branches were for sale throughout the city. A bouquet of them sat in a big stone vase in Michel's hall.

"You must remember," Eberhard said, pouring the Easter Morning muscatel, "our family comes from the East. Germany is an eastern country. We are in the West now, but historically we are an eastern people. We are not at home here in the centre of Europe." The wine was sweet. This wasn't wine. It was anti-freeze. Before the Wall fell, little wineries up in Baden still made wine like that—in Liliental (Valley of Lilies) and Bischoffingen, Vogelsang (Birdsong), Vogtsburg, and Schelingen, and all the hundred other towns lining the roads through the sandy vineyards and 400-metre peaks of Death's Head and Mount Katharina. The area is called the Kaiserstuhl—a hard volcanic upcropping draped with sand in the Rhine floodplain north of Freiburg. The emperor can sit there, on "The Seat of the Emperor," and stare up the Rhine to its source in the Alps. The cheaper blends of this *Badisch* are so sweet they stick in your throat—cough syrup, bottled in heavy glass bottles with wide bases, almost like champagne bottles, decked out with labels and decals glinting with silver and gold, about as decorated as a bottle of wine can be before it becomes a piñata. Wine like that is something you smash across the prow of a ship a Rhine barge, perhaps, hauling potatoes or coal up and down a river as green as an eel.

As we drank it and it dissolved our teeth, Eberhard told me a story—an example, he said, of how the family never did fit into the West. "We used to light the candles twice a year on the Christmas tree. The first time was on Christmas Eve, when Papa threw open the doors of the smoking room and the whole tree would be blazing with candles. We gathered around the tree and sang "O Tannenbaum." We watched the candles very closely. When they were burned halfway down, we snuffed them out. We had a candle-snuffer on a very long pole, which we used for that. It was a very great honour to be chosen as the candle-snuffer. You had to be very careful, and very quick—so that you didn't start a fire. We lit the candles again on New Year's Eve, when Mama and Papa had a big party and people were invited from all over People were singing and dancing and drinking champagne, and just before midnight the tree was lit. In about a half hour the candles started to die down and go out. They didn't all go out at the same time, but there was very little time in between. As soon as the candles started to die we gathered around the tree, and when there was only one candle burning you had to look quickly around the room and find your shadow somewhere in the room. The candle wouldn't burn for long. It would flicker with a rough flame and the shadows would dance. You had to find your shadow. It was very serious, because if you didn't, it meant that you would not be alive to see another Christmas. You would die during the year. Nobody does this in Germany. It is not a German custom, but we did it every year. It is something we brought back from the East."

I paged through the Dostoevsky. "*I know from bitter experience,*" Dostoevsky writes, "*how deceptively complete outer appearances can be; that sometimes a snake is hiding among flowers.*" I paged further. "*Look for happiness in suffering.*"

Oh, that's just great.

"Dostoevsky is as much a German as is Goethe or Beethoven," Eberhard added.

"Thanks," I said.

"Read it. Goethe said that what a man inherits from his father he has to work for." In German, the sentence works upon a turn of phrase; it is quite witty. Eberhard was not sure I had understood—and he wanted me, very clearly, to understand, so he added a comment of his own: "It is then you become an adult. You have to understand it and make it a part of yourself. Everything else is lost. It doesn't belong to you."

All right. Rules.

Every morning before school I sat on the bare wooden stairs leading to the basement. There in the light from one naked sixty-watt bulb I polished my black leather shoes to a high shine. They were tall shoes, like army boots. There were a few other simple rules in that house: we would never wear T-shirts, we would never wear jeans, we would never own a pickup, we would never touch a gun or even talk about one, we would never wear a shirt untucked or a pair of pants without a belt, we would always keep our hair cut short, part it on the left, and smooth it down with Brylcreem. Those were the rules. We would never ask to borrow our father's car when we were sixteen. We would name our firstborn son Hans. We would move away from home, and after two years we would move back and farm with our father.

The other boys in Cawston had a different introduction to the world. Their fathers had been fighter pilots, tankers, gunners, and infantrymen. Their history gave them guns as weapons for freedom—instruments of creation; they made you into a man. To my father, they were only weapons of destruction. When my friend Murray shot blue jays, when Dale came to school with a squirrel tail stapled to his hat, I was in awe. Those boys exuded male power. I explained that I wasn't allowed to have guns, because of the war. I took it seriously. The boys laughed.

As the years went by, my father broke his prohibition against guns. With deer eating his young apple trees under Puddin'head Mountain, eating his dream of the future, he bought a Remington 30-30 and a .22 and went out at night with Karl May to shoot them.

"Some nights, there were thirty deer out there eating the trees. I shone the lights on them. It was easy. There were so many one night you couldn't count them. I took a line on a big buck, shot it, and when I got to it, there were two dead deer lying there—with one shot. The bullet had passed right through one and still had enough force behind it to kill the second one."

That Christmas my father gave me a spring-action pellet pistol and two tins of lead pellets. The very next day, I set out to enter the world of woodpecker killing and crow blasting and quail hunting that I had escaped a decade earlier, when Davy Crockett was everyone's hero and we sang Walt Disney's songs of the Alamo while changing our sprinkler lines. I shot at the quail that hoo-hooed from the dead pruning piles, the starlings twittering on the power wires, the sparrows that flitted through the branches like leaves caught in the wind off of a cool fire, the pheasants that stalked through the grass just after dawn, red-necked, dressed in brocade like Chinese emperors, and I missed every one. After five hundred pellets, I finally hit a sparrow that was patient enough to sit on a dead branch long enough for me to get in three slow shots. The bird flew away with a scream, and a few feathers remained, floating down through the air. I was appalled. I went back along the edge of the hill. The elm trees we had planted along the ridge were twittering with gold finches. I threw the gun into the garbage, where it belonged.

The previous fall, my father had gone for a walk with his own father, in downtown Constance, among the 700-year-old houses: *built 1319, destroyed by fire 1467, rebuilt to the old plans, 1519, burnt to the ground 1783, rebuilt 1799,* painted right on the wall. Dr. Rhenisch bought a fur hat, a fur coat, and a Russian/German Dictionary. "This time the Russians are going to win," he said. "And this time I am going to be ready. I have seen them fight. They are merciless."

Just like citizens of the Interior, compromised between land and raw log exports, most German families have two histories. There is the public history, the one created in a few short minutes in 1945—to face the world, to explain what the members of the family were doing during the war—and the real story, the one that few in the family know anymore or ever knew or still care to remember. The first story, the story you tell your children, the one you tell the Americans when they haul you up in court to process your denazification papers, or tell the neighbours when you have them over for kuchen and coffee, is a fairy tale, about sacrifice and suffering, about innocent people being caught up in and destroyed by a terrible war, and your neighbours will nod their heads and tell the same wonderful, sad story. You shake your head at the suffering they have had to endure, at the vagaries of the world, and how it drags down a pure heart. It is an old lesson, and an important one. The Germans have been learning it for years.

I first heard this story in 1967. In this story, my grandparents joined the Party because they had to. Six months before the start of the war, Dr. Rhenisch was drafted as the head of a military hospital. He followed the Army east in 1941, stayed with them in Russia, and was with them, years later when in the retreat his hospital—a hospital! a noncombatant's hospital, dedicated to healing the injured!—was bombed by the Russians. When he got out of the Russian hospital, he had a silver plate in the back of his head, three silver vertebrae in his spine, and amnesia. By this time, the war was over and he was in a military hospital in France, but did not know his name, or how he got there. This story is a soap opera: when the hospital was blown up, Dr. Rhenisch had been declared dead; his widow, Charlotte, who had slaved away for the entire war as the only doctor in the city of Rastatt, the only doctor for eighteen thousand people, up at 4:30 AM, back home at 10:30 at night, walking eight kilometres to work and eight kilometres back past the concentration camp every day, for years, remarried and had an eighth child.

A year after the end of the war, Europe was still in ruins. There were piles of brick everywhere. The whole of Germany was on the move, taking trains in all directions, over rattling Bailey bridges, through bombed-out stations, looking for lost relatives, looking for a sack of potatoes or a few lumps of coal, and hauling it all back to whatever city the war had thrown them down in. That was how Dr. Rhenisch was discovered, in his hospital bed in France: an acquaintance from Kuppenheim came through looking for someone else and saw the great man there, the Herr Doktor, shattered by the war and the Russians, and said, very surprised to see the dead man, "Hans, what are you doing here?" and so my grandfather remembered who he was and went home. It was a miracle. When he arrived at the house in Kuppenheim, though, the miracle was over: the door opened and my grandmother stood there, a baby, my aunt Margot, in her arms. A man's voice called out from in back, "Who is it, dear?" Dr. Rhenisch didn't say a word. He placed his hat back on his head, turned on his heel, and walked away. He never set foot in that house again.

The second story is a secret story, the one you tell at the end of your life when someone asks and you don't care any longer, because it is all so long ago. This story was collected out of pieces here and there, from conversations in bars, with friends, words picked up on the street, and memories lived and relived, sifted and remade time and time again, until a story came out of them, memories remembered and memories of memories remembered, relived, reinterpreted, re-seen.

Okay. My grandfather joins the Nazi party in 1928, works as the regional doctor for the SA, the Brownshirts, who march violently through the streets in communal nostalgia for the land. That is the year in which his girlfriend, Charlotte, runs to Basel, Switzerland, to have her first child. For a woman in her position—unmarried—it would have been impossible in Germany: she would have been expelled from medical school. She knows nothing about babies. The nuns give her a five-day crash course on baby care and send her back across the border.

From 1928 to 1932, Freiburg University is a hotbed of Nazi-directed student agitations. The student newspapers swell with Nazi propaganda. By 1933, the Nazi party is in power, his nationalistically oriented fraternity, rooted in the Wartburg revolution, has been forcibly merged with the Hitler Youth, Charlotte, now Dr. Rhenisch's wife, has given birth to my father, their third child. The situation is desperate. My father is sick at birth and can't keep milk down. Desperate to regain his piece of mind, Dr. Rhenisch prescribes brandy. My father lives off that for two weeks. As Dr. Rhenisch now has a wife and three kids and as a graduate now is no longer eligible for a student's subsidy—in gold, no less, and not subject to inflation—he has no means of support. His solution is to call in his Party connections in an attempt to gain the only open seat in the faculty of medicine. As an intern he had participated on a pioneering open heart surgery team, and he wishes to continue with that kind of work, as a team leader or even a head doctor. He is very much in the shadow of the important doctors who were in Freiburg at that time: Sauerbruch, Aschoff, Rehm, Büchner. He does not have much of a chance. He has done too little research, and so is always handled patronizingly. His prospects are not especially rosy.

At this time, an opening presents itself. Late one evening a telegram arrives from his former fraternity brother Hans Kletti, who writes: "Hans, listen: here is the chance of your life, but you have to make a decision within three days. I am the lawyer for Schömperlin und Gast Ltd., the leading Mercedes factory in Karlsruhe. Schömperlin's daughter has married a general practitioner, Dr. Van Klef, who has just built her a big house in the form of a villa in a small village at the mouth of the Murg Valley, and he wants to sell it. His reason: in this "perfect isolation," in this wasteland, in this undeveloped farm village, where not a single road is paved and where cowshit and horseshit lie a centimetre thick on all the streets, this Mrs. Schömperlin just can't feel at home. She is used to going to the theatre three times a week, used to a grand house and to sumptuous surroundings. In that town she is bored to death. With a heavy heart, Dr. Van Klef has decided to give the place up, since his wife is totally against it." And thus, of course, the house is offered below its worth, as the matter is urgent. Kletti is in charge of the sale. The first person he thinks of is his fraternity brother in Freiburg, who is living like a monk as an intern at the university clinic. Although he has no down payment, Dr. Rhenisch receives a loan for eighty thousand Reichsmarks, co-signed by Kletti, and both Hans and Charlotte set up as country doctors and have a mural painted in their front hall. The fraternity? A descendent of the students at the Wartburg. Not surprisingly, by this time it has been swallowed up by the Hitler Youth.

Maybe I have become too distrusting, but the following conjecture still fits the facts, if that is what they are: the arrangement had been made within the channels of the Nazi Party, Dr. Rhenisch was directed to go there as it was not politically expedient to give him a post at the university, the difficulties of the loan were smoothed over by the Party, and through this act my grandfather was beholden. Even further conjectures still fit the facts: Dr. Van Klef did not flee because his wife was a fancy city woman and could not bear life in a conservative, Catholic village; rather, his sudden flight and his frightened urgency were politically motivated: either he was being ousted by the Party, was being blackmailed and had nowhere to turn in a state that now used blackmail as an open means of conducting government business, or he was Jewish.

Thomas thinks I have a wild imagination.

—

There are, however, still the facts: Dr. Rhenisch had a big portrait of Hitler in the house, a massive thing of a size designed for large public buildings. As the '30s progressed, he spent more and more time in political activity, and less and less time as a surgeon and doctor. He was head of the local Red Cross. The party built him his own hospital. He was head of a regional physician's association and still worked as regional party doctor for the Brownshirts.

"He had the only car in town," says my father. "That was no accident.

My mother used to go to Berlin with him on party business, where they lived the high life."

"My father was naïve," says Michel. "He believed that belonging to the Nazi party was the same thing as listening to Beethoven or Brahms, just an expression of pride."

My father: "Papa was on the German medical team for the 1936 Olympics."

Since Charlotte was regularly having children, for the Party ostensibly (in 1943, after seven children, she received a medal of motherhood from the government—a kind of copper-coloured iron cross), and was running her own medical practice out of the house, the children were raised by a succession of maids. The maids were Catholic girls from town, pressed into household service by the Party, just as the boys were pressed into the Hitler Youth. The children tormented the maids, and the maids never lasted more than two months. While the children ran wild around him, my grandfather spent all his free time—which was not much—playing the piano.

"There are two questions I would like to ask him," says my father: "'Why were we so ashamed to have a father called Dr. Rhenisch?' and 'Why did you turn around in the door like that and walk out?' But I can't ask. It is too late.

"We were wild, terrible children who grew up without parents. We did terrible things. No other children would have been allowed to do the things we did, but we were the doctor's children. You have to understand, when I was a boy we sang a rhyme, *Kaiser, König, Edelmann, Burgher, Bauer, Bettler.* You had the Emperor. Then the King. Then the nobles. That was the first group of people. Then, completely different, you had all the rest: burghers, the good solid, respectable citizens of the towns, and then the farmers. That was just about everybody. They were all so poor they didn't have anything. Then if you didn't fit into all that, anywhere, which was all the possibilities for people, then you were a criminal, an outlaw, a beggar, a *Zigeuner*—a gypsy. That's all there was to it. Papa used to say to me, 'I am a doctor and your mother is a doctor, because we are nobility. That is why we are doctors. That is our responsibility.' My brother Michael used to say, 'Don't play with those other kids in town. They are the proletariat. You use them as workers and soldiers, but not as friends.' Of course, I was not going to have anything to do with that. That got me into a lot of trouble with everybody, even with the peasants! That is what they taught us in those days. We were told it was very important. It is all a lot of bullshit. But that is why my father was respected, as the Herr Doktor. That is what that was all about. We would not have been able to do the things we did in that town if we were not the kids of the Herr Doktor and the Frau Doktor. There would have been a lot of trouble. But there wasn't! There was an allotted order in life. I grew up in the Middle Ages. For example, I did not go to the academic high school because I was smart. I was terrible at trigonometry. I went because I was the doctor's son. They took me out of school and crammed trigonometry into me for two weeks so I could pass my test. Some farmer's kid who was smarter than I was simply would not have gone.

"We hooked one of the maids up to 220-volt power once. We connected the wires up to the doorknob and hid, waiting for her to grab it. What a shock she had! You should have seen her!

"My father was respected as a doctor. He was very sensitive and gentle. He could play the piano like a genius. He would sit down and play it for hours and hours. I remember listening to him play when I was very small, as the sound flooded through the house. He was very gentle as a doctor, and everyone loved him as a doctor. He was even gentler and more sure and even more respected as a surgeon.

"But he could be a real son of a bitch."

My grandparents were not a good match. Charlotte was impulsive and easygoing, not especially feminine, emotional, and lazy. Dr. Rhenisch was working himself to the bone and wanted her to care for the house, with everything in order, and to be a support for his soul; wanted to be able to come home from a long day and share his daily troubles with her. He worked himself past the edge of his physical stamina, worked late into the night and went on house calls at all hours. In six years he paid back half of his huge mortgage. For her part, Charlotte wanted to be a doctor herself, not to play the role of an office girl. And she let the children run wild. Dr. Rhenisch broke into tears at the first whiff of emotion. He lived for his feelings. Philosophy and music affected him deeply.

"This picture I still see as I saw it when I was a kid," says Michael: "My father was certainly, as you'd say these days, full-proportioned, and the Brownshirt uniform had a leather belt approximately eight centimetres wide. Whenever my father poured himself into this uniform, I always thought of old knightly armour, which people used to have built up around them. The worst was the belt. That one took two women, one holding it on the left and one on the right, and pulling until the buckle made it around the stomach and my father with his last strength sucked in his gut and snapped the buckle together."

As Brownshirt officer and Red Cross director, Dr. Rhenisch entered a world of power that raised him higher than a position as minister in the government would today. His marriage became a straightjacket. He believed that he no longer had to follow the rules of acceptable behaviour, adopted a new lifestyle, and spent money lavishly. His circle of friends no longer included Charlotte. In September 1939, he was picked up by the army. Whenever he came home on leave, he was wearing a different uniform. At first he was a lance corporal in an ambulance brigade. The next time we saw him he was a team doctor, then he was a head doctor. And in his time as head of the reserve in Rastatt, he fell in love with a woman who served him in the Rastatt train station. That's how far he had to go to get a drink. As Eberhard explains, "It would have been unthinkable for a man of his class to stop in at The Blume, the pub around the corner in Kuppenheim, for a beer. It just wasn't done."

"She was good for nothing," says Michael. "Unlike all the others, he did not use her for a sexual escapade, but believed himself morally obliged to marry her. She was a vamp, a butcher's daughter from Constance, a kind of Marilyn Monroe, younger than he was and the greatest experience of his life. He idealized her completely." Her husband was the service manager for the Rastatt train station.

Hans and the woman had a child. Dr. Rhenisch felt it his duty to divorce his wife and leave his children, to stand by his new love. It was the talk of the town. Rastatt is not a big place. It wasn't long before news made it to Kuppenheim.

Charlotte reacted emotionally, and went to the leader of the regional reserve, General von Hornstein, who she knew socially. He knew already, and frowned on it: the woman had already passed through many hands.

"It would have been tolerated if Dr. Rhenisch had done as the others had," says Michael, "had gone with her once to Stuttgart or to Denmark, but marriage was against the sense of the officer's code."

Charlotte begged the general to transfer Hans so he could get over his silly infatuation. Von Hornstein went along with the scheme and transferred Dr. Rhenisch to Brünn, in what had until shortly before been Czechoslovakia, just south of his old stomping grounds in Kattowitz. As a sugar pill, he was given command of the Brünn military reserve. Suddenly, doctors from the high command had to be his assistants in surgery. The posting was held out as a reward for good service, but Dr. Rhenisch soon discovered that it had been made on Charlotte's request. Figuring she had sent him to the East to be killed, he pressed for a divorce.

"In truth," says Michael, "everyone knows that a reserve hospital with over a thousand beds is not set up in the trenches, but hundreds of kilometres in the rear. So no way did my mother want him to be transferred as a front-line soldier, with the probability, sooner or later, of being killed. That's absolutely not it at all: as I know my mother, all she wanted in her feminine way, was that he got away from this woman.

"Naturally, the result was completely the opposite."

Because of his terrible wounds, at the end of the war Dr. Rhenisch was sent to France on a prisoner exchange. There he was in hiding, unwilling—afraid—to show his face. He had staked everything on the Nazi Party, and could not return, either to Freiburg or to Kuppenheim. When an acquaintance from Kuppenheim walked through the hospital and recognized him, the gig was up. Once more he had a name—not a new name, but an old one. He shouldered it and went back, the door opened, his wife met him with a baby in her arms, and, feeling betrayed by her again, he put his hat on his head and turned on his heel.

He then went to face the Americans. For his denazification, he worked for them for a year as a doctor.

"It was stupid," my father explained. "He was completely harmless. The Americans just wanted to get free work out of him. People with lesser skills, who had been actually active in the Party, were released long before he was. It made him quite bitter."

At the end of his denazification, Dr. Rhenisch had a total collapse—his injuries were still not healed, he still could hardly sleep or move for the pain, and everything he had counted on and everything he had loved had failed. He hit rock bottom. Country, ethics, morals, dreams, personal life, national identity, the cities he knew and had loved, all were destroyed, shattered, burnt out. It must have been a terrible blow to him when his son Hans left the homeland, the *Heimat,* to go to Canada, to join the enemy, while he could only watch helplessly, damned to complete silence by his own entanglement with propaganda.

With this story, I thought I had come to the heart of the matter. I thought I had replaced the fairy tale with the real story of a man and his struggle through life—he was fallible, and tragic in a wider sense.

I was wrong. It was not the last story.

—

In the third story, nothing is clear. It is the spring of 1941. A seven-year-old boy with stomach problems is taken for tests by his father, a doctor, to the hospital where he works. The boy's name is Eberle. His father leads him into a bare white room in which sits an examination table, and asks him to wait there until he gets back. The boy nods shyly—he is, after all, afraid of his father. It is not a contemporary father/son relationship, with soccer practice and ice cream at the Dairy Queen. It is the way things used to be done. Suddenly, a different doctor opens the door with urgency, says a few words to the boy's father. The father looks worried and asks the boy again to stay there. Again the boy nods. The father slips out, the door closes, and the boy is alone in a cold white room.

The father does not return as he promised. When the boy is bored and feels forgotten and cannot stand it any longer, he opens a door to look for his father, not knowing what he will see, not even imagining what it might be. He opens the door into Hell. Hell is very close. Hell is a long, long room lost in darkness at the far end. It consists of rows upon rows of hospital beds, full of men screaming. There is blood everywhere. The men are wearing dirty uniforms and are terribly wounded. Nurses and doctors are shouting. The din is terrible. Hell is in Rastatt, on the Rhine river, not in Brünn on the Polish Border, where it should be. Hell is a triage station.

The boy closes the door and waits, for hours. In this story, the father is never posted to Brünn, there is no 1941 divorce in Prague, there is no absent father. He is there, right through the war. He spends every Sunday with his wife and children. There are photos, perfect German Propaganda Ministry photos, of the boy's mother in a long dress, blonde hair plaited back like Wagner's Sighilde, three children—a baby and a couple toddlers—a peach tree espaliered against the garage wall, and the father in his business suit, hair slicked back, looking down benevolently.

In this story, the viewpoint changes. Soon the boy is whisked away from the house, because it is so close to the Rhine. Like his brothers and sisters he is sent up for safety into the Black Forest. In his case it is to the home of Erwin Rommel, the Desert Fox—a social friend of his father. Rommel is away at the war and the boy lives in the formal house, full of rules, with Mrs. Rommel and the servants. It is very stiff. It is now the spring of 1944. The Allies are expected to land in France. The boy's brothers are singing an American marching song, just for fun, "We'll hang our washing on the Siegfried Line!" The American song boasts of the ease with which the GIs would conquer Germany. The German version is just the opposite:

> Yes, kid, you were too flippant when you talked
> about the big wash day on the German Rhine,
> but if you've also filled your trousers to the top,
> you don't need to ruin your day with crying.
>
> We'll soon soap you down from your head,
> and then we'll soap you up from your toes.
> When the Germans do their washing, kid,
> you won't ever need to wash your clothes.

One of Eberle's brothers is manning a flak gun on a bridge across the Rhine—on that line.

As one of Hitler's favourites, Rommel is assigned to prepare the coastal defences. Things are out of control. Count von Stauffenberg has engineered a coup against Hitler. He has enlisted the help of the senior officers of the German armed forces, all in top secret on pain of death. For his part, Rommel agrees to surrender to the Allies so that they can push through quickly into Germany and protect it from the Russians. All this is part of the story.

The boy's father holds a meeting in his house in Kuppenheim. Present are: Field Marshall Erwin Rommel, Dr. Med. Hans Rhenisch, and General von Hornstein. Except for those three men, no one knew what was discussed at that meeting, and they are all dead. There were, however, four men who knew that the meeting had taken place: the three men who sat in the smoking room with the curtains drawn, and General von Hornstein's chauffeur, who talked down at the pub. Soon General von Hornstein was hanging on a meathook in Berlin. Rommel was given the choice of suicide and a hero's death, or a trial and shame for his family. He chose to protect his family. Dr. Hans Rhenisch was sent to the Eastern Front—a death sentence.

The rest of the story is familiar: the bombing of the hospital, the wounding, the surgery, the prisoner transfer to France, the recognition, the return home, the baby, the wife, the hat, just as in the family photo from 1941, except it was the wrong baby, the turned heel, the no-going-back. All of it keeps coming up again and again like a recurring motif in a fairytale, a crossword puzzle crib of a story that you lay down, your head spinning, and pick up later and try to finish, again and again—a broken record of a story. The only thing that everyone agrees on was that it was impossible to return. You can't go home again. People are on their own.

—

"Those Christmases were terrible," my father said. "When my father was in Russia, during the war, he came home for a couple days and what could he talk about? He wasn't the same man anymore. He didn't come home for Christmas. We had a tree, and Mama had managed to save a few candle stubs, and we could only light them once, that's all we had. There were no presents under the tree. There wasn't anything to eat. It was awful. We all cried. That is how we spent Christmas. I don't want to remember any of this anymore. Now I've told it to you and I can forget it."

If, as Thomas and I suspected, Dr. Med. Hans Rhenisch knew more than other people, what did he know?

Doctors in Germany were prescribing euthanasia as early as 1933. The idea was to turn socialism completely on its head: an individual diagnosed to be of no value to the state was to be killed to improve the health of the state. God knows if Dr. Rhenisch was part of that racket, or if he pretended to follow along but bowed out in the end. That is how you did it: you gave a bow of deference to the audience. As detailed at length in Robert Lifton's book, *The Nazi Doctors,* resistance is a strange language with extreme social rules: any doctor who refused on moral grounds to carry out the killings prescribed by the state—like the excision of a cancer—for the health of the state, was punished by the same prescription. If he refused to do the work on practical grounds, however, if he said that he personally was too weak a person to carry out the task, he was relieved of all further responsibility for it, without punishment. He was clapped indulgently on the shoulders and sent back to his practice.

If Dr. Med. Charlotte Rhenisch knew more than other people, what did she know?

"Our mother was very weak about discipline," says Michael. "All week long she collected a list of our transgressions. It was a pretty long list! Stealing plums, teasing the neighbour's cat, driving our father's car down the road, knocking on doors and then disappearing, so when the old ladies came out there was no one there, and, after they had gone in, doing it all over again. Once a week, on Sunday, before dinner, our father sat down in the smoking room, laid the list before himself, and called us in one at a time. He looked at the list, and gave us one strike with the cane for every transgression during the week, then sent us up to bed without dinner. Then it would be all over for another week. You can imagine how little of an impression it made on all of us."

It took four of them to drive the car. As the brains behind the operation, Michel sat in the passenger seat, ran the shift lever, and gave directions. Hansel steered. Lottl ran the clutch and the brake, under Hans's feet. Eberle stood up and gave directions.

"It's Frau Sturmann!" Eberle yelled. They all ducked.

Frau Sturmann watched the car putt putt down the street, without a driver. That evening, she paid a visit to Charlotte. "Frau Doktor Rhenisch," she said, breathless at the door. Erwin Rose's big blue mural glared out at her like an eye. "Those children were driving the Herr Doktor's car!"

"Now, how could that be?" asked Charlotte. "They're just little children. How can they drive a car? They're not even big enough to see over the steering wheel!"

"I saw the car driving down the street, without a driver!" gasped Frau Sturmann.

"Frau Sturmann! I think you are imagining things." When Charlotte closed the door, she laughed.

That week, "Driving Papa's Car" appeared on the punishment list.

"I shot down three planes," Michael once told me in his post-war house in Freiburg, proud of how he had helped rebuild his city from the ruins, proud of the makeshift factory he had been working in since 1952, making binders for school children—an accidental life for a man trained to carve coats of arms into silver plates for princes and kings. "One time, it was a Canadian plane. It crashed just over the river in France. I got my squad together, and we marched across the bridge to capture any survivors. We were just a bunch of boys, fifteen and sixteen years old. When we got there, the whole crew was smashed up and dead, except there was one man missing. We found him in a barn a hundred metres away. We pointed our rifles at him and told him to come with us. I knew a bit of English from school, so I told him, 'The war is over for you.' He just laughed at us. It was so humiliating. He was a great big guy, like a football player, wearing a leather flying jacket and big boots. We didn't even have boots and our jackets couldn't keep out the cold. We didn't know what to do. He was supposed to be our prisoner, but we were the ones who were afraid. Finally, we all got underway, but he made us go in front, and he went in behind, laughing at us all the way over the bridge into Germany and calling out, 'Left! Right! Left! Right!' That was so humiliating."

My father's attempt to free himself from Nazism lasted for decades. When he tried to polish himself up, like Aladdin with his lamp, a shy, quiet boy rose from the spout, a skinny kid with blonde hair and green eyes, scarcely able to raise his voice above a whisper in his father's house. That boy was me. This is the one story my mother and father tell together. In this story, the temperature falls to thirty below zero Fahrenheit. At dusk, between the Penticton airport and the beach at Skaha Lake, the Volkswagen dies. The wind howls off the lake and over the tiny car, piling the snow against the snow fences at the end of the runway. As the red runway light blinks above her on a ten-foot post, my mother sits wrapped in a blanket, while my father walks back to Penticton through the blizzard. There is no other car on the road. There are no houses for miles. It takes him two hours to get back.

That was the day of my mother's twenty-six-week prenatal checkup. At 2:00 the next morning my father woke up. The whole craggy, harshly pruned orchard outside was silting full of snow. Snow was drifting into the driveway and packing down as hard as cement. Prunings raked jagged and black out of the edges of the drifts. The light was on and my mother was at the side of the bed, folding her nightgown into a suitcase.

"My god, what are you doing, woman?"

"It is time to go to the hospital."

"You have two and a half months to go. Go to sleep." And he did.

At 5:30 she was shaking him again. He opened his eyes. She was standing there beside the bed, in her winter coat, a hat pulled down low around her ears, her face red and flushed.

"You'd better warm up the car. We have to get to the hospital soon."

Five minutes later they churned out through the drifts. Their breath froze on the tiny windshield. The fumes of the gas heater flooded the car, without heat. The engine purred, high-pitched. They tore off through the storm to Penticton, at eighty miles per hour. That was top speed for a Volkswagen. Not for that car, though; it had a Porsche engine in it, dumped in sideways and re-geared. They slid out around all the corners and my mother kept crying out, "Slow down!", and my father kept looking over at her as another contraction hit her and she bit her lip and turned white beside him. All he could think of was his child being born there at Yellow Lake. He pressed his foot to the accelerator and drove faster. There was not another car on the road and they outraced their headlights in the early morning dark. The sun was only a faint glow of light over the White Lake hills and the radio telescope as they wound down the old stagecoach hill, then into the pale blue of the Okanagan and the blinking, red aircraft lights lining Skaha Lake.

They arrived at the hospital at 7:00. At 7:20 I was born, tiny, behind a curtain in the emergency room. I screamed. My father took one look at me, wrinkled, purple, with sketchy hair, eyelashes, and fingernails, and said

"That's not my son!" But I was. They named me Harold and Arthur, after two kings, as a spell to keep me living. It worked. Two weeks later they took me home. I was the first baby born in the Similkameen in the Centennial Year of British Columbia. I got a silver cup. The race was won.

Eleven months later, we had candles on our tree, which blazed like stars. This is my first memory. There is nothing in it except that tree, blazing in a dark room. It suddenly appeared in the house and I tottered up to it and fell down and got up and tottered up to it and my brother, almost two years old, came running in, laughing, past the woodstove.

As the years went on, I was socialized in the norms of my mother's country. I dreamed of trees and flowers. I went around with my mother, as she had tea with old ladies in town, collecting flowers for her flower garden. At home later, if I watched closely, I would see eagles, slipping along the cliffs in an updraft.

"You have eagle eyes!" my mother said to me, and I scanned the slopes even more carefully for the slight tear in the blue shadows that betrayed an eagle. I felt like an Indian brave on a rocky outcrop. I lit small fires out of dried tumbleweeds in the yard, and with an old gunnysack from my father's shed, practiced sending up smoke signals.

In the spring of 1969—when I was eleven years old—my father questioned my brother and me every afternoon at length about what had happened that day at school.

"You have to learn something every day," he said. "What did you learn today?" It felt patronizing. "Did anything happen at school?"

I wasn't going to tell him about the girls I had a crush on, the boys who wanted to beat me to a pulp, the boredom.

"Nothing," I said. I thought it odd that my father was in the house asking these questions, instead of being out in the orchard. Even when my brother and I had brought the mumps home from school and his throat swelled up like a balloon, he had just wrapped a cloth around his throat and went out working. I didn't trust this.

He grilled us for a few more minutes. When he was satisfied, he drained his coffee and went back out to work.

Afterwards, I rode my bicycle a mile down the road to move the sprinkler pipes on one of our farthest orchards. Every day an old man stumbled out from his orchard along the way. It looked more like the ruin of an orchard than a producing farm. He lived off of his trees by the grace of God, picking a little fruit here and there, nailing a sign to a post, selling a few boxes of apricots or plums to someone who might stop by. As I passed his orchard, he stopped me on my bike and asked me questions about my father and his business dealings.

That spring, children at school started calling me a Nazi. It felt shameful. I came home the first time and asked my mother what a Nazi was. She went all quiet. "Your grandparents were only Nazis," she said, "because everybody had to be. But that was it."

It didn't help. I still didn't know what a Nazi was.

Years later I was able to put it all together. I went into my mother's kitchen and helped her do the dishes. The orchard spread out in front of us, tossing in the wind. I asked my mother about those years.

"We received threats," she said. "*'You fucking Nazi! Your children will not come home from school.'*" It was written in a childish script. We figured out who it was, but we couldn't prove it. We watched you boys very closely in those years."

I told her about the man who used to stop me on my bike every day when I went past.

My mother looked very pale.

My parents had bought an orchard in a Veteran's Land Act settlement. They were the only German family on that side of the mountain. Everyone else had been in the war. Killing Germans.

Broken by the North, in 1955 Bruno's own search for Canada led him to the German community in the Okanagan, which he had left in '29. He took his shinglebolts along. He left his son behind, speaking West Talk, sitting with Louis Riel over tea. When my father set Bruno up with an orchard in 1963, newly planted among the horsetails of the Similkameen floodlands, Bruno brought the shinglebolts along again, and finally split them to roof his chicken shed and his house—as always, an old log cabin that he spruced up with some plywood and some lathes and a coat of paint on the old floor of the glaciers. Above it, the rock of the Similkameen mountains was sliced off and raw in the thin blue light. Icefalls hung from the lips of the hanging valleys high above the farm and glowed in the last light against the black slopes.

One day every year, the *Tannenzweigen*—fir branches—came from Germany in boxes full of Swiss chocolate and honey cakes. The branches were dried out from the six-week trip on the boat over the Atlantic. When we lifted them out, needles fell off with a soft patter like wooden rain and their scent flooded the room. For a few weeks there in the dark of every winter the house was alive. For a few weeks the old German forest was among us. The dream of the land was so strong that compared to that image of the German forest, the very real forests surrounding us were only pale shadows. For the Christmas of 1969, after thirteen years of marriage, my father took his bride home to Germany at last. My mother's only comment was that it was cold, and the store clerks were bossy. She ate fondue and liqueur chocolates, she complained about the coarse toilet paper, she taught Matthias, the stepfather, how to cook a turkey, and that was that. The turkey was my mother's favourite.

"They cook geese over there, and geese are so fat you have to cook them a lot, to get the fat out, but turkeys have no fat, so when they cooked them like geese, they came out dry and floury. So I showed them how to do it." Very matter of fact. Her only other comment was in mock indignation: "They don't heat their houses! And they expect you to have a shower!" She knew enough about that.

Thirty years later, I sat with my father, listening to Górecki's *Symphony of Sad Songs*—hymns of grief for the dead of Auschwitz building a transcendent church out of sound. We were sitting at my dining room table—made out of English oak by exiled Germans to European models in Pennsylvania in the 1880s. Pieces like that were usually made out of the ship the immigrants came over in—there really was no going back. Before us, the snow was falling, like a thin dusting of flour. The whole time we talked, for hours, only five millimetres collected on the railing of the deck. We drank mineral water, and for a moment, as we talked, and as Górecki's symphony played in the background, euphoric, all the years fell off of my father's shoulders and he was again the short, happy-faced kid he was in Kuppenheim so long ago.

"This is really beautiful music," he said. "Very beautiful."

The lights of the house across the lake were clear in the air. A nearly transparent snow was dropping between the spaces within the air—sifted by the air. The house was filled with the cathedral then, and our bodies as well.

"The thing about this music," I said, "is it's so sure it knows exactly where it's going and it goes there. It's like the way Gould plays Bach: whether it's right or wrong, he gives the illusion of playing the music exactly as he wants, and of leading it somewhere."

"No, there's something else about Gould that you might not know. That's not it about Gould at all. He would sit under the piano and drink coffee. He would have people over and have them play the piano and he would lie under the piano and watch it for hours. So he understood every nuance of it. It wasn't just the music he was playing, but the tool. When he was playing Bach he was playing himself. He slept under the piano! He was in love with it."

The snow was still falling. Dawn Upshaw's voice rode high and clean, while the music that had built the church around her began to beat with her breath. The world was the sound of a human voice, affirming, mourning, loving, crying out.

My father was speaking: "When I was eight years old I went with my mother to Prague, to see my father, for twenty-four hours. We stayed in a fancy hotel, and the whole time my father was distant, and removed.

"For Papa it was not a leave pure and simple. As the head of a military division, he had business to conduct there in Prague and we followed him.

"I was shunted out of the way for the weekend. It was all very awkward. My parents had a hard time speaking. It was very strained.

"On the way back to Baden Baden on the train, I asked Mama, 'What does Papa think about the war?' and she said the only harsh thing I have ever heard her say in my life: 'He thinks they are all assholes.'

"What my Dad did in the war I just don't know.

"When I was a kid it was 'Children should be seen and not heard,' and a lot of the time not even seen.

"He was a bastard, but when he came back from the war, he was also afraid.

"Those movies they showed us after the war, of the death camps, those got me really angry. There they were all the time telling me that I should feel guilty for what happened. They told me that I should be ashamed. Me. I was just a kid. I had absolutely nothing to do with any of that. I told myself that I was not going to feel responsible for any of it, ever."

The black window suddenly splashed over me, and the music built up its great cathedral of sound around us. Dawn Upshaw began to sing:

> My son, my chosen and beloved,
> Share your wounds with your mother.

> And because, dear son, I have always carried you in my
>   heart,
> And always served you faithfully,
> Speak to your mother, to make her happy,
> Although you are already leaving me, my cherished hope.

The air was a nearly transparent snow. The house was filled with the cathedral now, and our bodies as well.

> Where has he gone
> My dearest son?
> Perhaps during the uprising
> The cruel enemy killed him.
>
> Ah, you bad people
> In the name of God, the most Holy,
> Tell me, why did you kill
> My son?

The snow was fog. Dawn Upshaw's voice had become a cathedral. The whole tonal structure flooded around us and through us, like a hologram. Every atom of the house and every atom of our bodies vibrated. The light from the windows and the sound of the music floated out into the night for a brief distance around the house, as if the house was a ship anchored in a safe harbour on a dark northern sea. All around it in the darkness the snow vanished unseen into the water.

Family is for me a deep irony. As I listen again to this prayer for the peace of the souls tortured in the centuries-long Polish struggle for independence, I know that this freedom was freedom from my family and from the images of my family.

Thomas shares the burden. He grew up in Freiburg, the city that tortured Jews and burnt witches, the cathedral and university town, the town of the Gauleiters on the edge of the Black Forest, where the forest water runs golden in the open stone troughs rimming the streets. When I was learning to tell the difference between fruit buds and leaf buds at my father's side on the Similkameen benchlands, Thomas was growing to find it physically painful to listen to German folk music, and learned to live instead through the cultural artifacts that have been made out of that past: art, history, and philosophy.

In 1986, outside a used bookstore behind the Freiburg cathedral, Thomas flipped open an old magazine, then tossed it to me: 1943. The closing article was a piece on barbed wire, illustrated with pen-and-inks of Texas cowboys straight out of Karl May, fencing in wild, long-horned cattle. They were followed by broad, flat-washed etchings of trenches on the Eastern Front and endless tangles of wire. The tone was balanced, and conciliatory. My grandmother's patients read this magazine on the hallstand sixty years ago, under that big picture of Hitler. Thomas laughed. "Barbed wire used to be an important part of our national culture!"

Thomas and I stand before the same destructive act. The beauty of the shale cones, basalt columns, and cool green orchards of the Similkameen of my childhood is nothing, for between me and that land stands a leering challenge, suggesting that even the attempt to approach the land is coloured with repression, violence, and hate, that these are the direct consequence of 'land.'

That day in 1986, Thomas and I paced together through the musty hall of the cathedral. The arching roof was filled with the imposing silence of the simultaneous presence and absence of God in this world. Our footsteps echoed, throwing us back on ourselves and giving us nothing in our selves, nothing at all but that building which posed the paradox. Tall white candles, bought at the postcard kiosk across the square for one Deutschmark, burned, fragile, in long brass racks, in the dark by the tower door.

I have learned to dip my lips to the little moon-ships bobbing on the night-river. I have watched red-headed fish thrash out of the winter mud under the creaking ice as I walked over it, sending long cracks racing ahead the length of the pool. I have held my hands as numb as roots in the wind. These experiences and skills for interfacing with the earth are a form of power, but it is not a power that will allow either Thomas or me to return to our grandfather's city. The whole dream, the whole attempt to live in this earth, has been discredited for the two generations since our grandfather's time—and for eight, twelve, sixteen more before that—by the horror of what was done in its name.

I have a picture from the first day of the Great War. I found it along with the postcard from Werben and a collection of holiday postcards sent from Russia before the Revolution. Each postcard had its stamp torn off—that betrayal. The British Columbia government had just ransacked the old man's house in Naramata, looking for anything of value that it could sell to raise money to pay his keep at the Haven Hill Retirement Centre—the old colonial hospital among its acacia trees on the hill above Penticton. The social workers would be back the next day to rummage again through the drawers, dumping out the rat nests, piling the books in the middle of the floor, and carting the furniture away. The hospital was built on the hill, so that the contagion would flow downhill. This was colonial architecture. This is how you treated malaria in Uganda and the Sudan, where matted reeds clogged the rivers and men went mad. To the social workers, the postcards on the floor were useless old junk.

The postcard I found is a sepia-brown group of soldiers of the Imperial

German Army lined up on a street in Magdeburg. They are well fed, bursting at the seams, serious, marching off to the train station to embark for Belgium. Many of them wear handlebar moustaches. They look uncomfortable in their stiff caps. It is a proud photograph. Scrawled over it are the words, in ink, in a thin, spidery hand, "In front of our cigar store!"

Forty-nine years after that, in 1963, Auguste Leipe died in Magdeburg, in an old POW camp made into an old folks' home, when I was five years old and running down the dirt driveway in our orchard in British Columbia as pink peach petals tore off in the wind and lay on the puddles reflecting the sky. I was singing as I ran, belting out my modernity at the top of my lungs, announcing my belonging to the future and severing my ties to the past: "She loves you, yeah! yeah! yeah! She loves you, yeah! yeah! yeah!" I didn't know shit.

When Auguste struggled into Magdeburg, she had nothing left. All her possessions were abandoned in one ditch or another between there and Breslau, along with all the heirlooms of the other millions who fled with her: wedding dresses, Meissen and Rosenthal china, brass mirrors, woodstoves, ivory beer steins, hand-carved games of chess. Most likely, somewhere, in one of those ditches, soaked and swollen with rain, lay the family Bible. That is the one book that can make any definitive sense of what are otherwise just stories, the lies we tell ourselves to keep our chins up.

My friend Paul has a Bible quite likely just like Auguste's. It is also an East European artifact. Even falling to bits, its spine cracked, pages crumbling from being thumbed late at night with greasy, farmer's fingers, it is a masterful example of the printer's art. In its black leather calfskin cover, with its big woodcuts black as night and fear and its chunky, carved lettering, it speaks from the heart of death and propriety. This is not a Bible of John the Baptist, the holy fool baptizing travellers while grasshoppers chirred in the scrub along the River Jordan. This is not a

Bible of John the Apostle, who wrote of a God creating the universe out of Love. This is an Old Testament Bible, a Bible of Judgement and Fear, of hands chopped off of thieves and eyes gouged out of the head with a thorn. It is a Bible about reality, a Bible from a country that had seen war ride over it with a death's head, and had seen its children smitten with the black plague. This is not a Renaissance Bible, like the one King James gave to the English. It is a horror.

Paul got his dose of reality from his grandfather, who had started out his life as a German farmer along the Volga. Descended from one of those tens of thousands of Germans lured east by Peter the Great to bring wealth to his land by turning it into an industrious farming paradise, Paul's grandfather got the impetus to leave Russia when Stalin—who had upgraded Peter's program into communes and five-year plans—starved him out. Hanging on until the bitter end, Paul's grandfather was presented with one final choice: use all of his remaining money to bribe his way out from the black steel bars of a jail cell in Moscow, trusting a crooked jailor to be honest about a bribe, or to die that night. There were dozens in that cell. Most died.

When Paul's grandfather got to Canada, he went farming on the prairies. He was back again on the land. "Ah, the soil in the Ukraine," he said to me in 1981, as I pruned the apple tree in his backyard in Rutland, just down the hill from where Bruno and Martha put on their Steinbeck costumes back in the summer of 1929. Bees flitted from pink blossom to pink blossom. Next to us, the raspberries were budding out. The sun was warm as wood on our cheeks. Paul's grandfather spoke in a slow, solid, old-man's voice, a farmer's voice. You hear that voice so seldom anymore, but it was very distinctive, living in the vowels, clipping off the consonants, but most of all speaking very, very slowly. It was a voice prepared to wait. No one but a farmer could speak like that. "The soil was deep and dark. There were no rocks. You could travel a hundred miles and not find a single one. Not like here in Canada.

The prairies are full of rocks. The soil here is very poor."

It is just such a Bible that Auguste threw into the ditch. When you walk five hundred miles, and everyone is dying around you, and planes are diving at you and the bullets are spitting up on the road, you learn very quickly what is worth keeping and what you have to throw away.

I'd like to hold that Bible some day. I'd like to think that Auguste hadn't thrown it into the ditch, that she had left it behind in her apartment instead, that it wound up in a used bookstore in Poland, and is still sitting there, on a low, dusty shelf in a back room, behind stacked-up copies of *Pravda* and remaindered copies of the collected poems of Pope John Paul II. I dream that if I went there, to the Wrocław that Breslau has become, and scoured the streets and back alleys of the city, on both sides of the Oder, I would find Auguste Leipe's Bible.

What I have instead is a tantalizing, even maddening, taste. I have a story. This story is about Alfred, the crazy one, the one with half of the back of his head missing, merci beaucoup, playing jack-in-the-box with his wife and the insane asylum in Sweden. Alfred saw Auguste's Bible in 1914, just before he was shipping out to the Front. A Bible like that was not something you let your kids get their hands on, though. A Bible like that was as heavy as God's Word. You kept it under lock and key. In the back, between the last page of Revelation and the flowery gold leaf of the endpapers you laid every important family document, and they were with God, and God kept them safe and their memory was God's. Alfred remembered what he had seen in the back of that Book, though: hundreds of years of birth certificates, marriage certificates, and private letters, stamped with the seal of the King of Prussia, with red wax and red ribbons. As Alfred remembered them—with only half a head—they talked about a grant of land in return for service given; they were letters among equals. Alfred asked Auguste about that. He asked her, "What is all that?" and her answer as the keeper of the Bible, as the keeper of God's Word, was that he was too young to know about any of that. She slammed the book shut and put it away. She was quite agitated. That was the last the matter was ever discussed. But what does Alfred know really, and how much can his memories be trusted? He is the man with a hole in the back of his head. Who knows what leaked out? Or what leaked in.

—

The stories, mind you, refuse to go away. Years later, they showed up on the train in Smithers, underneath Hudson's Bay Glacier. The railroad had originally announced it was going to build its roundhouse on the dry, deep gravel at McAllister, up the line. By the time the land speculators got finished with McAllister, however, the railroad declined to buy them out. It wasn't an issue of being able to afford it. It was the principle of the thing. Four of a Kind beats a Full House. Hence the swamp. The Canadian Pacific Railroad drove piles down a hundred and fifty feet and perched the roundhouse on top of them. They filled in the swamp—sort of—and built Smithers on that. It was as pretty as Banff.

The stories came in the form of my great-aunt Martha, Bruno and Alfred's sister. She had come a long way from that lacy white dress in that dress-up picture in a photography shop in Breslau when she was sixteen—that high point of family pride when Alfred and Bruno were shipping off to save the Fatherland. The reunion in Smithers in 1953, those long thirty-nine years later, was damned close to rock bottom. Bruno had been farming up there in the shadow of the glacier for six years—if you can call it farming. Life was brutal.

Martha, Joe, and Hans were expecting a joyful reunion, with crisp linen on the beds and fresh flowers on the morning washstand and rose petals floating in a basin. Martha was expecting a curving driveway lined with lindens, fields golden with wheat or dark with sugarbeets stretching into the distance, outbuildings closing off a farmyard, buildings for the hired workers, servants at the dinner table dressed in black, and a position in the community—"Just like we used to have in the family," said Martha, "back before the family fell on hard times." I think she'd seen Auguste's Bible.

My grandmother had warned Martha over and over again that she could expect only a hard life in the bush, with no relief from the work. That's all they shared, too—a far cry from the photo I have of them at Christmas in 1926: Bruno, Alfred, their sister Martha, and their respective husbands and wives sit around a small table in front of a curtained window; my grandfather has a ukulele and my grandmother holds a guitar. Happiness is theirs. Alfred also looks festive, and his wife has a wry grin, while Martha and Joe appear stern and conservative. During those years they would all take the train for four hours down to Schneekopf in the Mountains of Giants on the Czechoslovakian frontier, walk up the slope for two hours, and ski back down for fifteen minutes.

When the Silesians stepped off the train into the willow swamps on the lower side of Smithers, the mountain loomed above them, its peak shrouded in blowing snow that was forming out of the air. A cold wind blew down over the mud of Main Street. Martha had completely misunderstood. When Bruno had written that he owned a farm in Canada, she had interpreted that in the only way open to her experience, although Bruno was just trying to impress the Canadian government enough with his solvency to let him bring her over.

The story goes something like this: a wealthy (or formerly wealthy) and powerful (or old and militarily powerful, that is to say well-connected) noble family fled the French Revolution (or earlier), for the Kingdom of Prussia (or Bohemia—borders changed), where they threw themselves on the mercy of (it seems, their friend) the king. That is sketchy, but reasonably clear. From there on in, however, speculation plays an ever greater role. There are two possibilities: first, that the king of Prussia (or Bohemia—borders change) did set them up, either on a pension, or on a piece of land in the new colonies along the Elbe, where the Leipes took up military service, and for which they were later rewarded with a noble title for their military successes; second, that they had fled France because they had already rendered those services (revolutions, guillotines)—in this case, the king invested them as peers of the realm as soon as they showed up at his door. Either way, the result is the same: political power, a close relationship with the king, a noble title, and a rich plot of land in Silesia, with fields of grain and peasant women starching the tablecloths. If this was true, in its hour of need the family had fallen on good fortune. I can't get out of my head the humiliating degree of ingratiation and bootlicking that would have been required to bring it off.

—

My mother was fortunate to have come from a working-class family, with very clear-cut ideas of social belonging. It helped her come unscathed through the dreams of former grandeur. "Tante was making it all up," she told me, and for her that was the end of the discussion.

—

The French Revolution also came home to roost in the tiny town of March, where Thomas lives, in the Rhine plain between the Black Forest and the Grauburgunder vineyards of the Kaiserstuhl. Tucked into a wall behind the church (sixteenth-century) is a cenotaph, in honour of the marching boys of 1914–1918 in their field grey: "They fought for the Fatherland; they died as heroes." There are ninety names on the list; the Fatherland must have pretty well cleaned March out. Back then, the town had maybe thirty houses, clustered below a hill of hard volcanic stone covered with glacial sand.

"They used to grow tobacco here," Thomas told me, pointing out a drying shed behind the city hall—a tall, narrow building, covered with slats. "It died out two generations ago. They rolled cigars. They weren't as good as Cuban ones, but March cigars were pretty famous."

"Maybe it was the war," I say. "Ninety boys dead, that's a lot."

"Oh, I don't think it was that."

I dunno. Whole stretches of British Columbia were completely cleared out by the war and never got back on their feet. You drive past them now and wonder how anyone could have thought of settling in such forlorn places: a few house trailers in Spences Bridge, a grand old courthouse in Clinton; Walhachin, Canoe, Invermere, Proctor, Harrop, Bowser, Needles—the list goes on: what looks like a failure of colonialism is really a failure of Empire, the ghost of a ditch filled with mustard gas cut across a boggy field in Flanders. The village of March looked like that to me. If they had been all the wrong boys, the ones who knew how to roll a good cigar, let's say, whole families would have died out by about 1939, and that would have been that.

Farther up the hill, Thomas and I came upon an old teahouse and tilted red sandstone statues covered with ivy, then out onto open fields of withered corn and mangels, dying in drought. The distant sky was brown with heat. I read the plaque in the teahouse: the castle was founded by a family fleeing the French Revolution. They must have been a sentimental lot, choosing this hill as close as they could get to their old country without actually touching it. On the hill, they built a miniature Versailles, with formal paths and stations of the Cross. They were trying to save a lost civilization. It gave me pause.

—

My uncle Gerd came the other way to the Rhine. He grew up in East Prussia, on the Russian Frontier. When he was five years old, he fled on foot in advance of the Russian army. The images of planes diving on the streams of refugees is still alive in him. I asked him whether he remembered a lot of people carrying stuff like family Bibles. He laughed.

"If there had been such a Bible," he said, trying to shift my thinking

Journeys Through a Dark Century ~ 297

to something useful as the big Black Forest clouds poured overhead along the edge of a weather front and a nightingale hopped from limb to limb in his apple tree, "it would have been one of the first things to go." Light and shadow tumbled over us. As he spoke, his hands moved and described his thoughts. "You just couldn't afford to carry anything that wasn't absolutely essential. All kinds of things were thrown into the ditch, or just dropped at the side of the road. You couldn't keep them."

So much for that.

Gerd had Mozart cranked up on the stereo—*Don Giovanni*—and the sliding glass door open so that the music could pour out over the grass. All the time that we talked, he kept time with his fingers on the white tablecloth. I asked him about the noble title and the papers that Private Alfred Leipe saw in the back of his mother's terrible black Bible.

"If you scrape deep enough in any German family," he said through the strains of Mozart, "you will find a castle, and a noble title, *and* a tragic story of how it was all lost. It is impossible not to. Every family has stories like that. They all use them to show how hard life is in the present, how it should have been better to them."

"Are they true?" I asked.

"Sure!"

Nine years later, I went with Gerd to the monastery of Maulbronn.

"Look at those windows lining the courtyard," he said. "The monks had a rule: no two things in the monastery would be the same. That first window on the left is Romanesque, but you can see in the next one that the round arch is becoming quite stylized, and the one next is pure gothic. This is where the gothic started." Gerd is excited and, although puffing hard with the exertion, is racing ahead from chamber to chamber. I stumble after him, barely able to take it all in before he wanders out of earshot and I have to find him by the serpentine echoes of his voice. In the room where the monks ate, in silence as they did everything in the monastery, I have a chance to turn around and around as the sound carries perfectly through the forest of pillars holding up the roof. The earliest capitals crowning the pillars are crudely cut, but the later ones are refined. Each one is carved with a different set of vines and leaves: the birth of the Rococo. Gerd drags me over to a pillar bathed in light from the windows. "This is why they call the wine they grow here *Elfenfinger* wine," he laughs. "The working monks would be half-starved, overworked, and in a daze from having to say their prayers every four hours around the clock. The administrative monks had it somewhat better. The Abbot would pour some of the local wine into this basin set into the pillar (he touches it), and it would dribble down the crack (he traces the crack). The monks were allowed to touch the holy wine with their fingers and lick it off. They said it tasted so good that it was 'eleven finger wine'! It started to get out of hand; the abbots had to limit the amount of wine they were pouring down that crack. That's how hard they had it here then."

Over lunch, Gerd poured me some *Elfenfinger* wine. It was sour. If you didn't serve it ice cold, it would tear the lining out of your throat, all the way down.

—

Back in 1995, we found a family of "lost" Leipes. For us it was like finding an abandoned city in the empty quarter of Brazil, where explorers disappear without a trace. These lost Leipes weren't exactly from the other side of the River Oder—that would have been a real find—but they *are* cousins, four times removed. That's good enough for two families that had always thought they were the end of the line. Ironically, the link that closed the family circle was Alfred's letter concerning the German post office. Wild.

The Leipe story starts off like an old Western, in black and white—a saga about four brothers making their fortunes across the West, say: a cattle rustler, a gunman, a shopkeeper, and a sheriff with a tragic past. Reasonable enough: Westerns, after all, came out of the transplantation of Jewish culture from Kattowitz, Riga, and Lödz to New York, and from New York to the Hollywood desert: the stories of John Wayne and Roy Rogers and the Cartwright Family are straight out of Silesia and Poland and Latvia—the lost brother, the wise rabbi, the dirt-poor shoemaker with the beautiful daughter—just with cactus and Ponderosa Pine and rattlesnakes instead of Cossacks and borsch and fog rolling in from the Vistula. The Cossacks, mind you, came through hardly scathed: the parts of the czar's soldiers with their horses and their tall black boots, stomping out villages for the Empire, were given to Geronimo and his braves, whooping out of dry coulees as John Wayne hid behind rocks.

Bruno thought so little of his cousins—or their four fathers—he never mentioned them. Having spent my childhood curled up on the floor, below the level of Bruno's pipe smoke, while my head spun and he talked communist theory until the cows came home, I'd bet my last shekel that his silence was based on political grounds: one of those cousins *was* enough of a Nazi to hold an Ancestral Passport. Those were thick documents, listing fathers' and mothers' birth, christening, and death, and fathers' mothers and fathers' and mothers' mothers and fathers, in proof that a family was Aryan for at least five generations. Not everyone got one of those babies. Those who did worked for the government. Dr. Rhenisch had an Ancestral Passport—the Jews absent, because the women of the family had married them, and so had flown the coop, thank God, but still rumoured: Karl Marx for one. Ironically, once Silesia was lost, once Berlin was flattened back to the brick age and rebuilt as steel and glass, after all baptismal records went up in flame, those passes are all that are left of public record.

Frank went back to Leipe-Petersdorf and found the old family house right where Bruno had left it, still sheathed in black slate, sitting alone on a corner of a forlorn and lifeless street.

"It is the most depressing place I've ever seen," he said. "Nothing has changed since the end of the war." He clenched his teeth. His face trembled. He spat the words out. "Nothing." He fixed his eyes on me. "The bullet holes have still not been repaired in the walls. Nothing has been painted. If a house was blown up, it has not been rebuilt. Factories are still standing, their windows empty where the bombs blew them out. The people all wear the same black clothes, and the same hats. They walk along without smiling. I stood on the corner where my mother's house was. All down the street the houses stand against each other: number 14, number 15, number 16, and there, on the corner, where number 17 should have been, where my mother lived on the second floor, there's only a vacant lot. They have done nothing. When the bomb fell on Mom's building, it blew out the windows in number 16 across the street. They are still boarded up. They have done nothing." He paused for emphasis. "Nothing."

The lost Leipes had also heard stories of the family's noble past: tales of betrayal, a saga of a slow falling-off from wealth and prestige to sheer penury—first removed from ownership of the land, then from a peasant life on it, and finally to the urban working-class life of the late industrial revolution, eating a few burnt potatoes from a cast iron pot on a cast iron stove, cooked over dirty coal.

They traced names on a map: Leipe, Leip, Lip, and imagined the family stretching back to the castle Czech Lipa north of Prague, and from there to Imperial Rome. According to their research, Czech Lipa was founded by a Roman. When the Empire fell, he stayed on, and created Europe—a kind of small-scale Byzantine emperor, continuing the work of the Empire long after the Empire itself had collapsed.

The library that contains these stories consists of one book: the Bible Auguste maybe threw into a ditch back in 1945 when the war drove her and her carefully folded documents out. This time, there were no French with whips and there was no Freikorps. Instead of guns in their luggage, people had only the clothes on their backs.

The Marshall Plan, the Red Cross, the Displaced Person's Camps, the Wirtschaftswunder, the Cold War, and the terrible memory of the extermination camps, all came together to me on the edge of the beech trees on a hill above Karlsruhe, with its radiating streets below laid out like Versailles, all converging on Karl the king's castle—his rest, his keep, his country barracks. He would have gone hunting up on the hills where I sat on Sybille's terrace on Hoover Street, in an old Red Cross development now used to house academics who have come over from the East. The flimsy umbrella gave little shade. We drank strawberries soaked in champagne, a delicacy from Silesia, and ate turkey and macaroni—a casserole out of *Redbook*. We talked about art. My sparring partners were a retired nuclear engineer from Leipzig, and a retired Coca-Cola printer from the Ruhr. It was a family event.

Mr. Coca Cola: "No one should be allowed to stage Goethe in anything other than period costume, exactly as Goethe would have done it. Otherwise they should not be allowed to call it Goethe. The things they do on stage are not art. One must show respect for tradition. If one is going to create, one must know everything that has ever been written, and then add to that."

I was pouring back considerable quantities of strawberries, because it was so damned hot. Mr. Coca Cola was trying to make the point that the new Germany, the one in which people pretended, poorly, that there was no West or East, needed to become German again by taking on upper-middle-class values. He was pointing out that there should be no revolution in art, that cultural continuity was the key to the survival of Germany. He wanted, in other words, to replace the communist ruins of the East and the slapdash American industrial cities of the West with German elegance.

Mr. Uranium: "Exactly." He was sounding this conversation's double-bass.

Mr. Canada: "No one has ever created anything by following that principle. You must be allowed to invent." I had just been through the museum mill: German, Egyptian, Roman, Greek. In Natzweiler-Struthof, though, where one night 150 members of the local Resistance were shot one by one in a little room to the side of the furnace—just down the hall from the dissection chamber with the tidy porcelain trough for the blood—those museums made sense: this was Rome.

It was the dissecting table that really got me mad. From the sarcophagi of Egypt, with the Pharaoh's relief carved in stone on the lid, to Roman sarcophagi, with the deceased's painting on the lid, to the knights of Cologne, Speyer and Eisenach, carved in relief on the lids of their coffins, to the bishops of Cologne and the saints of St. Gallen set in gold cases, their bones decorated with jewels, to that damned dissecting table in Struthof: the line of design was pure and unbroken. The third-century Syrian pedant Iamblichus talks about the mysteries of the Egyptians, how God is present in perfection, how the more perfect an artistic—sculptural—shape, the more of God is present in it: it radiates God like Radio Free Europe somewhere off the coast of Holland, rocking in a storm, while the BBC tries to jam it from the Dover Cliffs. In the Greco-Egyptian Museum in Berlin, I had seen God in sculptural shapes like that, and saw how they had changed, from the cube that was lightly carved into a seated form of the dead, to the cube that was removed from around the dead but still projected from him, and then to that damned dissection table with its white porcelain tiles and green stand, in a bright room full of windows next to the jail, with its solitary confinement cells, with their tiny doors full of slits. In Natzweiler-Struthof, there was no longer any need for any honouring of the dead, any magical object to carry the body to the land of the dead: the memorial, the engine of god, had become the place where a real, living body, could be dissected, until its soul left it and it was thrown into the camp cesspit.

Don't get me wrong. This is not a German problem. This is everyone's problem. Every day, every hour, we have to return to a culture, and a language, that is rebuilding the camps in its mind. It's not that Mr. Coca Cola and Mr. Uranium are Nazis. They aren't. They are decent, generous, talented, and loving men. The culture, though, our inheritance, which has officially suppressed, cynically manipulated, or fed off of the lives of people who have given their histories and bodies to the earth, is another thing.

Twenty years ago, my cousin Andrea left the city of Zurich and moved out into a small town beyond the suburbs, where she has raised four children, at times in an abandoned factory and at times up in the mountains in an old farmhouse without running water or power. She calls it her Heidi house. The factory was so they could leave the System behind and live simply and lightly on the earth without paying taxes. The house up on the mountain was so that their children could attend the village school. When I last visited, Andrea's daughters, Bärblin and Cleo, were twelve and fifteen. They wanted to go to university, but because of their rural schooling they did not get good enough marks on their exams to enter academic high school. In an attempt to bring themselves back into the twenty-first century, they planned to spend a year taking the train every day into Zurich, to attend a special school, where they would study daily to retake their exam. Their future depended upon it: all job placements in Switzerland fill the needs of the state. To the state it does not matter whether Andrea's daughters live and breathe an academic life: it gets the workers it needs, period.

I wanted to take them home.

It's an old story. When my mother was in elementary school in Smithers, in 1947 and 1948, she spent half of every day in Grade 8 teaching the Grade 1 class, because she was the only student in her grade, there were few materials for her, and about the only career open for a bright girl was teaching anyway. When I was in high school in Keremeos in 1974 and 1975, she fought unsuccessfully for some quality of programming. That was the year I taught my Grade 12 math teacher calculus—and trigonometry (and in fact the whole course). He had the answer key, with every step of every answer for every problem, and still could not make sense of it.

"Well, boys," he said one day, setting down his book at the front of the room. "What did you get for question number 3? I couldn't figure it out." I had spent three hours the night before on that damned number 3. I showed him. One day he came in, opened his book to the chapter on calculus and said, "Boys, I haven't studied calculus since 1938, and I wasn't much good at it then. You'll have to be patient." I ignored him.

He was also my chemistry teacher. One day he interrupted my attempts at making spatial models of atomic structures by showing me how to make elephants and giraffes instead, and gave me a mark for successfully completing the lab assignment that he had interrupted with his zoo. In the same year, my law teacher cancelled our law course halfway through the term because too many of the students were failing. He gave the course a less threatening name, with half the assignments and no final exam.

When my daughter Anassa went through high school in 2002 and 2003, her social studies teacher covered the First World War by telling his students that the battle of Stalingrad was an important battle in that war, and covered the Second World War by showing them the movie *Saving Private Ryan*. I saw red. I went in and talked to him that day.

"How is it?" I asked him, as he sat behind the desk in his Vancouver Canucks hockey jersey, "that twenty Americans, who had been in the war for a few days, could defeat one of the elite regiments of the German army, who had been fighting for five years? How is it that every American shot killed a German, but those Germans had to shoot two hundred bullets to kill a single American? That isn't history. It's propaganda."

I was beginning to sound like Bruno.

Every time our family gathers around a dining table, whether it is our table on Christmas Eve, with Riesling in the glasses and a goose on the platter and the girls sparkling in their dresses, or my parents' farmyard kitchen table, with tomato-barley soup and warm bread, my father holds up his hands to either side and says, "Excuse me," quietly, if someone has already started to eat, and laughs lightly. We then put down the serving bowls and our forks and spoons and knives, stop pouring the wine or apple juice, and hold hands in a circle around the table. Then my father lifts his hands and says, "Seid fröhlich!" and lowers them, and we follow suit around the table, and let go. *Seid fröhlich* means "Be joyful" in German. In our family, we don't say Grace, but we do say that prayer.

I always assumed it was a German custom, but when five-year-old Anassa tried it around Eberhard's table in the Ruhr, he assured me that it most certainly was not. He had never heard of such a thing.

"Perhaps it is something from the East," I suggested.

"No. No one does it. It's not German."

It was a puzzle, which was only solved for me in the fall of 2003 in Castlegar. I was having lunch with Nora, the daughter of Fritz and Trude Pruesse, who had shared Bruno and Martha's first year in the Okanagan, and who had taken pity on them when, shell-shocked and impoverished by the North, they had come down to Penticton in 1955, on the first holiday in their lives since the kayak trip down the Rhine thirty years before. By that time, Trude's mother, Omi, or Granny, was living with them above Skaha Lake. The three women wasted no time: they got together and decided that it would be a wonderful thing if Bruno and Martha moved south to manage Fritz and Trude's orchard, to save them from their Northern folly. Fritz could even build them a little house on the lake. By this time, Bruno was obviously not in disagreement. Fritz even built a little house for him overlooking the lake, and gave him the title of "hired hand."

"Bruno was such a poetic man," Nora said. "Do you have any of his poetry?"

"I do," I said.

Nora laughed. "We really enjoyed having Bruno and Martha around." She pronounced it "Martte." Then she reached out for us all to join hands. We did, and she said "Seid fröhlich!" and we dropped our hands and the meal commenced.

Now it was my turn to laugh. "Where on earth did that come from?" I asked. "I've been trying to find out where it comes from for years."

"You do it in your family, too?" She beamed. "That's wonderful. It was my father. He had been reading Socrates—or was it Plato? No, I think it was Socrates. And he read that Socrates used to do that with his disciples. Before they ate anything, he would have them hold hands and say a prayer to Joy. My father thought that was a great idea, so he just translated it into German!"

— —

Memory is important. Mr. Coca Cola got that much right. On the shore of Lake Geneva with my cousin David and his friend Werner, Anassa and I watched swans swimming on the still blue water. Very few people were out. It was just too hot. Werner is a Maitre D' in a big hotel in Zurich, and a member of David's guild. These are old Zurich families. Werner served us strawberries and coffee on his balcony overlooking the lake. As the swans swam past, and the cool of the water flowed over us, I told him my dream for Dresden.

"It is a ruin," I said. "Have you seen it?"

He nodded. The Alps rose up behind him in a blue wall. "Yes, it is terrible."

"I have a plan," I said. I was pacing my thoughts to my footsteps. "If you rebuilt it with glass, you'd draw the power back out of the river, into the city. It would come alive again, but you'd have to do it with glass. You'd have to have the same houses that were there before, the tall Renaissance houses with their sculptured doorways, and the narrow alleys and winding streets. The place would be full of the sun and open to the weather. When a cloud passed by, it would flood through all the rooms of the houses. When it rained, the houses would be water. You could even bring in the designs from the Meissen China, little floral elements of coloured glass, for accents. You could bring in a lot of elements from china."

"Do you know Sir Norman Foster?" asked Werner, putting a hand on my arm, interrupting me. "He rebuilt the Bundestag in Berlin. Have you seen it?"

I stopped walking and turned to face him. He was outlined in shadow against the tiny blue waves of the lake. I could make out his lips, but his eyes were dark, unreadable.

"No," I said.

"Well," said Werner. He had caught my excitement. "He won a design award to build it. It had been destroyed in the war, and the Communists left it to sit there for fifty years. His design to rebuild it was to make it completely out of glass. It would be vulnerable to the air, and transparent."

"But that's just what I thought!"

Werner smiled. The waves lapped gently at the stone of the promenade. "You should go and see it," he said, softly. "It is the only way," and he stressed that, "the only way to honour the destruction that came from the bombers, that came from the air."

I saw myself walking through those glass streets in Dresden, that city that now has all its suburbs but no city at the core. The streets were narrow, twisted this way and that; the houses were bright, like a Venetian glass necklace, or a cut-glass chandelier at a fancy ball. At night the streets were dark, while the houses poured up into the sky with light. Flowers bloomed inside the glass.

We passed into the shade of a plane tree, planted in 1903. "I think if you can make a completely new city," I said to Werner, "then you can get past the German problem of trying to put the country back together again as it was in 1914. That can't be the only way there is to be German. There's too much history there. It has to be something new. It has to be something that people build together." We passed out from underneath the plane tree. The glare of the sun off of the cobbles made me squint. The world was white. I stopped and turned to face Werner. "Tourists would come by the millions Dresden advertises itself as the Florence on the Elbe, but it's just a joke. This would be real. People would come."

"I'd go," said Werner.

We walked on, along the promenade, David, Werner, Anassa, and I, past black iron statues of Miles Davis and Sammy Davis Junior and Louis Armstrong, set against the glare of light over the alps. As a morning breeze ruffled lightly through our loose shirts, I realized what had gone wrong with our conversations in Dresden and Karlsruhe: I had been speaking as a Canadian, but Eberhard was reading me as an American. I was offering a third way, neither the return to the past, which was all that was left of European Europe, nor an American rush into the untethered future with an axe to the ropes and a pole to push you off of the dock, but a third way, a middle way: growth with honour, tradition not with the freedom that can lead only to the exploitation of tradition, but with the freedom to re-imagine, which is what a whole generation had struggled to give to me, as the only kind of freedom that could be passed on. It was the first time in my life I have felt Canadian. I was proud to have that place within me, and very, very sad. It hurt me to see Eberhard so conflicted, and to be able to do so little for him. Canada is not, after all, running the world. America is. Against that rush to the future, Eberhard was setting the past, and clinging to it, like a drowning man in the North Atlantic as the Titanic went down and he started to grow very, very cold.

Anassa and I continued our tour across Switzerland. Up above Lake Constance, in the Abbey Church in St. Gallen, we found Adam mounted on one wall of the nave, staring across the congregation and the arches decorated with thousands of stylized golden apples—a yellow, Swiss variety called *Glockenäpfel*, "bell apples," by the looks of them—towards Eve, on the opposite wall. The happy couple were carved from a light, polished wood—beautiful. As I took notes of the stations of the Cross around the perimeter of the church, my cousin Sabine, an evangelical pastor, sat on the pews, in silence.

We came back at 1:00 for a guided tour. The guide was about eighty years old, spoke, or rather sang, Swiss German, and sounded as if he had lost part of his tongue to a stroke. In the church, for some reason, his voice echoed twice for every word he spoke. It was as if there were three of him singing at the same time. It was hard to follow. I had to consciously block out the echoes. Sabine came up beside me as we waited for the rest of the group to file down the narrow stairs to the crypt, where the Irish monk, St. Gallen himself, was buried. He had come in the year 612, and only stuck around because he was too sick to leave. He stayed for twenty years. He couldn't have been that sick.

"Do you go to church?" Sabine asked me quietly, from over my shoulder.

"You know," I said, "I tried that. If I lived in Europe, I'm sure I would, but in Canada the relationship between Church and culture is completely different than it is here. I tried when I was twelve years old. It was so painful. I couldn't stand it. I have had to find my own way."

"We all have to find our own way," she said quietly. "As it says in the Gospels: if you look, you will find the truth."

—

My way is to make a city of glass out of the ruins. Water and light move up into the branches of the city and bring it to life.

You are standing in that city.

—

I have a picture. We are in the mountain house above Wald. Andrea and me are drinking tea—it has taken her a half hour to light the stove, and five minutes to slip out to the garden and pick mint leaves for the pot.

"I am terrible with this stove!" she laughs. "I usually get someone else to light it for me."

I have been watching Anassa and Cleo convince each other to play music together. Cleo gets out the sheet music, and lays it on the piano; Anassa sits on the stool. As Andrea comes in with the teapot, Cleo unpacks her viola, looks over Anassa's shoulder, and begins to play.

They play for half an hour, Bartók and Mozart, in half-tempo, as they grow used to each other's musical voices. They play so earnestly—Anassa's sweet piano fingering, halting on the chords, and Cleo's strong, broken voice on the viola come together to form a music that keeps Andrea and me captivated. Something that was always apart has come together. Something has been made whole. We both notice that. I catch Andrea's eyes, and they are smiling—dark eyes glinting with devilishness.

There is a strength there that takes me off guard, but I recognize it, and I respond to it.

There are two types of men: those who believe in time and those who take up space. There are no other possibilities. I have known this for many years. I just didn't know how deeply, irretrievably, I knew it. What was missing was the courage to stare straight at what I knew and to draw conclusions.

Welcome back to the land.

The Incola Hotel and the S. S. Sicamous, 1934.
SKOOKUM PUBLICATIONS

HAROLD RHENISCH lives in 108 Mile House, BC. He won the Confederation Poetry Prize, 1991, the *Arc* Poem of the Year Award, 2003, and *Arc* Critic's Desk Award for best long poetry review, 2003, and most recently the *Malahat Review* Long Poem Prize, 2005. He has been a seven-time runner-up in the CBC/Tilden/*Saturday Night* Literary Contest and won the BC & Yukon Community Newspapers Association Award for Best Arts and Culture Writing, 1996. His non-fiction book *Tom Thomson's Shack* was shortlisted for two BC Book Prizes in 2000.